Rethinking Prison Reentry

Rethinking Prison Reentry

Transforming Humiliation into Humility

Tony Gaskew

LEXINGTON BOOKS
Lanham • Boulder • New York • London

Published by Lexington Books
An imprint of The Rowman & Littlefield Publishing Group, Inc.
4501 Forbes Boulevard, Suite 200, Lanham, Maryland 20706
www.rowman.com

16 Carlisle Street, London W1D 3BT, United Kingdom

British Library Cataloguing in Publication Information Available

Library of Congress Cataloging-in-Publication Data

Gaskew, Tony.
Rethinking prison reentry : transforming humiliation into humility / Tony Gaskew.
pages cm.
Includes bibliographical references and index.
ISBN 978-0-7391-8312-0 (cloth) -- ISBN 978-0-7391-8313-7 (electronic)
1. African American prisoners. 2. African American men--Social conditions. 3. Crime--United
States--Sociological aspects. 4. Criminals--Rehabilitation--United States. 5. Discrimination in crimi-
nal justice administration--United States. I. Title.
HV9469.G37 2014
365'.608996073--dc23
                       2014023757

Printed in the United States of America

Contents

List of Figures

List of Tables

Preface

This book was written for anyone who believes in the reality of redemption, reconciliation, and social justice for incarcerated students. It's for an audience that gets up every morning, from a variety of professional and academic backgrounds, and understands they can do a better job of self-actualization in order to educate the public on the cruel and unjust realities of the criminal justice system. This book is written for those who are currently incarcerated or have served a prison sentence, and who have looked repeatedly in the polished metal mirror inside of a cell and said to themselves "enough."

This book also serves as a cautionary warning. We must begin to educate incarcerated black students who are trapped in a counter-culture of crime, about who they really are and what they really can become, despite the uncomfortable realities of racism, white supremacy, white privilege, and the manifestations of the politics of shaming, self-segregation, and transgenerational learned helplessness. If not, black children, the only hope to humble the criminal justice system into reform, will continue to pay the social debt inherited from their incarcerated black fathers. It is my hope this book plants the seeds of a pedagogical revolution, where prison educational programs begin to serve as academic runways to strengthen the heart, mind, and spirit of its incarcerated student body. It's for the many people just like me, who, when they see an incarcerated black male, they actually see a black male student who happens to be incarcerated.

Last, but definitely not least, I am writing this book to remind those who live the collective black American experience, have been exposed to their "cultural privilege" and have transcended and reconciled life's many humiliations into the saving grace of humility, to never forget one of the most fundamental universal truths: I am my brothers' keeper.

Acknowledgments

In the middle of writing this book, my eighty-two-year-old dad fell ill and was hospitalized in Chicago. As I left from Pennsylvania, all I could think about was my dad's incredible life's journey. He had survived the nihilism and violence of inner-city Chicago since he was twenty-one years old; however, he would spend most of his adult life telling me stories about his journey as a "country boy" growing up in a segregated Jim Crow Louisiana. When I walked into his hospital room, he was sitting on his bed laughing, echoing the familiar "Hey man, glad to see you" while extending his arm for a handshake. Over the next six hours I listened to him tell me stories; a complete oral narrative of nearly eight decades of his "collectively lived" black American experience. I didn't say a word. I just listened. In each of his stories, he would always remind me to "never quit on black people" and "to always tell them the truth." I am blessed and very fortunate to have a publisher, colleagues, students, friends, and a family who also support his wish.

I would like to thank Jana Hodges-Kluck, Jay Song, Natalie Mandziuk, along with everyone at Lexington Books and the Rowman & Littlefield Publishing Group for providing me the written platform to express my truths to a wider audience. My unwavering gratitude goes out to Dr. Livingston Alexander, President, University of Pittsburgh (Bradford). Your support the last eight years has "put me on the map" and I will never forget it. To Dr. Dani Weber, your critical and straightforward editing and commentary was a breath of fresh air. To one of the brightest criminal justice reformers I know, Dr. Lisa Guenther at Vanderbilt University. Your philosophical insight was invaluable. I would also like to thank each of my incarcerated students, program participants, and program facilitators over the years. Each of you has contributed to the "authentic voice" of this book. A special thanks goes out to the entire executive staff at FCI McKean for trusting and believing in my pedagogical vision over the past six years. Your faith will impact generations of lives.

Finally, to my biggest supporters, the entire Gaskew family. To my brothers, Walter and Jim, my son, Adonis, and my wife, Desiree. To my dad and mom, Walter and Nellie Gaskew. God bless you both for sacrificing everything in order to break the cycle of hopelessness. So many owe you their lives.

Introduction

The most powerful weapon in the policing armory of the criminal justice system that has destroyed any hope of maintaining the balance between crime, justice, and the truth comes in the form of two applied standards of procedural law: (1) The Mental State Requirement; and (2) The Public Authority Defense. In fact, these judicial precedents are so powerful that the incredible safeguards guaranteed by the Bill of Rights, including the Fourth and Fifth Amendments to the U.S. Constitution that have historically held the criminal justice system in-check, are defenseless against their power.

After almost thirty years in the business of crime and justice, I've come to one clear and undisputable truth: the overwhelming majority of our nation's citizens have no fathomable clue how the criminal justice system really operates. For the most part, this includes a significant segment of our white American population and based on historical precedent, they never have to learn. You see, the *Mental State Requirement* allows a police officer, within the performance of his official duties, to participate in criminal activity and not be charged with a crime because he lacks the specific intent or "mental state" (Joh, 2009). The *Public Authority Defense* also known as the law enforcement authority defense, which operates under the legal arm of the common law defense, permits law enforcement agents working under the color of the law to commit crimes and engage in criminal behavior for the purpose of gathering evidence of a crime (Ross, 2004).

In sum, these two cornerstones of legal precedents provide police officers the constitutionally protected right to look directly into the eyes of its citizens and lie to them within the pursuit of justice. After a while, everyone forgets what the truth actually is, including the criminal justice system. To clarify my point, over one million sworn law enforcement officers around the country have the ability in the full performance of their duties to use deceit in an interview, buy drugs, sell drugs, use drugs, manufacture drugs, deal in stolen property, transport, trade, and distribute automatic weapons to convicted felons, print counterfeit money, launder money, engage in sexual acts with prostitutes, commit perjury, etc. Elizabeth Joh's *Breaking the Law to Enforce It: Undercover Police Participation in Crime* refers to this policing power as "the practice of authorized criminality" (p. 157). Jacqueline Ross' *Impediments to Transnational Cooperation in Undercover Policing: A Comparative Study of the United States and*

1

Italy noted in *United States vs. Murphy* 768 F.2d 1518, 1528–29 (7th Circuit 1985), which involved an FBI sting operation against corrupt Chicago judges in which the agents perjured themselves in court:

> The court reasoned that "in pursuit of crime the Government is not confined to behavior suitable to the drawing room. It may use decoys, and provide the essential tools of the offense. The creation of opportunities for crime is nasty but necessary business. (2004, p. 575)

I know some of my readers might be thinking, "Well, if you're not committing crimes then you have nothing to worry about." However, I wish it were that simple. There is a *triad of culpability* when it comes to crime and justice in America: (1) of those who commit crimes; (2) of those who enforce criminal laws; and (3) of those who stand by and do nothing. Based upon my own experience in the profession of crime and justice, the simple fact is that everyone commits crime at some point in their life but not everyone is arrested. Anyone who says they have not subjected themselves to the crimes of underage drinking or the use of marijuana, including myself—well, need I say any more?

Thus, the concept of justice becomes an *abstract discretionary power* ripe for abuse. Again, I reiterate how the majority of people are "clueless as to how the criminal justice system really operates." You see, the criminal justice system is not just some blind faceless social structure, that is, a police department, a courthouse, or a prison that dispels justice like an ATM machine. The criminal justice system is actually the people who work within its *cultural privilege*. That's right; when you pull back the curtain similar to the Wizard of Oz, all you discover is that it's just everyday people making the discretionary choices of whether someone goes to jail, receives a prison sentence, or just goes home—each of which is a life impacting decision. Those are the same people who laugh, cry, bleed and have the innate ability to both love and hate. Those are the same people, just like you and me, who may possess a bias, who see the social construction of race every day when they come to work and who, based on their physical and mental senses, make predetermined judgments based on this bias.

If you don't believe me, take a few minutes and complete an Implicit Association Test (IAT) on race, at the Harvard University weblink: https://implicit.harvard.edu/implicit/. The people who work in the criminal justice system know that a racial bias exists at every single level of the justice system; however, they either choose to acknowledge the issue but ignore the consequences, or the more hideous option, deny its very existence because they can no longer distinguish a lie from the truth.

Just ask the racially disproportionate percentage of the 2.2 million who are housed in our jails and prisons, the 4.8 million on probation or parole, the 13.5 million who are arrested each year, or the 41.2 million who receive speeding tickets each year who have a much better applied understanding of how the criminal justice system really operates (Center for Constitutional Rights, 2009; U.S. Department of Justice Office of Justice Programs Bureau of Justice Statistics, 2011b; U.S. Department of Justice Office of Justice Programs, 2012a; U.S. Department of Justice Office of Justice Programs, 2012b; Federal Bureau of Investigation Arrest Statistics: 1994–2010, 2013c; Federal Bureau of Investigation Uniform Crime Report, 2013b; National Association for the Advancement of Colored People, 2013).

The criminal justice system has developed a Du Boisian double consciousness regarding the culpability of crime and justice when it comes to black Americans. It has been using the specific judicial weapons of the socially constructed lies noted above and an almost endless onslaught of supporting case laws in policing, courts, and corrections to demonize black males for so long that the justice system can no longer see through the smoke and mirrors of its own lies to the truth of the protracted damage it has caused in the black American experience. However, black Americans are just as culpable in this web of lies. Many just sit back and silently watch one out of every three young black men accept their acting role in this theater of lies. As a *black counter-culture of crime* grows daily across this country, sustaining many of the negative stereotypes that ignorantly are being cemented into the fabric of the black American experience, incredibly, there is a sizable portion of black Americans that perpetuate these socially constructed lies by describing this same counter-culture as simply "victims of society."

Black Americans cried foul regarding the results of the Trayvon Martin case, with nationally prominent voices and laypersons alike baffled at how they would be able to explain the verdict to their black children and how they would educate their *black children* on the "real criminal justice system." I wonder how many of the same black parents educated their children on the realities that an entire generation of black men living in a counter-culture of crime, coupled with a blindly inept, unjust, and biased criminal justice system, was in truth responsible for the death of Trayvon Martin and the acquittal of George Zimmerman. Hell, how many black Americans knew that George Zimmerman did not have to categorize himself under the racial demographic of "white" because the FBI's Uniform Crime Report (UCR) automatically places all Hispanic/Latino Americans under this racial category. The black people who live and work in some of these communities across the nation know that a black counter-culture of crime, with every destructive element it brings to the black American experience, exists; however, they either choose to acknowledge the issue but ignore the consequences, or the more hideous option, deny its very existence because they can no longer distinguish a lie from the truth. If this sounds like a broken record, it is.

This book seeks to break the cycle of the socially constructed lies faced by so many black men who fill our nation's prisons and jails and are trapped in a black counter-culture of crime, through the simple concept of owning the truth. In this book, I will introduce the *Humiliation to Humility Perspective* (HHP), a prison-based education pedagogy that consists of five connective tenets designed to address the *politics of shaming, self-segregation,* and *transgenerational learned helplessness* that have served as insurmountable psychosocial obstacles for so many incarcerated black males attempting to make the successful transition back into owning their respective lives. Within this pedagogical framework, black males are able to transform the *humiliation of criminal offender* to the *humility of incarcerated student* and never look back. HHP advocates that prisons and jails across the nation also transform the paradigm from the *humiliation of correctional facilities* to the *humility of correctional learning centers* (CLCs). These "incarcerated students" must be able to transcend their role within the black American experience by owning their truth; understanding their connective history and *black cultural privilege* (BCP); learning to process the criminal justice system; knowing the true victims of a *black counter-culture of crime*; and finally by exploiting their duty to remain free and to start making their own life choices.

History teaches us that incarcerated black men have a cultural DNA, an indestructible historical and cultural legacy of a *collective lived experience,* that is, lived individually but gathered and shared as a whole, as in a black collective consciousness, that can withstand any man-made humiliation, and the intellect to potentially alter the entire black American experience as we know it. We need to look no further than Malcolm X as an example; however, these traits need to be awakened and cultivated. HHP seeks to serve as a pedagogical "blue print" for this purpose. Because as Fanon (1952, pp. 228–229) declared, there is only one true right, "that of demanding human behavior from the other," and one true duty, "that of not renouncing my freedom through my own choices." For way too many years, incarcerated black men have been making decisions without fully understanding all of their choices.

However, articulating this "truth" has its challenges and limitations when one looks through an academic lens. First, my thoughts, behaviors, and words are those of a black man within the collective lived black American experience and everything that this encompasses both tangible and intangible. First, I am unapologetically a black American man and I believe the most authentic method to understand, study, and examine the black American experience is to live within the socially constructed racially stratified label of being black. As noted by Zuberi and Bonilla-Silva (2008, p. 7), "Race is not about an individual's skin color. Race is about the individuals' relationship to other people within society . . . within this construct, the person of color does not exist outside of his or her otherness." I realize how that may sound, especially to the countless white male and female researchers and occupants of the Ivory Tower who have invested years of participant observation, fieldwork, and cultural immersion into whatever phenomena they've tried to explore and define within the concept of *blackness*; however, at best all they can produce is an *avatar* understanding and that's simply not good enough. There are just way too many intangible aspects that encompass the lived black American experience that can never be understood, described, or owned by seeing it through the eyes of the socially constructed lens of white privilege. Second, the lived black American experience does not offer the convenience of an "ethical escape plan" or a conclusion "expiration date" that are prerequisites for many ethnographic research designs because in order to authentically understand the black American experience, one must understand that there is no golden parachute; black Americans can never walk away from or escape back into a separately defined reality other than that of the socially constructed black race. Those are my truths, based on an almost fifty-year journey as a black man living within the realm of the black American experience.

However, as a social scientist who argues for the intrinsic powers of the "lived" methodology as being the best fundamental research approach available for studying the black American experience, I must also admit it has clear limitations. My understanding of the unique narrative of the world and every person in it can only be viewed through the filter of my own lived racially stratified experiences as a black American man. This "veil" was not my choice but one that American society constructed and labeled as part of my distinct and proud history. I recognize that my *blackness* can be so robust at times that it has the potential to "suffocate" the invaluable truths of others. Thus, I can never authentically understand what it is like to interact in this world as a white male or female, without first filtering it through my own sense of blackness. Although my multi-racial ancestry within the prism of blackness has provided me and so many others an intimate "communal window" into the realities of being an "outsider" with the unique ability to describe the social construction of *whiteness*, ownership into this club is by social invitation only; thus I have no right to attempt to accurately define the collective truth of its occupants. In fact, using the methodology of the "lived experience," I do not even attempt to provide an "authentic voice" in this book from the perspective of a black female that supports the quest for reconciliatory liberation from the criminal justice system and the black counter-culture of crime.

For example, according to the Sentencing Project report *The Changing Racial Dynamics of Women's Incarceration,* black women represent nearly 30 percent of all females incarcerated in state or federal correctional facilities. As well, black women were more than three times as likely as white women to be incarcerated in prison or jail. However, from 2000–2009 the rate of incarceration declined 30 percent for black women, while the rate for white and Hispanic women has increased 47 percent and 23 percent respectively (The Sentencing Project, 2013a). This significant "drop-off" is not the same for black men (less than 6 percent); thus the often invisible factors that would cause the rate of incarceration for black females need to be explored in-depth, and in their own unique voice. My lived experiences as a black man provide me limited specific insight into this phenomenon. Statistical data regarding incarcerated black females can be found anywhere; however, the "authentic voice" of the incarcerated black female can only be found within her own lived experiences.

That being said, I would like to point out that the socially constructed label attached to the black male is so powerful and pervasive in its historic ugliness that it many times consumes the separate and unique voices of not only incarcerated black women, but those of any race or ethnicity, making the subjugation of the black male the most accurate reflection of how the United States defines the concept of justice. This is the reason why James Baldwin (2010) was so inherently confident in his own *blackness* to be able to describe the social construction of *whiteness*:

> Whether I like it or not, I cannot only describe myself but, what is much more horrifying, I can describe YOU. . . . No one has pointed out yet with any force that if I am not a man here, you are not a man here. You cannot lynch me and keep me in ghettos without becoming something monstrous yourself. And furthermore, you give me a terrifying advantage . . . that whereas you never had to look at me, because you've sealed me away along with sin and hell and death and all the other things you didn't want to look at, including love, my life was in your hands, and I had to look at you. I know more about you, therefore, than you know about me. I've spent my life, after all—and all the other Negroes in the country have had to spend their lives—outwitting and watching white people. I had to know what you were doing before you did it. (pp. 11, 14, 15)

You see, ever since twenty Angolans landed in Jamestown in 1619, the policing of the black American male has set the standard of how justice will be applied to all men and women regardless of race, ethnicity, or creed. The policing of the black male sets the "social tone" for the policing of the rest of the nation, that is, white men, black women, white women, Hispanic men, etc. "Terry Stops" are not an accidental enforcement strategy but are defined by structural forces that have legislatively identified and labeled the urban "black male" as the gatekeepers of the crime within the "American experience." According to trial evidence obtained in *Floyd v. City of New York*, between 2004 and 2012, approximately 2.35 million black males were "stopped & frisked" by police officers in the self-described "capital of the nation" New York City. Just to give some perspective, that figure is greater than the number of black Americans residing in the cities of Detroit, Birmingham, Memphis, Savannah, Baltimore, and New Orleans combined (U.S. Census Bureau, 2013d). Although *Terry v. Ohio* legally permits police officers based upon the articulation of reasonable suspicion, the ability to "detain and pat-down" an individual for officer safety considers looking solely for weapons, less than 1.5 percent of total 4.34 million stops in New York City over the past decade has ever result in the seizure of a weapon.

In fact, according to a report by the New York State Attorney General's Office (2013), *A Report on Arrests Arising from the New York City Police Department's Stop-and-Frisk Practices,* in roughly less than one-tenth of 1 percent of all "stop and frisks" were any firearms seized, and just 0.1 percent led to an arrest for a violent crime. Additionally, less than 3 percent of all arrests resulting in the use of the "stop and frisk" tactic ever resulted in a criminal conviction. NYPD Commissioner Raymond Kelly justifies his agency's actions, noting that black males commit over 70 percent of the city's violent crimes and deserve extra police scrutiny, while garnishing a majority support for this tactic from voters separated along racial lines (Susman, 2012). However, over the past decade approximately 2.15 million innocent black men have been illegally "detained and frisked" by NYPD using the case law application blessed by the Supreme Court of the Unites States, exposing them to the "socially constructed lie" that is controlled, operated, and owned by the criminal justice system. If someone wants or needs to understand the foundation of America's past, present, and future regarding the concept of applied justice, whether examining the roots of its economic prowess through slavery and the act of learned helplessness or exposing its greatest psychosocial fear regarding the social construction of race, it can be found in its treatment of the black male.

Throughout each chapter, I do my absolute best to separate the conceptual realities of "my truths" from "the truths"; however, these lines become very blurred. Although the *Du Boisian* "veil," or what I refer to as my *blackness,* allows me to see the world through a set of individual eyes, society has determined that the reaction and treatment of my blackness become part of a collectively lived and racially stratified shared black American experience. As a black man who has operated as an insider within the criminal justice system for the majority of my adult life, I do not get a "pass" from its socially constructed lies. I am still followed by undercover security officers nearly every time I walk into a store. In elevators, white females still clutch their bags and do everything in their power not to make eye contact. Police officers still give me what I define as that *nigger stare* whenever they drive by me. As well, my education does not protect me from these racial truths, because for the most part I'm the "most educated person in the room" during these encounters. You see, these truths have become simply part of the shared black American male experience, so "my truths" have become intertwined into "the truths" of so many black men.

I only hope the reader understands that the universal nature of that which I describe as "my truths" in this book is not a matter of hubris but

one of *life transformative humility*. The same type of humility is described
by James Baldwin in *The Cross of Redemption*:

> You will learn a certain humility, because the terms that you have
> invented, which you think describe and define you, inevitably collide
> with the facts of life. When this collision occurs—and, make no mis-
> take, this is an absolute inevitable collision—when this collision occurs,
> like two trains meeting head-on in a tunnel, life offers you a choice and
> it's a very narrow choice, of holding on to your definition of yourself or
> saying, as the old folks used to say, and as everybody who wants to
> live say: Yes, Lord. Which is to say yes to life. Until you can do that,
> you've not become a man or woman. (pp. 73–74)

Within this shared concept of humility, I don't expect the criminal
justice system to change because to put it quite frankly: (1) The culture of
white privilege embedded within the justice system will never be able to
empathize with the true essence of the black American experience; (2) the
profits generated for the correctional servitude of one out of every three
black males is a price the justice system cannot afford to lose; and (3) the
majority of the two-thirds of the black Americans who have absolutely
nothing to do with the criminal justice system will continue to remain
silent enablers, because they somehow feel uplifted and comfortable
about their own *blackness,* as long as there is a clearly demarcated public
enemy to blame for the "social sins" being committed on, for, and within
the black American experience: the incarcerated black male. You see,
black Americans need a "social scapegoat" as well. If not, they would be
forced to admit that "Malcolm not Martin" had a much more accurate
vision of the future plight of the black male, mass incarceration, as many
continue to allow themselves to be defined within the narrow prisms of
the politics of shaming, self-segregation, and transgenerational learned
helplessness (Cone, 2003). Many of the *two-thirds* continue to waste their
time and energy blindly hoping, dreaming, and praying that one day a
nation that was built and has profited on the subjugation of the black
American experience will "judge them by the content of their character
and not the color of their skin" (King, 1968b) instead of embracing the
real struggle: the need to speak the truth.

Thus, I have directed my attention to the third party of this triad of
culpability: the *black counter-culture of crime.* It is my contention, based
primarily on my faith in the spirit and resilience of the black American
experience, that if the black men who sit at the center of this New Jim
Crow know, understand, and own the truths of their existence they
would work to end the mass incarcerations of themselves and their breth-
ren. In this book, I introduce a new pedagogical framework for incarcerated black men, many of whom are trapped in a black counter-culture of
crime and who, like over 95 percent of all inmates in the nation, will be
making the transition from prison back into their respective commu-

nities. *Rethinking Prison Reentry: Transforming Humiliation into Humility* describes an applied prison-based pedagogical theory, the *Humiliation to Humility Perspective* (HHP), designed to transform incarcerated black men into *black students who are incarcerated*. The transformed "incarcerated students" must be able to transcend their role within the black American experience by owning their truth; understanding their connective history and *black cultural privilege* (BCP); learning to process the criminal justice system; knowing the true victims of a black counter-culture of crime; and finally exploiting their duties to remain free and start making their own life choices. Inspired by the Bell Hooks pedagogical family of "radical cultural engagement," this book seeks to address the transgenerational cycle of mass incarceration by focusing on the "lived experiences" of those who have been historically the most disproportionally impacted by this nation's war against humanity and social justice: incarcerated black men.

This book seeks to confront the issue of race, crime, and justice head-on by critically examining the underlying connective result of long-term structural and direct violence on the psyche of the black American experience: transgenerational learned helplessness. It explores the growth of a black counter-culture of crime that has created modern-day killing fields across urban neighborhoods in Chicago, while at the same time addressing how race has become an unstoppable economic force and political tool used to enhance the social construct of white privilege. This book seeks to illuminate the inherent redemptional powers of *truth* and its role in transforming humiliation into humility.

Each chapter in this book addresses a separate tenet in the *Humiliation to Humility Perspective* (HHP). The first chapter provides an overview of "my truths" of transforming humiliation into humility. One cannot expect incarcerated black men to transform into incarcerated black students until they find the "reality of truth" that is often hidden in the continued fog of socially constructed lies. So, I reflect on the truths of my personal, professional, and academic background as well as my collective lived experiences as a black American male. I also cover the HHP pedagogical tenets, framework, and design. The goal of this chapter is to illuminate the redemptive power of owning the truth, and to inspire incarcerated black students to understand that their journey to reconciliation and freedom can only begin with the discovery and ownership of their own truths.

Chapter 2 seeks to inspire intellectual accountability for incarcerated black students to own the collective knowledge of their *black cultural privilege* (BCP). It explores how the *essence of blackness* can be found in an era of mass incarceration. It examines the damage that the institutionalized campaign and unquestioned acceptance of *black inferiority* and *white superiority* have played in the lives of incarcerated black students. It discusses the growth of transgenerational learned helplessness, and challenges its hold on the black American consciousness by confronting and owning its historic foundation: slavery. This chapter describes how BCP allows incarcerated black students the ability to successfully navigate the rich legacy of an African past with the evolving and indestructible nature of their glorious black American present.

Chapter 3 turns our attention to educating incarcerated black students on how to process the criminal justice system within a collective lived black American experience. It examines why the three components of the criminal justice system, policing, courts, and corrections, the symbolic *Great White Shark*, has always had an insatiable political and economic appetite for black men. It explores how a *black counter-culture of crime* has surfaced as the de facto national identity for many incarcerated black students, perpetuating the socially constructed lies that continue to redefine the black American experience. This chapter also describes how a culture of *informanthood* has ravaged the body, mind, and spirit of incarcerated black students attempting to make the transition from humiliation to humility.

Chapter 4 examines how black male children have been inheriting the *social debt of mass incarceration* directly from their incarcerated black fathers. It emphasizes that the most important role an incarcerated black student can play in his life is that of a father. Breaking the transgenerational cycle of mass incarceration falls on the incarcerated, as only a black man who has lived within the confines of governmental servitude has the owned truth that can keep his own black son from the mouth of the shark. In closing, Chapter 5 reflects on the last educational tenet of transforming humiliation into humility: the freedom to make choices. For way too many years, incarcerated black men have been making decisions without fully understanding all of their choices. Only by intellectually inspiring incarcerated black students on the importance of owning their own lived truths, and the truths behind their black cultural privilege, the criminal justice system, and the true victims of their involvement in a black counter-culture of crime, will they finally be able to own their life choices. Confronting the cycle of humiliation provides incarcerated black students an opportunity to culturally liberate themselves from the *politics of shaming, self-segregation,* and *transgenerational learned helplessness,* embracing the universal power of redemption, reconciliation, and humility.

ONE

The Killing Fields of Chicago

Dear reader, I begin my book with a confession and a cautionary warning. As a little boy, I knew very little about the truths of my own *black cultural privilege* (BCP), the criminal justice system, my own victimization, and most of all, my choices in life, growing up within inner-city Chicago. As I became a young man, I discovered that the world, including my very own life, was not going to be seen through a set of rose colored glasses. In fact, I was taught that the "invisible elephants in the room," racism, white supremacy, and white privilege, were going to be attached to my black American experience whether I liked it or not, and that my only real choice was how I was going to manage them.

I know some of my words in this book are not going to sit well with some people, including black Americans like myself. However, what I've learned in this quagmire of crime and justice in America is that there is a *triad of culpability*: (1) Of those who commit crimes; (2) Of those who enforce criminal laws; and (3) Of those who stand by and do nothing. The truth of the matter is that, although this culpability is not equally distributed across these three groups, each plays a role in continuing the cycle of criminal justice servitude for black men. My intent as a life-learner has always been to inspire a critical debate about how these three interconnected dimensions have impacted the black American experience. I believe based primarily on my faith in the spirit and resilience of the black American experience, that if the black men who sit at the center of this *New Jim Crow* know, understand, and own the truths of their "collective existence" they would work to end the cycle of mass incarcerations for themselves and their children. For as African historian Molefi Asante (2003, p. 1) says, "A people without an appreciation of the value of [their] historical experiences will always create chaos." You see, in the end the

11

lives of everyone—the victims, the police, and the perpetrator—all equally matter.

I understand that my assessment of the ever-growing "black counter-
culture of crime" that one out of every three black males finds himself
cycling through in his lives will be questioned by black Americans. In
fact, some will critically suggest that my criminal justice career has made
me severely jaded towards my own race, and that maybe my NAACP
card should be revoked for life. However, these same black Americans do
absolutely nothing as their very own children and grandchildren kill
each other at a record-setting pace, filling our nation's jails and prisons to
the brink with unclaimed doctors, authors, poets, professors, and engi-
neers. I would strongly encourage them to read with an open mind Martin Luther King's *Where Do We Go From Here? Chaos or Community* (1968a),
and ask themselves if they *really* know who their children are, and what
their children can *really* become once those children discover their true
nature as cultural icons.

Some of my colleagues who are practitioners in the criminal justice
field will try to characterize my criticisms of the justice system as the
"angry black man syndrome" that seems to have infected the minds of
many educated black men around the country. In fact, I feel that as a
former black law enforcement agent, I have earned the right to critique a
system that I've voluntarily contributed to. I would hope that the infectious widespread cynicism within the criminal justice culture, which is
understandable considering the negative environment law enforcement
officials find themselves in daily, has not destroyed their sense of social
justice nor their ability to conduct an honest assessment of the very justice system that has caused so much senseless suffering directed at communities of color. I would hope they would understand that the criminal
justice system sits as the epitome of "white privilege," blinding even the
most sincere and genuine advocates of justice to the destructive outcomes
of their solemn oath to serve and protect, and would recognize its detri-
mental consequences on the historical black American experience. As
well, in an era where communities of color around the country have
dangerously less faith and respect for the criminal justice system than
ever before, with a record-breaking number of documented complaints of
officer misconduct, falsification of reports, excessive force, racial profiling, unreasonable search and seizure with Terry Stops, coupled with the
disproportionate mass incarceration of people of color nationwide largely
due to the *War on Drugs,* how could any criminal justice practitioner in
the country not admit that our current justice system is in a state of racial
dysfunction? No one can deny this fact. I would encourage criminal justice practitioners read Charles Ogletree's *The Presumption of Guilt* (2012)
and Tom Burrell's *Brainwashed* (2010) just as a starting point to measure
the "damage assessment" the criminal justice system has had on the collective psyche of the black American experience.

Some of my academic colleagues will question my pedagogical theory, the *Humiliation to Humility Perspective* (*HHP*), because it is not supported by the type of hardline empirical data that conforms to the so-called evidence-based practices that they themselves have supported and benefited from. They will be dismissive if there is not specific data indicating that the recidivism rate has fallen for my HHP audience, not quite understanding the need for a paradigm shift that requires us to stop measuring a successful prison-to-community transition on what I label as the *staying out of prison* (SOP) model. Instead, we must focus on building the "sustainable whole person through truth" who will then be able to offer more to himself, his children, and his community than a minimum wage job and a counter-culture that is lost in shame, anger, and alienation.

The fact is, the overwhelming majority of my academic colleagues in the discipline of crime and justice have no idea what the "collective lived black American experience" entails, with a robust 80 percent living under the academic comfort zone of white privilege. Many have no idea what it's like to live a lifetime of making choices about whether to confront the who, what, where, when, why, and how of racism, white supremacy, and white privilege or to hide behind the fear of being labeled a "black radical" if you choose to stand up for your blackness. Many have never placed handcuffs on a black man, acted as legal counsel for a black man in court proceedings, supervised a black man on probation, managed a black man in a correctional facility, or actually ever stepped inside a prison setting and engaged in a face-to-face conversation with an incarcerated black man. Many have never experienced the level of critical engagement that takes place between a black post-secondary educator and an incarcerated black male student. Many sit very comfortably behind a desk and the safe world of "academic chicken hawking," producing journal articles and books by the dozens, informing criminal justice practitioners and the black community alike "what they're doing wrong and what they should be doing for the successful reentry of black male offenders." I would challenge my academic colleagues to apply the perspective of the very first expert on black American crime, W. E. B. Du Bois, and what he learned during and after his ground breaking scientific work *The Philadelphia Negro*. (1899)

I would offer to my academic colleagues that the *lived* experience is the most accurate statistical tool available to understand the holistic black American experience, such as my own *lived* experiences as a black male, my *lived* experiences as a black practitioner within the criminal justice system, and my *lived* experiences as a black social scientist involved in educating black incarcerated students. I would suggest that my *lived* experiences as a black male involved in countless critical discussions with career correctional professionals, offenders, ex-offenders, along with other justice advocates over the past twenty-five years, sits at the essence of empirical research. I would also encourage them to read Tukufu Zuberi's and Eduardo Bonilla-Silva's *White Logic, White Methods: Racism and Methodology* (2008). I would argue that presenting statistical data that examine the plight of black Americans involved in crime and justice is completely empty and void of meaning without first accepting the reality that the collective lived experience of black Americans is owned by black Americans.

I would hope that my academic colleagues would be up to the challenge of taking the time to do as follows: (1) invest their *very own lives* to go inside the prison walls many pontificate about with their publications and inside their classrooms; (2) learn to communicate with incarcerated black men as post-secondary college students and not as research participants; (3) learn to work with incarcerated black students on creating new and innovative prison-to-community transition initiatives, adopting a pedagogy founded on the principles of self-actualization, counter-hegemony, and culturally responsive teaching; and (4) learn to inspire curriculum and programming that are inclusive and not dismissive of the collective lived black American experience. For in the end, it is crucial to recognize that the lives of incarcerated students trapped in the black counter-culture of crime are just as important as the police officers or the victims of their crimes.

I do confess, this is not an objective examination of the criminal justice system and the black counter-cultural "merry-go-round" that hundreds of thousands of incarcerated black men find themselves in while preparing to reenter into their respective communities each year. It can't be. As a black man who was raised in a city surrounded by a black counter-culture of crime, a former police-detective possessing a unique understanding of the internal mechanisms of the criminal justice system, which is often intentionally hidden from general public view, especially to people of color, and currently as a tenured university professor armed with a PhD along with the academic freedom as a social scientist to expose and voice the often "invisible truths" of structural violence, how can I be? I have witnessed first-hand how black fathers and their sons who are vested within the black counter-culture of crime, can destroy a black community. I have witnessed first-hand how a black community can be conditioned to ignore the criminal behavior of its very own black men, contributing to its very own collective suffering. I have witnessed first-hand the ugly outcomes that the criminal justice system, specifically the *War on Drugs*, has levied on the black American experience. I have witnessed first-hand how the criminal justice system, instead of serving as the beacon of freedom and justice, has helped perpetuate the cycle of oppression in the black American experience. Unconscious macro and micro forms of racism, dehumanization, marginalization, and white privilege all exist as undercurrents of a social institution that advocates that "lady justice wears a blindfold." The reality is, *lady justice* doesn't simply take a peak, she often removes the entire blindfold and uses optical enhancers akin to the Hubble Telescope most of the time. I have witnessed first-hand how all parties involved in this *triad of culpability* deny their role in the cycle of mass incarceration. This is the primary reason why the black American experience, as it relates to crime and justice, can never be understood without the lived experience.

I confess that academically I'm very selective about how I nourish my body and soul regarding African Diaspora and Pan-Africanism, choosing primarily to digest the selective historic erudition of John Henrik Clarke, Derrick Bell, Chancellor Williams, W. E. B. Du Bois, William Leo Hansberry, E. Franklin Frazier, Booker T. Washington, Marcus Garvey, Carter G. Woodson, James Baldwin, Lerone Bennett, and others of similar philosophical flavor. I also admit that the ideas of Maulana Karenga and Molefi Asante shaped my worldview regarding the importance of always remembering that the black American experience, although it continues to transform based on social and political paradigms, must always do so centered upon the foundation of its own historical African culture. I consider these black intellectuals modern-day "fortune tellers," predicting with the utmost accuracy, almost up to a century ago in some circumstances, the plight that black males would find themselves in today if they did not discover the educational *truths* about themselves and their ancestral journey. Remember, every black American intellectual today received their "academic DNA" from many of these scholars. Finally, I confess that I am unapologetic that I find inspiration in the words and deeds in the likes of black men such as Malcolm X, George Jackson, Huey P. Newton, Bobby Seale, Eldridge Cleaver, or even the writings of Stanley Williams. I would not be the man I am today if it were not for *The Autobiography of Malcolm X*, *Soledad Brother*, or *Soul on Ice*. The temptation to paint their voices as only the "music of incarcerated black revolutionaries" is not only academically short-sighted, but it is comparable to the dangerous historical mindset that still perpetuates the belief that Christopher Columbus discovered the Americas.

Now, my cautionary warning. Today, there is no need to create any new forms of white supremacy in order to keep the criminal justice system full of young black male bodies. Clearly, there is irrefutable evidence to support that black men were intentionally and institutionally demonized and treated as subhuman when we look back at America's ugly history with race and injustice. Did slavery, the black codes, and Jim Crow set the stage that we have today regarding mass incarceration and the black counter-culture of crime? You bet it did. Does racism still exist in the criminal justice system? Yes, yes, and yes, dating back to its historical roots, as does the arrogance of white privilege among its millions of professionally employed gatekeepers of justice. To even suggest that the likes of J. Edgar Hoover, the top law enforcement officer in America for almost fifty years, did not use the incredible powers of the executive branch of the U.S. government and the FBI to criminalize the black American experience, or to even suggest that today's *War on Drugs* is not directed against black Americans, borders on intellectual and moral ignorance.

However, although securely in place, today there is no need to have all of these race-based criminal justice structural biases functioning in order to keep the "prison franchise" running efficiently. The cumulative effect of a 400–year mindset of racism, white supremacy, and white privilege along with its attached catalogue of structural injustices, and its remarkable ability to hypnotize and distract the black community from "keeping its eye on the prize," has allowed the rich historical legacy of the black American experience to become erased from the hearts and minds of today's urban black males, transforming some of them into a scared, intimidated generation, capable of some of the most gruesome acts of cultural destruction and crime imaginable. Black communities are then either forced, or in many cases, choose to turn over their young black fathers, sons, brothers, and cousins into the open arms of the criminal justice system to be raised into manhood. As Paulo Freire (1970) predicted decades ago, "the oppressed have become the oppressor." I have seen black men and their wildly popular and universally accepted "anti-intellectual counter-culture of gangsterism" simply walk right into the mouth of the criminal justice system with arms extended and with no form of resistance, like lambs for the slaughter. In fact, today black men are responsible for imprisoning more black men, including their very own sons, than J. Edgar Hoover ever dreamed of in COINTELPRO or any DEA sting operation in the history of our nation, with this black counter-culture of crime infecting them and any other black male in their vicinity with unchanneled anger, shame, humiliation, and violence. My father once told me, "The word *nigger* don't mean shit . . . say *nigger* 100 times and see what happens . . . nothing . . . it has no power unless you as a black man decide that it does." With my father's very own words of wisdom, I will begin my truths.

THE WILD 100s

The greatest gift my parents ever provided me, and there were many, was their *cultural DNA*. I don't mean this in terms of some biological essentialism, but rather from an edifying perspective. That's right, a sort of "cultural survival gene" that has withstood the burdens of structural and direct violence that often sit at the core of protracted psychosocial humiliations. They educated me on my multi-ethnic and multi-racial black American identity and culture. They taught me that the power of my truth originated in the awareness of my *black cultural privilege* (BCP), which served as my gateway to respect for and connectivity with, not fear of, other cultures. They educated me to be an *unapologetically black*. They raised me on the 1960s ideological philosophy preached by *Sly and the Family Stone's* "Everyday People." I was raised under the umbrella of "different strokes for different folks." I was educated on the "one drop rule" and what that meant from a historical, cultural, and social perspective, in relation to other races and ethnicities (Davis, 2001). I was allowed to explore my *blackness*. That coveted yet rarely discussed part of my cultural DNA has permitted me to see through the invisible "social veils" of structural violence, racism, civil, and economic injustice faced by many black Americans, and described by W. E. B. Du Bois (1994) in his social masterpiece *Souls of Black Folk*. This same *cultural survival gene* has allowed an entire people not only to survive the worst set of transgenerational crimes ever perpetuated on human beings, the genocide of the African Holocaust, but to transform the shame, anger, and hopelessness that have attached themselves onto an ongoing series of institutionalized humiliations over the past four centuries, into the *transcendent humility* required for the type of global success never imagined for a people. I was taught to speak the truth and stand up to racism, white supremacy, and white privilege. I was taught that those who used these "three invisible elephants in the room" to attempt to marginalize my blackness had one of three responses when confronted, to deny, to deflect, or to distress, and none of these responses would determine my destiny. I was taught the inevitable fact that there would be a black President of the United States of America one day, long before Barack Obama arrived on the national radar, solely because of my cultural DNA. You see, I'm a fervent believer in my cultural survival gene, for it has been my invisible secret weapon my entire life. In fact, every human being who has ever suffered life's many humiliations carries with them a hidden and often invisible *cultural coping mechanism* that was forged by the journey of their ancestors who all survived long-term systemic oppression, hardship, and marginalization, but the humiliated do not know how to tap into its amazing transformative qualities of humility.

Once you understand this fundamental concept, it's easy to explain how a person, regardless of race, ethnicity, gender, or religious affiliation, raised in an environment of poverty, crime, violence, and utter hopelessness, not only evades the trappings of this climate, but transcends these *humiliations* and goes on to thrive in the personal and professional success of *humility*. But its transformative power can only be "tapped into" by educating, understanding, knowing, and owning the *truth* of "who you really are" based on one's history and *collective cultural life experiences*. This truth cannot only be taught but must be *discovered* by some of our young incarcerated black men today. Sadly, some black men, like my father, are only able to discover their truth within the solitude of incarceration. This was the first of many truths I would uncover in my life's journey, and it is one of the first truths that I share with every Federal

Bureau of Prisons (BOP) offender that I've come into contact with as a post-secondary instructor over the past six years. I let them know that each of them also has the *cultural DNA*, but that for the most part, it lies dormant, waiting to be awakened and put to use. This book seeks to help awaken this *cultural survival gene* specifically for incarcerated black men.

You see, there is no other way that I can explain surviving my life journey. Growing up a black male, invisibly poor, I was surrounded by predatory wolves in one of Chicago's most violent urban settings, the "Wild 100s," many of whom eerily shared the same racial profile that I, along with approximately 40 percent of the current U.S. prison population, possess. Unlike what is portrayed in our popular entertainment culture, urban black poverty is not glamorous or exciting, but humiliating. It breeds the type of cultural nihilism that permits the universal acceptance that urban black Americans, whom Huey Newton (1972) referred to as the "Inner-Third-World of America," would prefer to sell drugs, rob, and murder each other by the thousands. Since the 1980s, over 100,000 black American men were murdered at the hands of other black American men (U.S. Census Bureau, 2012). According to the U.S. Department of Justice (2011c):

> Blacks were disproportionately represented as both homicide victims and offenders. The victimization rate for blacks (27.8 per 100,000) was 6 times higher than the rate for whites (4.5 per 100,000). The offending rate for blacks (34.4 per 100,000) was almost 8 times higher than the rate for whites (4.5 per 100,000). (p. 3)

THE SMOKE AND MIRRORS OF CRIME STATISTICS

The above statistics sound despicable, right? They make a strong case for the mass incarceration of young black males, correct? However, truth be told, in large part most Americans, including black Americans, have been hoodwinked. Today, there are more young black men enrolled in college than incarcerated (American Council on Education, 2012). In fact, black college educated men like myself are not the exception but the invisible cultural norm. According to the U.S. Census Bureau (2010), the number of black men currently enrolled in post-secondary education is 1.241 million versus the 844,600 (Minton, 2010; Guerino, Harrison, and Sabol, 2010) who are incarcerated in prisons and jails across the country. My desire within the *Humiliation to Humility Perspective* (HHP) is to transform the psychosocial reality of these 844,600 offenders trapped within a *black counter-culture of crime* into 844,600 *black students who happen to be incarcerated*.

In fact, according to the FBI's Uniform Crime Report (2013a), white Americans commit and have historically committed more crimes than any other race in America. The notion that we are a "nation of black crime" is one of the greatest myths ever perpetrated on the black American experience. Statistically, 7 out of every 10 crimes in the United States are committed by white Americans. Out of the thirty or so arrestable "offenses charged" catalogued by the UCR, white Americans were arrested by an almost 2 to 1 ratio in every single category, including rape, burglary, aggravated assault, motor vehicle theft, drug and weapons violations, white collar crimes, driving under the influence, and all offenses against family and children. The only offense categories that blacks led the nation in were gambling and robbery arrests. Statistically, although whites held a very slight edge in murders at 4,261 in 2010, blacks were not far behind at 4,209. In fact, according to the UCR data, in 2011 blacks led the nation with 4,149 arrests for murder, committing 49.7 percent. The demonization of the entire black American experience in the eyes of some white Americans is found in the single UCR category labeled "Murder and nonnegligent manslaughter." It has been used as the lead talking point, past, present, and future, to describe what is wrong with everything black; however, it's all smoke and mirrors once you take a closer look.

Although I use the term "black-on-black violent crime" to describe the selected behavior of some black men in this country throughout this book, let me be very clear; according to U.S. Department of Justice (2011c) statistics, since 1980, 84 percent of white Americans killed every year are killed by other white Americans. White-on-white violent crime actually lives in the same reality as black-on-black violent crime. Crime has always reflected an intraracial paradigm.

As well, although the concept of "black proportionality" is consistently used to "explain away" the crime rates of white Americans and to demonize black Americans, what we as social scientists in the field of criminal justice have consistently failed to clearly explain is that UCR data by design is the worst measuring device for crime because it only reports an outcome or effect, which for the most part is not even statistically accurate, and it does not account for the causation. In football, this is akin to counting a game-winning touchdown while ignoring the ten offensive holding penalties that led to the scoring drive. As a social scientist, this is akin to a researcher not recording or considering how or why the independent variable (IV) has been manipulated, yet continues to measure the response within the dependent variable (DV) as statistically significant.

The people who scream the concept of *black proportionality* at the top of their lungs in regards to crime refuse or fail to take into account the reality of racism, white supremacy, and white privilege (IV) and its impact on the black American experience (DV). They refuse to accept how the 400 year cumulative impact of institutionalized poverty and unequal access to employment, education, justice, and healthcare opportunities are significant variables in creating the black counter-culture of crime.

They refuse to acknowledge the UCR has always had five major scientific weaknesses regarding its credibility and reliability: (1) It reports only "self-reported crimes" by local and state police agencies; (2) it reports only the most serious crime offense in the incident; (3) it does not collect all relevant data; (4) all crimes against the United States of America (federal crimes including drugs, immigration, etc.) are omitted; and (5) it reveals more about police behavior than it does criminality (Regoli and Hewitt, 2008).

Such critics refuse to acknowledge that the overall statistics on black-on-black homicides (93 percent) are skewed because of the large number of urban drug-related killings. According to the U.S. Department of Justice (2011c) from 1980 to 2008:

1. Black victims were over-represented in homicides involving drugs, with 62.1 percent of all drug-related homicides involving black victims and 65.6 percent by black offenders. By comparison, 36.9 percent of drug-related homicide victims were white and 1 percent were victims of other races;
2. Compared with the overall percentage of murder victims who were black (47.4 percent), blacks were less likely to be victims of sex-related homicides (30.4 percent), workplace killings (12.5 percent), or homicides of elders age 65 or older (28.6 percent); and
3. Black offenders were less likely to be involved in sex-related killings (43.4 percent), workplace homicides, (25.8 percent) or homicides of elders age 65 or older (41.9 percent) compared to their overall involvement as homicide offenders (52.5 percent). (p. 12)

As well, most homicides were intraracial:

1. 84 percent of white victims were killed by whites, and
2. 93 percent of black victims were killed by blacks. (p. 13)

The same critics refuse to acknowledge that if the Uniform Crime Report considered "self-inflicted homicides" as a statistical category, the concept of "black proportionality" would never be uttered again. According to the American Association of Suicidology (2010), there were 38,364 self-inflicted homicides in 2010, which today stands as the tenth leading cause of death in America at a cost of $34 billion annually. White Americans were responsible for 34,690, or 90 percent, of all self-inflicted homicides. In fact, white males were responsible for 27,422, or 72 percent, of all self-inflicted homicides, with the highest rate in the nation (22.6 percent). Since 1986, 796,672 self-inflicted homicides have been committed in America, and if the rates have stayed consistent, white Americans have been responsible for 717,004 of these violent deaths. This does not include the estimated 800,000 suicide attempts each year. In fact, the suicide rate for white Americans jumped 40 percent between 1999 and 2010, while there has been little or no change for people of color.

They refuse to acknowledge that in stark contrast, black Americans have the lowest self-inflicted homicide rate in the nation (5.1 percent). Given the four centuries of inhuman degradation, structural injustice, oppression, and discrimination faced by black Americans, how can this amazing unknown phenomenon be explained? According to research by the University of Miami and by other social scientists around the nation, black Americans have a higher sense of self-esteem, individualism, and collectivism. Black Americans have better coping mechanisms for dealing with stress (Burns, 2006). In other words, as I've already noted in this book, black Americans have a "cultural survival gene" like no other. When incarcerated black American men realize this undisputable fact, arguably many will never intentionally seek to destroy their cultural legacy again. Black-on-black violence is not an individual crime but a collective one, perpetrated by black males who have been "hoodwinked" into a black counter-culture of crime, brainwashed by the legacy of racism, white supremacy, and white privilege.

However, where are you going to hear these truths? The reality is that while there are far too many black men in the criminal justice system—nearly 30 percent of the entire black adult population in America when we add those on probation and parole, and at significantly higher rates than other races and ethnicities in the nation—even more black men have chosen to sustain their incredible legacies inside of a college classroom than within the confines of a prison cell. Unfortunately, for many Americans, including black Americans, it is so much easier to accept an image of a young black male with saggy pants, exposing his underwear, a mouth full of "bling" with a gun in his hand, than one wearing a college graduation gown and a degree in hand.

You see, the Southside neighborhood that I called home for almost twenty years, the Roseland community, or what is commonly referred to as the "Wild 100s," sits at the heart of the violent killing fields that exist in Chicago today. The first several years of my formative childhood I was a social prisoner in one of the many "urban ghetto cages" that Chicago built to house its poorest residents: the Harold Ickes Housing Projects. However, living in Roseland ended my childhood innocence; in fact, I saw my first shooting, armed robbery, drug sale, and murder, all before the ripe old age of twelve. I witnessed first-hand "black-on-black violent crime" long before scholars coined it as a term of endearment for the plight of some young black inner-city men across the country. I was a participant/observer in the *Code of the Street* described by Elijah Anderson (1999) long before his ethnographic travels in West Philadelphia. The *Wild 100s* taught me the four basic rules of how to survive living in a poor, violent, urban black community: (1) Never get lost, (2) never find yourself in the wrong place at the wrong time, (3) never travel alone, and (4) never hang around anyone who will get you killed.

Empirically, there can be little doubt that the inner-city nihilism faced by countless black communities across the country today was a condition originally triggered by a combination of modern historical structural forces. Julius Wilson (2009) describes five structural conditions from the 1960s and 1980s that had a profound impact on inner-city poor black neighborhoods:

- Federal transportation and highway policies shifted jobs from the black inner cities to the white suburbs.
- Home mortgage financing limitations, in which race has always been a factor, left many blacks isolated and condemned to living within the confines of inner-city neighborhoods.
- Urban renewal and the building of freeway and highway networks destroyed the pedestrian patterns and economic opportunities for many inner-city blacks. Many black Americans could not then and still cannot today afford to purchase an automobile for transportation to jobs that are often ten to fifteen miles away from their inner-city residence.
- New fiscal policies drastically limited the federal aid funding to cities such as Chicago, Washington DC, St. Louis, New Orleans, and Detroit. One glance at the unemployment rates for black males, which is nearly triple the national average, along with the incredible rate of violent crimes such as murders, leaves little empirical doubt about the result of these policies.
- Inner-city blacks were left far behind as the labor market shifted from an industrial to a computer-based, high-tech work force. (pp. 144–145)

Cultural factors have also contributed to the negative plight of poor black inner-city life. Wilson (2009) added that two cultural forces played a major role: (1) national views and beliefs on race; and (2) cultural traits, i.e., shared outlooks, modes of behavior, traditions, belief systems worldviews, values, skills, preferences, styles of self-presentation, etiquette, and linguistic patterns—that emerge from patterns of intragroup, e.g., "black on black" interaction, in settings created by discrimination and segregation and that reflect collective experiences in those settings (pp. 14–15).

From an insider's perspective on crime and justice, it's the cultural forces that seem to have the most profound negative impact on the lives of incarcerated black men today, intentionally impeding successful efforts in the prison-community transition. During numerous conversations and observations with Bureau of Prisons (BOP) offenders, I have discovered that a significant segment of incarcerated black men not only understand the global and domestic negative race-based stereotypes associated with being raised in a poor urban environment—e.g., that black males are inherently violent, have all served time in prison, hate the police, sell drugs, have a handgun tucked away in their waistband, impregnate multiple women who then raise fatherless children, belittle the benefits of a formal education, and live only for the "bling" in/on their mouths, necks or cars—but that they choose to embrace these negative stereotypes as part of an alternative "black counter-culture of crime" that they've created in order to establish an identity and gain respect among peers within their own "underground criminal community." To make my point clear, there is a segment of the black male population currently in and out of prison who embrace the negative race-based stereotypes created to demean the black American experience, and who have attempted to make these ugly, intolerable, and demonizing images of young black manhood an accepted part of the overall black culture in America today. Based on my lived experiences, a clear segment of incarcerated black men will never accept the incredible historical legacy and cultural responsibilities that come with their *black cultural privilege* (BCP). They are lost in this black counter-culture of crime and do not want to be found. I understand that sounds horrible but it's the truth. As I will further illuminate throughout this book, the incarcerated black men who refuse to accept their BCP responsibilities are the worse type of traitors, because they seek to destroy the "collective spirit" that sits at the core of the black American experience. When urban poet Tupac Shakur said, "a *'nigger'* is a black man who hangs from his neck by a rope on a tree and a *'nigga'* is a black man who hangs a big gold chain from his neck," he spoke volumes about the disparate voices within the modern-day urban black American male diaspora.

I AM MY BROTHER'S KEEPER

The greatest critic I have ever met regarding this black counter-culture of crime, which was an integral part of the environment in my early life in Chicago, was also a black male, extremely violent, who could barely read or write, had an alcohol problem, and had been a one-time felon himself. This person was my dad. He was not a thug or a gangster by today's media hyped standards. His reputation for violence in our neighborhood was notorious, but this had very little to do with many of the criminogenic excuses you see today. He was simply reacting to the reality of a life in a country that despised his very existence. He was a poor black man who lived in the warped universe of Jim Crow, first in the highly racially segregated south and later in the more progressive thinking north. He was part of the "Great Migration" that brought over 5 million black Americans from states such as my dad's rural environment of Louisiana, to the big city ghettos of Chicago, only to find the "same shit" (my dad's words) he tried to leave behind.

Unlike many of the misguided black men today, my dad and his cultural generation had reason to be very angry. *Plessy v. Ferguson* (1896) and legalized segregation ruled as the law of the land. My dad and other black men did not read about white supremacy in a book or see it on television; it was part of their everyday "collectively lived experiences." They were not even considered citizens in the applied sense of the word. Jim Crow ensured my dad could never vote, go to school, use the same restroom, or eat in the same restaurant as his white male counterparts, and more importantly for him, he could never secure fair employment. My dad was forced to drink out of water fountains that read, *colored only*. My dad understood the significance of social and political equality and its enduring impact on the black American experience. He was raised in an era where you heard the revolutionary echoes of "black is beautiful" but saw the realities of police dogs and water hoses being used to subjugate the black American experience. However, my dad and other black men like him had a quality that separated them from their incarcerated counterparts today: their children were everything.

For the most part, incarcerated black men today do not put their children first. Again, I understand that sounds overly generalized and harsh; however, I was taught to speak the truth to black men. In fact, many incarcerated black men do not possess any parental bonds with their children at all. History repeats itself with the reality that some black men today simply "breed" children, similar to the plantation slave mentality described in the narratives of Frederick Douglass (1995). I would argue that many of the black men and women who currently have sons who are incarcerated have failed them as parents. This becomes painfully obvious as generation after generation falls into the servitude of incarceration. When I share these feelings in front of incarcerated black students, some immediately leave the classroom voicing profanity in my direction. What many don't understand was that my dad was one of those men at one point in his life, and if he could change and become a parent, so could they. My father was mentally and physically prepared to be treated as a second-class citizen as long as he could find a job to raise his children, because he understood that his humiliations would allow my brothers and me the humility required to a better life. I witnessed how angry and bitter he became enduring this journey for his children. He knew that his personal dreams would be sacrificed for his children. He didn't long for the "toys" of fast money, jewelry, cars, or even the identity-based respect and power so many black males yearn for today. He just wanted a chance to give his black children an opportunity for the great equalizer among the world's oppressed: an education. Looking back today, thank God I had my dad in my life.

I'm not quite sure when my father's behavior turned criminal, but I can tell you when it ended: the day I witnessed him being arrested. As several Chicago police officers banged on the front windows of our house, my dad calmly looked at me and opened the front door. As the officers rushed inside, I screamed for them to "let him go." After handcuffing him, the officers gave me that all too familiar *nigger stare* that every black man in America is conditioned to recognize as part of the warped social construct of white privilege. As my dad later explained to me, this was the most humiliating moment in his life. This was the first time I had ever witnessed him look toward the ground instead of making direct eye contact with me. He made no excuses for his behavior and shared the truth of his crimes with me later, as he decided to move forward in his life. As my dad would later tell me, "I just wanted to raise my boys and make sure they had a better life than me"; he refused to define his legacy, and more importantly the legacy of his sons and his culture, as one centered on the black counter-culture of crime. He became my personal hero and my only life mentor. Afterward, he obtained a job as a janitor, which he kept for several decades until he retired, at a private parochial school he and my mom forced me and my brothers to attend, in order to secure our access to a better life. He always preached for me to finish my education and go into the field of criminal justice, even at a very young age. My dad told me that as a black man in America, I had no choice about whether I wanted to be involved in the criminal justice system. It was simply a given. He added that the only choice I had in the matter was either "learning from the system" or "being taught by the system." My dad told me his "sacrifices" gave me choices and that most of my friends would have the criminal justice system make this choice for them.

Although he could barely read and write himself, he mandated that I read books and sharpen my academic prowess at a very young age. When he recognized that the inner-city environment could potentially take his sons, he confronted it with violent words and deeds. If anyone in my neighborhood attempted to place me in a situation that he deemed "would jeopardize my future," many who were other black men, he reacted with unbridled violence and contempt toward those individuals. He would rather die from the hands of another black man or kill another black man before he allowed his sons to be servants of the criminal justice system. My dad taught me what "real" black-on-black crime meant.

On weekends, he would open the school gymnasium, as a safe haven, and allow all the young black men in the neighborhood to play basketball all day, even though, if it had ever been discovered by his employers, he would have been terminated. He taught me how to be a 1960s style social revolutionary, an activist, and a caretaker of social justice. He taught me how to be my brother's keeper. He taught me to prepare myself to die for my children if necessary, because sometimes black dads have to die to save their children from themselves and their environment.

Today, when I go back and visit my dad in Chicago, we often talk about my Roseland neighborhood friends who were killed and swallowed up by the *War on Drugs* and imprisoned since the early 1980s. We also talk about all the ones he personally saved by just opening up a gym door and giving them *access* to hope. My dad taught me how to transform humiliation into humility, and he inspired me to channel the socially constructed shame and anger that come with racism, white supremacy, and white privilege into a vehicle of social justice and education. In every way, I'm the person my dad taught me to be and an extension of his own dreams.

THE WOLF

Fast forward to 1993 and I'm a police-detective assigned to the Melbourne Police Department's Special Operations Unit, working as a member of the Department of Justice's (DOJ) Organized Crime Drug Enforcement Task Force (OCDETF). Funny thing, but as a police officer assigned to a federal drug task force, I still looked at myself as a predatory wolf, similar to those who stalked my childhood neighborhoods when I was young, but just hunting a different type of prey. My territory was the Middle District of Florida, and I was very good at my job. In fact, in 2001 I was named the Region IV Narcotic Officer of the Year. My highly tuned "cultural survival gene" provided me with street instincts that simply gave me an unfair advantage, especially with urban black males trapped in a counter-culture of crime. Although I never officially kept a body count, I was easily responsible for the arrests and incarcerations of thousands of black males during my law enforcement career, who, just like me, grew up in marginalized violent communities living under the code of the street (Anderson, 1999). You see, in federal criminal investigations, the most important facet in the entire enforcement process was the post-arrest interview or proffer, where you had an opportunity to convince offenders to cooperate and provide information on others involved in criminal activities, in order to obtain a reduced prison sentence. I was a great interviewer because the person sitting across the table was often a young black man just like me, and I could relate to his unchanneled anger, fear, shame, and cultural humiliation.

Anyone who works in the law enforcement culture, and yes, it is very much a culture, and whoever tells you that being a black male police officer does not have its own unique challenges regarding issues of racial stratification is being disingenuous at best or living in a state of complete denial at worst. You witness first-hand the institutional and systematic displays of racism from police officers, prosecuting and defense attorneys, correctional staff, judges, and worse, you witness the despicable lack of executive-level leadership and courage to address these issues, yet the criminal justice system does not skip a beat. You have an intimate backstage pass to explore one of the most sought-after and "exotic" research subjects ever studied in the behavioral and social sciences: the role of race in the criminal justice system. Yet, very few if any black police officers ever bother to seek these answers. Matters of race, crime, and justice are thrown in your face on a daily basis, yet the policing culture attempts to condition black officers to filter it out, in order to perpetuate a universal "collective colorblindness." Complicating matters, I truly believe the overwhelming majority of my white colleagues in the criminal justice field were not racists; however, when they witnessed racist behavior from others in my presence, they would often not lift a finger to stop it, assuming it was my sole responsibility as a person of color to lead the charge against racial injustice. This is the same exact narrative I heard shared by many of my fellow black police colleagues throughout my career, which I discovered, was a subculture within a culture. For the many living outside of this black policing subculture, it is almost impossible for me to put into words the incredible pressure that you live and work under as a black male police officer. Nobody can relate to your world. You can face issues of racial injustice from fellow white colleagues and solidarity from black colleagues internally, while at the same time, you are utterly despised by and alienated from the majority of the external black community that depends on the money generated by their family members involved in the black counter-culture of crime. At the same time, you receive accolades and enjoy the perks of being a law enforcement officer within the white external community.

THE BLACK POLICE OFFICERS' CODE

One of the first truths you learn as a black male police officer, if you choose to open your eyes and ears wide enough, is that the criminal justice system is flawed in its original design because it reflected the racially oppressive and marginalized beliefs of a society and government of an America in its infancy stage. Thus, because of these flaws at birth, the justice system continues to unfairly impact the lives of people of color in unimaginable ways today, helping to perpetuate a cycle of counter-cultural self-destruction that has imprisoned one-third of an entire generation of black men. As well, and for the most part, there is very little that a black police officer individually will be able to do to end this cycle. Alexander (2010) was somewhat critical in her overall assessment of police officers of color and their complacent role in the *War on Drugs* when she wrote:

> Profound racial injustices occur when minority police officers follow the rules. It is a scandal when the public learns they have broken the rules, but no rules need to be broken for the systematic mass incarceration of people of color to proceed unabated. This uncomfortable fact creates strong incentives for minority officers to deny, to rationalize, or

to be willingly blind to the role of law enforcement in creating a racial undercaste. . . . If the caste dimensions of mass incarceration were better understood and the limitations of cosmic diversity were better appreciated, the existence of black police chiefs and black police officers would be no more encouraging today than the presence of black slave drivers and black plantation owners hundreds of years ago. (p. 237)

I wish it were so simple. First, black police officers are not just police officers. I am also a black father, a black husband, a black intellectual, and a black American. My socially constructed race transcended every level of my being, both when I was on or off duty. I too, like many other black Americans across the country, have been illegally targeted by the criminal justice system, racially profiled on I-95 in Florida driving my police department issued Range Rover with my noticeable dreadlocks on countless occasions. Even as a university professor today, my locks and skin color continue to serve as *cultural reasonable suspicion* to stop me every time I drive my 2013 Cadillac SRX on I-86 in New York State. The police never see the father, husband, former cop, or PhD when they stop me, but the black man they believe is transporting drugs or guns. The police see the same black man who has been arrested thousands of times previously in our country, matching the exact same physical profile as myself. How can I be angry at just the police because they are not acting alone in this shameful crime? Truth be told, black men who have been caught trafficking drugs and guns and who live within the counter-culture of crime are just as culpable as the police officers that conduct these unlawful stops. As a black father, husband, and American, I am ashamed, angry, and humiliated that my son's historical legacy, his black cultural privilege, is being handed over to an uncaring criminal justice system and, more hurtful, by an undermining, statistical handful of generationally lost black men trapped in a counter-culture of crime.

Second, black police officers simply feed off the racial complacency of not only the criminal justice system, but also of black communities alike. This racial complacency is spurred by the reality that all communities, including black communities, encourage police officers to make arrests. In the overwhelming majority of drug investigations and subsequent arrests I've made primarily on black males, it was the very same black communities where these men resided that made the initial incident complaint; however, these same communities would be the first to voice their disgust that too many black men were being targeted and arrested. Clearly, these same black communities understood that the only mechanism that police will use to address criminal incidents in the black community is to effect an arrest on their black father, black brother, or black nephew? To scream that a racial injustice has occurred after the fact is not only transparent to black police officers but reeks of the type of hypocrisy that serves to feed the *triad of culpability*. I hope this book will help clarify the transgenerational harm and suffering the black counter-culture of crime creates within the collective consciousness of a black community.

Finally, although the majority of black male police officers I came into contact with during my career clearly understood the holistic racially oppressive nature of policing, how can anyone defend the overt actions of black men engaging in collective crimes that harm their very own black community? I have never arrested a black male in my career or even known of any who specifically sold drugs in order to pay for the college education of their black brother, sister, mother, or cousin. I'm not saying that drugs are not sold as a means of obtaining life's many necessities, but for the most part they are not sold for some community or family-based philanthropic endeavor. That is a Hollywood myth and the simple reality is, whether black, white, brown, or yellow, many people sell drugs because they have an addiction to money, and communities, including black communities, must understand and respect this truism. As well, black male police officers see first-hand the vile direct impact that some black men who engage in criminal behavior have on their own communities, especially on their families and children. Do you really expect black police officers not to make an arrest knowing these facts? In fact, many times in the criminal justice system, black male police officers are the only entity that sincerely cares about the wellbeing of black men and black communities across the country. Truth be told, profound injustices occur when black male police officers "don't" actively involve themselves in the criminal justice system. Black male police officers learn to become "mitigators" within the criminal justice system: to enforce the law with a keen understanding of how the criminal justice system contributes to racial stratification, and to choose enforcement strategies that inflict the least amount of systemic damage, if at all possible.

BECOMING A NEIGHBORHOOD MITIGATOR

I am often asked primarily by other black Americans and always by incarcerated black students at FCI McKean, (only because I believe some whites are way too uncomfortable), if I feel distraught as a black man for contributing to the mass incarceration and the creation of the *New Jim Crow*. I have been referred to as an *Uncle Tom,* or a *House Negro* by several incarcerated black students involved in my post-secondary programs because of my former law enforcement career. However, it's a great question and I always applaud the incarcerated students who are courageous enough to ask it. It deserves to be addressed, regardless of the context of the message or the messenger. Without hesitation my response is always the same. I give them a "real talk" response and request that they agree to listen to my explanation. I tell them that I worked for the 95 percent of the American population who were not involved in the counter-culture of crime. I tell them that I worked for the 70 percent of all black Americans who were not involved in the black counter-culture crime. I tell them that I believed this concept then and believe it to this day. I tell them that if they were involved in the counter-culture of crime, whether black, white, Hispanic, or Asian, they were "fucked."

In my Roseland neighborhood in Chicago, I personally witnessed black males "terrorize" the community with violence, literally holding people hostage within their own homes. I witnessed children forced to live their lives within the confines of a bedroom instead of playing basketball at Palmer Park, because it was controlled by black gangs. The only type of people that would stand up and confront the type of young black men who would use violence to control a community would be other violent black men like my father. They were the *neighborhood mitigators*. I would watch my father interact with "street hustlers" and lay down the rules of engagement, protecting my brothers and me from their violence and more importantly, their influence. My friends who did not have a father or a father-figure quickly fell prey to these "street wolves" and their bullshit fake black counter-culture lifestyle. My father and other men similar to him were the only thing that stood between "black victimizers and black victims." The problem was, these "neighborhood mitigators" got too old, were killed, or moved their families away from the area, leaving the wolves to tend the sheep. As my father continually encouraged me to go into law enforcement and become a *mitigator* to "protect the sheep from the wolves," he cautioned me that the other black men would despise my very existence and accuse me of doing the "slave masters' work." I was reminded that the only people who were capable of fighting the Africans involved in the Atlantic slave trade were other Africans. I was reminded that it was the moral duty of Africans to go to war with other Africans involved in the slave trade. I was reminded that upwards to one million African and black Americans were killed fighting those involved in the slave trade, and that by fighting the wolves, I might be killed as well. I vowed to become a mitigator, just like my dad, at any cost.

Thus, during my law enforcement career I have *never* arrested a black man for a drug or weapon violation in my life where another black man (father, brother, uncle, cousin, friend, etc.) had not betrayed him, and the entire black American culture, by supplying him drugs to sell or a handgun to use, thus becoming the gatekeeper for indoctrinating him into the *black counter-culture of crime* and perpetuating crimogenic conditions. I have *never* lied on a police report, falsely testified in front of a federal grand jury, or misled a prosecutor and judge, in order to frame a black man for a crime. I *never* made my money, and policing is a career with great employment benefits, by "culturally victimizing" my own black community, unlike many of the young black men whom I arrested. I have *never* used my incredible powers as a law enforcement agent to intentionally disrespect or belittle the family or community members of a black man who was in my custody. Finally, I *never* lost my sense of humility when faced with a counter-culture of black men who, if given an opportunity, would have made my son fatherless in the pursuit of their own underground economic and social addictions to money and identity-based "hood fame." What made me different? My self-actualization and awareness of humiliation and humility. This meant establishing a *moral duty* as a criminal justice professional to treat everyone, especially black men, regardless of the nature of their crime or whether they used lies, deception, and manipulation as a criminal defense, with the same respect and dignity as if they were my own father. I admit that finding *humility* is not an easy task for any police officer who has lived and experienced the destructive *humiliation* a black counter-culture of crime can wreak on a black community; however, for me this was applied social justice.

My policing career involved many years examining the black counter-culture of crime discussed throughout this book, and to be truthful, there was an accepted and mutual contempt, between the policing culture and this black counter-culture of crime. I tried to explain to black men trapped within this counter-culture of crime that my job, while acknowledging the historical truths of the overt and covert acts of racism and structural violence that have epitomized the criminal justice system over the past century, was to protect the true victims of their behavior, black children, so they would have an opportunity to pursue their dreams and rightful *black cultural privilege* (BCP). I explained to them that I was a *mitigator*. The only way that could be done was to incarcerate the "dream-killers," be they black, white, brown, or yellow.

I would argue that many of the self-appointed self-described *dream-killers* in the black community whom I've arrested share one central common characteristic with many of their victims: they themselves are black men. Again, I am not trying to minimize the horrific social and psychological impact that government-supported racism, oppression, and structural violence have had on young black males because I lived in that reality; however, truth be told, black men actually do commit crimes and have played a very destructive hand in perpetuating this counter-culture of crime and victimization within the black community (Dyson, 1996; West, 2001). Damn, I know that sounds cold and distant but we have to stop lying to our very own black men, especially those who are incarcerated.

I tell them the truth about what they are doing not only to themselves, but what they do to the cultural image of every black American from a global perspective. The only people who can end the genocide of black men and restore the true legacy of the black American experience are the dream-killers. The problem has been convincing these incarcerated young black men to invest in themselves and their black communities, contributing to the global advancement of the arts, sciences, humanities, and social policy. This book serves to provide a pedagogical framework, using the *Humiliation to Humility Perspective* (HHP), for transforming *dream-killers* into *dream-makers*. Reflecting back, some of the best times of my professional and personal life were as a police officer, solidifying life-long friendships and memories that are simply unforgettable. However, it will always be soiled with the distant yet tainted aroma of injustice if I remain silent and do not contribute to a constructive dialogue centered on collective redemption and social justice.

THE BLACK INTELLECTUAL

Teaching has always been my calling, which I think is a natural extension of the lived black American experience. In my courses today at the University of Pittsburgh (Bradford), criminal justice majors often tell me that they sit in class and daydream about future careers as police officers. Funny, but when I was a police officer, I daydreamed about a future career as a university professor. I always thought of myself as an artist in many ways, and I was keenly aware of the impact I could have nurturing the intellectual and spiritual growth of college students in the social sciences, especially in regards to the three-dimensional relationship between race, crime, and justice. My lived black experiences, as a practitioner, observer, and scholar in the criminal justice system, coupled with my self-actualization skills that have allowed me to connect each of these paradigms, have left me with an incredible social canvas upon which to paint. As a people who understand their amazingly rich historical legacy and life journey, from the birthplace of humanity to the incredible struggles of the institutionalized inequities of oppression, marginalization, and structuralized racism, black Americans know the great equalizer that falls under the mantle of education. Black Americans, at least at one point, understood that *education* is more than just a word. It encompasses everything black Americans have been denied since twenty Angolan Africans arrived on the shores of Jamestown, Virginia, in 1619, and everything black Americans need to re-take their rightful place in global history. For countless black Americans, education has always been the framework and setting for social justice movements, ranging from the Black Panther Party to the Nation of Islam, fighting the protracted conflicts associated with the universally destructive force of a Fanon-styled colonialism.

Fast forward to 2013, and I'm a tenured professor at Pitt. As one of only seventy or so tenured black American professors in the academic discipline of criminal justice in the country, as well as one of fewer than fifteen or so black American criminal justice program directors in the country, I seem to have gone from one racial subculture in policing to an even smaller racial subculture in academia. The Ivory Tower shares many of the same racial injustices I witnessed within the criminal justice system: very few black male university professors within and outside of my academic discipline; poor representation in executive-level administrative positions; race-baiting peers who hide behind the cloak of liberalism; and a dearth of black men to serve in the role of academic guides. It has always amazed me how so many white professors flex their "academic middle finger" at the criminal justice system because of its unjust propensity for the mass incarceration efforts regarding people of color, and at the same time, they mirror the exact same warped agenda of race and class domination under the umbrella of *white privilege* in academia. The term "qualified" is operationally defined to promote racial exclusion instead of inclusion in regards to hiring and promoting black faculty members. However, this does not provide a ready-made excuse for me to ignore my duty to promote social justice within the academic ranks. As a black intellectual with tenure, I have the unique ability to effect transformative change within the criminal justice system by way of the Ivory Tower's sacred tenets of scholarship, research, and community outreach. That said, everything is not what it appears.

LEARNING MY TRUE DUTIES

In graduate school and even later during my doctoral studies, I was never reinforced to understand my true duties as a black intellectual: to use scholarship in order to advance the understanding and plight of the collective lived black American experience. As a social scientist, my doctoral emphasis at NSU was conflict analysis, where I focused my research in the areas of crime and justice. I was taught how to conduct research and produce scholarship, follow models of classroom instruction, and recognize the importance of service to the university; however, not a single lesson was taught from the pedagogical perspective of the lived black American experience. None of my professors ever told me that as a black intellectual, my journey within the Ivory Tower extended far beyond the very basic requirements of tenure and promotion. I was going to have to discover this invisible fact on my own. I used to wonder whether it was because all of my professors were white and had no idea of the internal complexities of navigating academia for black scholars, or they simply did not care enough about the advancement of black scholarship. In fact, over a span of seven years or so, the dearth of course booklists that promoted any specific Afrocentric erudition or black American authors gave me incredible pause to my commitment to a career in academia. It amazes me even today how one could academically process the concept of "conflict resolution" at the doctoral level, yet not have a single black American male faculty member in the program, and not inherently take a critical examination of the black experience in America from the perspective of a black American male author. It's not that my doctoral readings did not provide scholarly insight into the destructive root causes of direct, structural, and protracted acts of institutional violence, but they simply lacked the depth required to express the collective narrative of the black American experience. Fortunately, my exposure to African Diaspora and Pan-Africanism during my early formative academic years, coupled with my professional career in criminal justice, allowed me to integrate the lived black American experience into my doctoral studies.

Like many other aspiring black male scholars before me, my *reinforcement* came from exposing myself to the plethora of historic works of black American intellectuals such as W.E.B. Du Bois, E. Franklin Frazier, and John Henrik Clarke. Their collective narratives lit an intellectual fire in my soul that has never been extinguished, and forever cemented into my psyche the steadfast moral obligation as a black scholar. Du Bois (1903a) stated:

> The Negro Race, like all races, is going to be saved by its exceptional men. The problem of education then, among Negroes, must first of all deal with the "Talented Tenth." It is the problem of developing the best of this race that they may guide the Mass away from the contamination and death of the worst. (p. 33)

According to Frazier (1920):

> The new spirit which has produced the New Negro bids fair to transform the whole race. America faces a new race that has awakened, and in the realization of its strength has girt its loins to run the race with other men. (p. 71)

Finally, Clarke added in the Wesley Snipes (1996) documentary, *A Great and Mighty Walk:*

> Powerful people cannot afford to educate the people that they oppress, because once you are truly educated, you will not ask for power. You will take it.

Due to the dearth of black professors, even as a new tenure-stream faculty member back in 2006, I found myself automatically becoming the *de facto* voice for "everything black" at UPB. Black student organizations and clubs will demand your time, energy, and guidance. Some of your colleagues will automatically lose interest if they discover your research agenda is focused too much on black American diaspora or they label you as a "black radical." Administrators will attempt to bully you into serving as a member on as many committees as they can find, in order to simply promote a face of diversity. Fortunately for me, I had four things going for me. First, I entered academia as a very seasoned professional and had developed excellent time management skills. Second, I was a veteran at being a black man in a majority white American career field, so my level of intimidation was at zero. Third, I had already developed the highly sought-after skill of politely saying, "No thanks." Finally and the most important, the campus president was a black man, was highly experienced in the "ways" of academia, and provided me with the type of guidance that became invaluable during my tenure-stream journey. In fact, I would not be where I am at today without his guidance. He supported and encouraged me to pursue my academic research interests without hesitation, knowing they focused on uncomfortable issues of social justice. He unwaveringly supported my community-based endeavors, where I spent a great deal of time outside of the classroom building a relationship with FCI McKean. In fact, a psychologist by discipline, he spent a good amount of time sharing his thoughts about the three dimensional relationship between crime, justice, and race during many of our conversations.

THE HUMILIATION TO HUMILITY PERSPECTIVE (HHP)

I'm academically cut from the *Frazierian* model of research, inspired by E. Franklin Frazier's classic work *The Negro Family in Chicago* (1932). To examine the black experience in America, which I perceive is my moral duty, you must work within the connective "lived" dimension, past, present, and future. Only then can you inspire a *true* plan for action and dynamic change within the black American experience. As Malcolm X (1965) said:

> I for one believe that if you give people a thorough understanding of what confronts them and the basic causes that produce it, they'll create their own program, and when the people create a program, you get action. (p. 118)

The goal of this book is to introduce a new pedagogical theory, a "blue-print" for an inclusive post-secondary formula that can be used as a foundation for a successful prison-community transition for incarcerated black men. This book seeks to break the cycle of the *socially constructed lies* faced by so many black men who fill our nation's prisons and jails, by confronting the black counter-culture of crime, through the simple concept of owning the truth. It is designed to transform the mindset of black criminal offenders into *black students who are incarcerated* and to encourage prisons and jails across the nation to also transform their paradigms from *correctional facilities* into *correctional learning centers*. My pedagogical framework, the *Humiliation to Humility Perspective* (HHP), was forged over three decades of ongoing scholarship, self-actualization, and critical discussions with black men trapped within a counter-culture of crime, incarcerated black students, incarcerated black students who have successfully made their transition back into their respective communities, prison staff, police and probation officers, prosecutors, and judges from local, state, and federal criminal justice perspectives.

OWNING ONE'S TRUTH

HHP was designed to shift the responsibility of reentry, if that's what we choose to call it, onto the incarcerated student's own truths, and wherever that takes him. Because at the end of the day, the transition from government correctional servitude into collective community redemption is an individual journey, and one that requires the knowledge of choice. How can anyone make real choices if they don't know the truth? Within this context, I hope to inspire a critical discussion of the criminal justice system and of its relationship with incarcerated black men involved with the prison-community transition process. I wanted to create a pedagogy that would transform the ugly label of the *black male offender* to a *black male student* who happens to be incarcerated. I wanted to provide an educational formula to address the accumulated effects of the *politics of shaming, self-segregation* and *transgenerational learned helplessness* that have served as insurmountable psychosocial obstacles for so many incarcerated black men attempting to make the successful transition back into owning their respective lives. I also wanted to create an opportunity for incarcerated black students to use the power of knowledge to become a *sustainable whole person by truth,* leaving the historic lies of the past that were active co-conspirators in their previous lifestyle of crime, and to create topics for their future university class assignments, dissertations, journal articles, or books.

With the HHP, I envision a criminal justice system that acknowledges that only through *truth* can this social institution begin to rebuild the reputation of the black American experience that it had such a critical role in destroying. A system that understands the true concept of justice is found in redemption and reconciliation from everyone impacted by crime. This truth would acknowledge the existence of a 400–year-old structural and institutional war that has been levied against the physical and mental state of black American males. Only acknowledging this truth would force the much needed reform of the criminal justice system. Truth would end the race-based *psychosocial fear* of the justice system that black Americans have been historically conditioned to bear. Truth would inspire one third of all black males who are currently servants of the criminal justice system, to make their first real choice: to live as a free man in body and spirit or accept being part of the "three fifths" compromise and stay the property of the United States of America. Truth would effectively end the black male counter-culture of crime that we have today. Truth would empower the justice system to become true partners of social change, by working with the black community to address issues of crime as well as by creating a correctional process that uses culturally responsive post-secondary college educational opportunities to keep formerly incarcerated black men at home with their children: a system that would understand and respect the truth of transforming *correctional facilities* into *correctional learning centers*.

You see, what the criminal justice system has failed to recognize is that the successful prison-community transition for incarcerated black men entails more than appropriating job skills, providing technical training, creating resumes, offering drug and alcoholic treatment, completing a GED, and implementing all the evidence-based behavioral modification programs you can dream up. Because at the end of the day, American history has taught us that society has never taken the success of any of these factors into consideration in their treatment of black male ex-offenders. In fact, American history has taught us that black men who have never seen the inside of a prison cell or probation office, and who have done everything this country has asked of them educationally and professionally, continue to face discriminatory hardships based on one central factor: the nation's fear of black men. The fear of black males has generated millions of discussions, talking points, CNN specials, and countless journal articles and book publications; in reality, however, these conversations haven't gotten us one step closer to surmounting this man-made barrier. The fear of black men runs so deep that black Americans needed *Brown v. Board of Education*, the Civil Rights Act, and the Voting Rights Act just to be considered asymmetrical "legal citizens" in this country. What we painfully learned as a people is that, when structural institutions define one's cultural history, something that is part of everyone's natural birthright, the only thing accomplished is a legacy of humiliation for those who are being oppressed. For one-third of all adult black males, this humiliation, whether societal-based or self-inflicted, has led them into the welcoming arms of the criminal justice system. The HHP attempts to *fill the gap* between the "tangible basic skills" one can learn in any prison reentry program, and the "intangible spiritual injustices" such as shame, self-segregation, and the loss of dignity, respect, and hope, that await every black man as psychosocial obstacles once he removes himself from the physical confines of correctional servitude.

The last six years or so serving as a post-secondary educator, volunteering in the implementation of reentry initiatives at the Bureau of Prisons (BOP) Federal Correctional Institution (FCI) McKean, have provided me with unparalleled insight into the interconnectedness between race, crime, and justice, but also into the vital role post-secondary prison programs can play in inspiring reconciliation, self-actualization, and transformational social redemption. Every incarcerated black man owes to himself, his children, and his community these three "gifts of humility," for the true consequence of his crimes has levied the greatest social cost:

destroying the legacy of *black cultural privilege* (BCP). This is the same type of humility Stanley "Tookie" Williams tried to earn regarding his crimes perpetrated as a black man, and for the result of his crimes against the black community. As he sat on death row clearly knowing he would be executed, Williams (2004) wrote:

> My redemption is a continual process of change that promotes day-to-day improvement in my life. No one can give redemption to me; no one can intercede on my behalf. I have to earn it myself. Even now, attempting to clarify this experience, I fall short. I don't expect anyone who's not had this sort of experience to comprehend it or be able to relate to the redemptive struggle by a condemned man. I have swum in the gutter among the dead, but had the fortitude to step out of the filth, wash off, and walk among the living. Redemption is not a discriminable commodity based on classism, elitism, political favorism, gender, race, creed, or color. Redemption awaits everybody . . . this prison environment is not a reflection of me, nor am I addicted to its deadening and vicious manipulations. (pp. 302–303)

EPIC FAILURE

Located in northwest Pennsylvania, FCI McKean is designated as a medium security facility housing approximately 1200 male inmates, with an additional 300 male offenders in the adjacent minimum security satellite prison camp. When I taught my very first Victim Impact Program class in 2007 as part of a reentry initiative at FCI McKean, I was provided with the curriculum lesson plan created by the Department of Justice Office of Victims of Crime (2013). In fact, I had never taught an educational program within the confines of a prison before; my only contact with federal offenders had been that on the opposite end, investigating and arresting them for drug and weapon offenses as a law enforcement officer. However, I was very comfortable in federal prison settings, having spent a great deal of time at the Coleman Federal Corrections Complex in Florida interviewing offenders who were cooperating with criminal investigations.

Within minutes of reviewing the comprehensive lesson plan, I immediately knew why so many reentry programs, although started with very good intentions, ultimately failed. It was comprised of thirteen individual training units, which included written assignments, group activities, and DVDs. The majority of the training units focused on understanding the impact of criminal offenses such as burglary, robbery, sexual assault, homicide, etc.; however, I immediately noticed three pedagogical red flag issues: (1) Drug trafficking and immigration violations were missing from the training units. This gave me great pause, because the overwhelming majority of the 200,000 plus federal offenders held in the custody of the BOP, over 60 percent in fact, were incarcerated for either drug or immigration offenses. (2) Not a single word in the lesson plan considered the personal characteristics or culture of their primary audience, other than the fact they were all "offenders." The offenders were considered pedagogically "neutral" regardless of any cultural or ethnic nuances. Again, this was alarming considering that over 72 percent of the BOP population was either black or Hispanic (Federal Bureau of Prisons, 2013). However, I did notice a photo in the "Introduction" section depicting two sets of holding-hands, each of a white person, being used as a symbol for victimhood. And finally, (3) the language and tone of the entire lesson plan was designed to keep its audience in an "offender's mindset" instead of just serving as an educational tool that advances critical thinking and critical engagement on the historic cycle of victimization. For example, the "Getting Started" section states:

> Welcome to Victim Impact: Listen and Learn. This program helps you to learn about the impact of crime on victims. You will have opportunities to learn information and skills that benefit you. The program challenges you to begin to focus on other people . . . people you have harmed. This is not a class about sentencing laws or offender rights. The focus is on victims. Although you may already think about the people that you have victimized, you may not know what it feels like to be victimized yourself. During this program, you will participate in activities, watch videos, and hear victims speak. You will see and hear directly from victims about how their lives have changed. (p. 1)

After giving this some additional thought over a period of a few days, it became clear to me that this lesson plan was intentionally designed to avoid the "invisible three dimensional elephant in the room," race, white supremacy, and white privilege. It's almost as if, if you ignore the issue, it's not an issue. How can you have a prison-based educational program on victim impact and not formally address the impact of race within the context of crime and justice? As well and more importantly, the pedagogical framework of the lesson plan was designed to maintain and enable the *politics of shaming* mindset produced by a "you vs. me" paradigm. If the goal is to create an effective and transformative learning environment, the climate must address and treat the audience as "incarcerated students," not "criminal offenders." This is the same type of careless educational environment that has crippled the learning experiences of young black males across the nation for generations (Gay, 2010). This is quite easy to understand if the people designing and implementing the programs are not culturally responsive educators. However, with only a couple of days before the start of my first class, and with no other options, I felt like a man preparing to walk the proverbial plank.

To be quite frank, as I stood in front of the first fifty to sixty federal offenders who were predominantly black, I was embarrassed. Embarrassed that if I followed this lesson plan and pedagogy verbatim, I would not only be regurgitating the same type of generic behavioral modification hype that had done little or nothing to address the black counter-culture of crime, but also a pedagogical framework that did not address the "transgenerational learned helplessness" that has infected so many young urban black males over the past three decades. Just to be clear, I've discovered that the overwhelming majority of BOP offenders are so grateful that any "civilian" educator would invest their own time to speak to them, that the content of the program often becomes secondary. And yes, the race and gender of the educator do matter for a variety of issues, both from an individual and institutional perspective. In fact, my experience suggests that most of the post-secondary educators in prison programs are white females. Although I will touch on this theme later in the book, these motivations are better left for another research endeavor. But at the same time, please don't be fooled. The often high illiteracy rates reported in prisons among offenders *do not* correlate with a low aptitude for learning and comprehending even the most complex schol-arly material. I've witnessed graduate-level erudition among BOP incar-cerated students with nothing more than GEDs. I will also amplify this theme later in the book, when I discuss teaching an Inside-Out Prison Program course.

After all of this, did I continue to follow the self-proclaimed evidence-based Department of Justice victim impact program protocol? You bet I did, and the awkward, half-asleep distant stares, mixed with responses riddled with an undercurrent of sarcasm and, more importantly, a cli-mate of educational fear, told me everything I needed to know. A "cli-mate of fear" is indicative that the participants don't want to say any-thing critical about the content of the program, fearing that it will offend the educator and would cause them not to return. So, for the most part, the overwhelming majority of incarcerated students will tolerate "bull-shit content" because they simply don't have a choice in the matter. I was determined not to follow this pattern and spoke to the participants dur-ing the final week of the program, a mixture of what I would term *30 percenters and 70 percenters* again, and asked them what they really thought of the program. I wanted to engage in a critical discussion on every aspect of the course. Thankfully, I built just enough trust where the incarcerated students could be open and honest. They told me the pro-gram and its curriculum were a fraud, just another gimmick they had seen and heard many times their entire lives, from police, attorneys, fami-ly, and fellow street hustlers. Their survival instincts told them to simply "tune-out" the message and the messenger regardless of its intent, but to tolerate it because it got them out of their cells.

I learned many very important lessons in this "epic failure" that would be instrumental in the development of my pedagogical theory, the HHP. Based on my conversations with incarcerated students, most pris-on programs are demeaning and are created to speak generically at them, not to them, and often address issues that are not relevant to their own unique lived experiences. I learned seven fundamental pedagogical truths in implementing a successful prison-based educational experience: (1) Connect the content of the curriculum with the *truths* and lived experiences of the incarcerated student audience. Incarcerated students need to be critically engaged by acknowledging and respecting their cultural nuances. (2) Prison-based pedagogyies subconsciously perpetuate the behavioral modification model of "adolescent servitude," addressing the incarcerated students as if they were disruptive children who will be placed into time-out or will have their cartoon privileges revoked if they do not behave. In other words, the tone should always address them as adults, whether the contextual message is perceived as good, bad, or indifferent. (3) Prison-based pedagogies are fundamentally designed around the premise that the incarcerated student is perceived as an abstract social problem from birth, and needs to be somehow rescued from himself. You must ensure the message is loud and clear to incarcerated students, that they are the *key* to ending the cultural cycle of psychological and physical incarceration. (4) Don't insult their intelligence. Prison-based pedagogies are designed from a perspective of illiteracy. Incarcerated students want to be intellectually inspired and challenged within the academic paradigm and will thrive in such an environment. (5) Most curriculum is largely designed by "outsiders" with the "inside" audience having very little *true ownership* of the final product. Make sure incarcerated students are not only part of the curriculum discussions, but get their "sign-off" on all issues, giving them equally cited credit for any new concepts, ideas, or themes. (6) Never avoid the topic of racism. In fact, your pedagogical framework should take into account racism, white supremacy, white privilege, and the historical impact of these social constructs on the relationship between crime and justice. And finally, (7) Remember that your audience will be "incarcerated students" not "criminal offenders." Implement a pedagogy that addresses the realities of this psychosocial dynamic and educational climate.

THE PEDAGOGICAL RACIAL GAP

I was determined not to make these same mistakes. First, I needed to rediscover my pedagogical framework. Others have found motivation on their prison-based teaching experiences, using the works of Paulo Freire, Michel Foucault, or similar followers of critical pedagogy to frame the dichotomies inherent in facilitating any academic program, but these would not suffice for me. I needed to create a new and specific pedagogical framework. One that addressed a unique pedagogical "cultural code" (Hooks, 2003). My student audience was incarcerated black men, and without diminishing the works of Freire and other similar scholars of critical pedagogy, those scholars do not know or understand the collective lived black American experience. In fact, Freire openly acknowledges his pedagogical limitations, seeing America only through the eyes of his own white maleness (Freire, 1970). Similar to traditional educational settings, one of the most glaring questions that continue to remain unanswered in classrooms behind prison walls is the pedagogical approach that best serves the needs and interests of the incarcerated student. In fact, there is a pronounced scarcity of educational literature and research about prison-based post-secondary education pedagogy, specifically as it relates to incarcerated black male students.

Clearly, the most educationally disadvantaged population in the United States is housed in our nation's jails and prisons, where the disproportional "faces and voices" of those incarcerated are black males. Today, over 830,000 offenders, nearly 40 percent of the 2.2 million people incarcerated in our nation's prisons, are black men (West, Sabol, and Greenman, 2011). According to the most recent census of state and federal correctional facilities, 35 percent of our nation's nearly 4,600 correctional facilities offer prison-based post-secondary education (PSE) programming; however, less than 9 percent of the estimated 100,500 offenders enrolled in prison-based college courses are black men (Harlow, 2003; Erisman, and Contardo, 2005; Stephan, 2008; Spycher, Shkodriani, and Lee, 2012; American Correctional Association, 2007). The exact reasons for the low black male participation are unknown because of a critical dearth of scholarship in this field; however, cautionary lessons learned nationwide suggest two primary barriers: (1) poor academic performance; and (2) a lack of critical engagement on the part of black males.

Nearly soxty years after *Brown v. Board of Education*, a significant portion of black males are still not graduating from high school. According to the Schott Foundation for Public Education (2012) roughly 52 percent of black males graduate from high school within four years, nearly 26 percent behind white males. Notwithstanding the "school to prison pipeline" phenomenon that has become a social institution for black males nationwide over the past four decades, the academic prowess and intellectual potential of incarcerated black male students is challenging all of these assumptions. Based upon data from the *National Assessment of Adult Literacy Prison Survey*, incarcerated black males who have a high school diploma or GED/high school equivalency certificate, and who academically qualify to enroll in PSE courses, have higher literacy scores on all scales than non-incarcerated black males living across the nation in the general population (Greenberg, Dunleavy, and Kutner, 2007). As a post-secondary educator working with the BOP FCI McKean, I see that this type of academic achievement is commonplace. I would challenge anyone who participated in my upper-level *ADMJ 1365: Reentry and the Offender* course and not leave thinking to themselves that some of the brightest students in the country are urban black males residing behind bars. Intellectual prowess among incarcerated black male students is not the problem.

However, the educational connectivity between critical engagement and pedagogy raises concern. Since the start of the correctional "Golden Age" in the early 1970s, the critical pedagogical movement has been infused into the foundation of post-secondary prison programming (Corcoran, 1985; Ryan and McCabe, 1994). The most distinguishing claim of the Freirean approach is that it is both "a form of cooperative educational practice and a form of collective educational action" for its practitioners (Forbes and Kaufman, 2008, p. 27). Critical pedagogists suggest that such practitioners not only encourage a learning environment that recognizes micro- and macro-level power imbalances that create oppressive social structures both on the "inside and outside" of the classroom, but that they are also moved to change these power imbalances.

An ever growing body of literature has raised some serious questions and supports a tempered skepticism of the "critical pedagogical movement," largely due to the field's dismissive analytical inclusion and application toward race and racism (Bell, 1992; Foster, 1997; Irvine, 1988, 1990; Lynn, 1999; Leonardo, 2005; Rossatto, Allen, and Pruyn, 2006). In the mid-1970s, motivated in large part by the inequalities of racism ingrained into our nation's legal system as applied to black Americans, Derrick Bell developed what is known today as Critical Race Theory (CRT). Bell suggested that "we use a number of different voices, but all recognize that racial subordination maintains and perpetuates the American social order" (Delgado and Stefancic, 2005, p. 83). Critical race theory scholars argue that

> CRT, as an analytical framework for addressing issues of social inequity, can be utilized as a way in which to uncover the racism embedded within American social structures and practices. More importantly, critical race theorists seek to reveal the hidden curriculum of racial domination and talk about the ways in which it is central to the maintenance of white supremacy. (Lynn, 2005, p. 129)

Bonilla-Silva (2005) suggests that the critical pedagogical framework is filled with foundational limitations regarding the conception of race and racism because its followers accept that: (1) Racism is excluded from the foundation or structure of the social system; (2) Racism is ultimately viewed as a psychological phenomenon to be examined at the individual level; (3) Racism is treated as a static phenomenon; (4) Racism is labeled as irrational and rigid; (5) Racism is understood as overt behavior; (6) Racism today is viewed as a remnant of the past historical racial situations; and (7) Racism is analyzed in a circular manner (pp. 3–6). *Reinventing Critical Pedagogy: Widening the Circle of Anti-Oppression Education* takes a critical tone at the dearth of black scholars as inclusive participants in conferences, meetings, and classes, as well as of being published authors and primary leaders within the critical pedagogical field. Allen (2006) goes on to suggest that most in the critical pedagogy community, who are primarily white, seem perfectly content with an academic audience that mirrors their own "faces and voices," adding:

> This troubles me deeply. How can the critical pedagogy community claim to be on the side of the oppressed when the members of the two most historically oppressed groups in the United States (and throughout the Americas), Blacks and Indians, don't show up to our events or have a strong, leading presence in critical pedagogy scholarship. . . . I would say that critical pedagogists, consciously or not, have been somewhat dismissive of all of those groups that . . . are defined as the "collective Black" or those who are treated if they were Black . . . [thus] if you ask those who consider themselves to be critical pedagogists to name the leaders in the field, the chances are great that most of the names will belong to Whites . . . the point is Black aren't the primary leaders in the field; thus they aren't the major source of intellectual and political inspiration. But this situation shouldn't surprise us. I can't recall anyone in the community seriously asking, "Why aren't more Blacks . . . or dark skinned people of color leading the field of critical pedagogy?" (pp. 4–6)

Therein lies the inherent pedagogical problem. Based upon statistics that are provided by one of the largest post-secondary prison college education programs in the country, the Inside-Out Prison Exchange Program, as well as the demographic make-up of university professors nationwide, it would be very safe to conclude that the overwhelming majority of prison-based college educators are white Americans. According to Van Gundy, Bryant, and Starks (2013) and data obtained from The Inside Out Center (2013) over 70 percent of the 464 educators who completed the National Inside-Out training since 2003 were white females. This data accurately reflected my own Inside-Out training experience, where I was the only black male in attendance, with the overwhelming majority of the remaining participants being white females. Although this book will not examine this phenomenon, this finding alone begs for further research into the dynamics of faculty race and gender complexities within prison-based post-secondary college programs. As well, based upon conversations with other prison-based college educators nationwide, which I admit is completely anecdotal, the overwhelming majority reported on programs that are supported by almost exclusively white college faculty members who claim a critical pedagogical theme. Supporting this assertion, according to *Black American Males in Higher Education: Research, Programs and Academe*, fewer than 6 percent of all nationwide university professors are black Americans (Frierson, Wyche, and Pearson, 2009; Taylor, 2009, p. 224). If we subtract the 60 percent of the black professors employed by historically black colleges and universities, these numbers would drop closer to 3 percent. Nearly 40 percent of our nation's prisons and jails are filled by black males; however, if we accept national trends, at best roughly 4 percent of our nation's prison-based post-secondary college educators are black men (Taylor, 2009, p. 230). I am quite confident this was not the *Du Boisian* applied vision of the "talented tenth" (Du Bois, 1903a, p. 30).

Thus, the question becomes, "Can white post-secondary educators bridge the cultural gap that links the 'collective lived black American experience' to the discourse of racism, white supremacy, and white privilege, as well, address the politics of shaming, self-segregation, and transgenerational learned helplessness, to properly engage incarcerated black male students?" If the dysfunctional history between black males and the educational system is any indication, without any new pedagogical reform and guidance such as HHP the answer is clearly, no. As McMillian (2003) notes, "African American male students are particularly vulnerable to disengagement" (p. 28), and once they are disengaged, an educational climate is no longer important to them. I would argue that the institutionally supported constructs of racism, white supremacy, and white privilege that spur psychosocial humiliations, sit at the root of this disengagement, and that incarcerated black males have a special relationship with those race-based social constructs—a relationship that is filled with a deep level of anger, hate, mistrust, and protracted shame because they have become the living by-products of 400 years of structural violence. Lynn (2006) described the broader disengagement of the educational system toward black Americans:

> As history shows, this system of education has not served African Americans well. Ex-slaves and their children were taught to read the world with a European culture that denigrated other forms of communications and learning. Schooling extended the arm of the slave master in the sense that it was a vehicle through which whites could continue to transmit Eurocentric values and morals to the oppressed, namely, African and Native Americans. More important, education and schooling in America continued the deAfricanization or acculturation process to ignore their culture and their history and to accept EuroAmerican culture as their own. (p. 118)

Woodson (1933) adds:

> The same educational process which inspires and stimulates the oppressor with the thought that he is everything and has accomplished everything worthwhile, depresses and crushes at the same time the spark of genius in the Negro by making him feel that his race does not amount to and never will measure up to the standards of other peoples. (p. xix)

A recently published research project by the University of Pennsylvania, *Black Male Student Success in Higher Education: A Report from the National Black Male College Achievement Study*, highlights that engagement is the key to success in post-secondary education for black males, specifically citing the following: (1) Resolving masculine identity conflicts; (2) negotiating peer support for achievement; (3) developing political acumen for success in professional settings in which they are racially underrepresented; (4) developing strong black identities that incite productive activism on predominantly white campuses; (5) acquiring social capital and access to resources, politically wealthy persons, and exclusive networks; (6) crafting productive responses to racist stereotypes; and finally, (7) overcoming previous educational and socioeconomic disadvantage (Harper, 2012, p. 14). Now, imagine a white college educator who epitomizes the social construct of white privilege applying these black cultural factors of engagement to the lived experiences of incarcerated black males, controlled by a white dominated power structure of a correctional facility, without any pedagogical guidance.

In order to embrace the psychosocial diversity of incarcerated black male students, educators must be mindful of their particular cultural needs. Culturally relevant pedagogy is nothing new to academia, as Gay (2000) describes:

> Using the cultural characteristics, experiences, and perspectives of ethnically diverse students as conduits for teaching them more effectively. It is based on the assumption that when academic knowledge and skills are situated within the lived experiences and frames of reference of students, they are more personally meaningful, have higher interest appeal, and are learned more easily and thoroughly. (p. 106)

In fact, Cooper and Jordan (2005) emphasized that the black male experiences in educational settings will be greatly improved once traditional norms of teaching have been reevaluated and restructured, adding, "if comprehensive school reform is to serve as a vehicle to promote greater academic and social successes for African American males, norms about race and culture must be explicitly addressed" (p. 8). Prison-based educators must be committed to understanding the enormous social and psychological complexities with regard to incarcerated black males and must be willing to transform their pedagogical approach to adjust to their students' needs. Ignoring the lived experiences behind the structural constructs of racism, white supremacy, and white privilege and assuming that incarcerated black male students will do the same is not only unrealistic, but an applied continuation of these perverse conditions. Prison-based educators must understand that there is more to educating incarcerated black men than just delivering academic instruction. Improving the engagement of incarcerated black men is contingent on understanding the 400 years of the politics of shaming, self-segregation, and transgenerational learned helplessness accrued within the collective lived black American experiences they carry with them into the classroom.

The intellect of incarcerated black males is not limited to the erudition of programming curriculum, but extends to questioning the very social constructs of the invisible three-dimensional elephant inside the prison college classroom: racism, white supremacy, and white privilege. Incarcerated black students question their very participation in the prison-based education programming in which they are currently enrolled. Incarcerated black students do not have the social fear of "black identity dysfunction" faced by black intellectuals described in the Carter G. Woodson (1933) classic, *The Mis-Education of the Negro*. The warped and discriminatory applied outcome of the criminal justice system on the "lived" experiences of incarcerated black males, which Alexander (2010) codified as the *New Jim Crow*, has removed any fear of the psychosocial ramifications for their intellectual inquiry into matters of race and social inequity. They want to engage in an open, honest, and continuous discourse as to the who, what, when, where, why, and how regarding racism, white supremacy, and white privilege as it relates to their own lived black American experiences. They want to be acknowledged as "incarcerated students" who are transforming themselves from the label of "criminal offender." Incarcerated black male students require a pedagogy that will inspire this transformation. The HHP seeks to fill this pedagogical gap.

MY PEDAGOGICAL INSPIRATION

I found pedagogical inspiration in the work of one of my original "spiritual" academic guides (spiritual because I only met her through her writings), bell hooks and her work *Teaching to Transgress: Education as the Practice of Freedom*. I was originally introduced to this writing almost two decades ago, and it shaped the type of educator I hoped to be one day. What I truly admired was that as an academic, with everything that goes along with that social construct, she unapologetically expressed a pedagogical framework within the unfiltered black American voice. In fact, this same virtue, the expression of the *unfiltered black American voice,* is what attracted me to the literary works of the many African and black historians, scholars, and activists who shaped my life and who eventually shaped my scholarship regarding the black American experience. Hooks' pedagogical audience was blacks, and so was mine.

hooks (1994) describes true education as the "practice of freedom," and as facilitators of this process, we must create a pedagogical climate where our audience becomes part of the learning community. She stressed the importance of creating an "engaged pedagogy" where both the teacher and student can incorporate their own unique "voice" into the classroom. She stressed that a classroom environment was "the most radical space of possibility" where the concept of self-actualization, from the perspective of both teacher and student, can be used to fuse the connection between "ideas learned in a university setting and those learned in life practices" (pp. 12–15). She defined critical thinking as a "process learned by reading theory and actively analyzing texts" under the bigger umbrella of our day-to-day interactions and experiences as people (p. 20). Finally, she placed an emphasis on not being afraid to engage in critical discussions on the uncomfortable truths of racism, white supremacy, colonialism, etc., and to inspire a "counter-hegemonic" spiritual intellect (hooks, 1994, p. 4).

As well, in *Teaching Community: A Pedagogy of Hope*, Hooks (2003, p. 93) emphasizes the need for educators to address the 400 years within the "politics of shaming" and "self-segregation" in the black American experience. kooks (2003) writes:

> When educators evaluate why some students fail while others succeed they rarely talk about the role of shame as a barrier of learning . . . embedded in this notion of freedom is the assumption that access is all that is needed to create the conditions for equality. The thinking was let black children go to the same schools as white peers and they will have all that is needed to be equal and free. Such thinking denies the role that devaluation and degradation, or all strategies of shaming, play in maintaining racial subordination, especially in the arena of education. . . . African Americans have suffered and continue to suffer trauma, much of it the re-enactment of shaming. The self-segregation black folks do in integrated settings, particularly those where white people are the majority group, is a defense mechanism protecting them from being the victims of shaming assaults. (pp. 93–94)

What made this programmatic failure at FCI McKean so personally disturbing for me is that I have routinely incorporated the pedagogical practices described by Hooks since my inception into academia, including every criminal justice course that I teach at the University of Pittsburgh (Bradford). My goal has always been to create a "counter-hegemonic" learning environment in my classes. However, in the case of my classroom experience at FCI McKean, I violated the central tenet of *trust*. I failed to trust in my audience, in this case black criminal offenders, to be able to intellectually reciprocate the transformation into *incarcerated black students*. Afterward, I had to take a second look at myself, at the type of critical self-actualization demanded from everyone, not only those involved in higher learning, but also at the entire criminal justice field. I learned a great deal about myself from this experience and not only became a better educator but a better human being committed to the tenets of social justice. To this very day, occasionally when I enter FCI McKean to facilitate a post-secondary program, I forget that incarcerated students are in my class and pay the price through a dysfunctional and uninspired academic exchange. This new mindset is fluid and requires a continuous and deliberate pedagogical reassessment from even seasoned prison-based educators.

For black men, historical pedagogical issues which enabled the collective nature of educating "cultural lies" sit at the heart of a long track record of humiliations, whether enduring the physical bars inside or the psychological bars outside of a prison-setting. Du Bois (1994) wrote:

> How does it feel to be a problem? They say, I know an excellent colored man in my town; or, I fought at Mechanicsville; or, Do not these Southern outrages make your blood boil? At these I smile, or am interested, or reduce the boiling to a simmer, as the occasion may require. To the real question. How does it feel to be a problem? I answer seldom a word. And yet, being a problem is a strange experience, —peculiar even for one who has never been anything else, save perhaps in babyhood and in Europe. (p. 1)

I swore to myself, even if it meant never teaching an educational program inside of a prison-setting again, I would never: (1) Advance the generic agenda of another person or entity simply because they used the comfortable buzzword "evidence-based;" (2) Create an atmosphere that addressed the incarcerated student as a problem; or (3) Participate in a program that would not allow the audience an *authentic voice* in the development of the curriculum, and the ability to transform into "incarcerated students." When my first victim impact class ended, I requested permission from the FCI McKean executive staff to create and implement my own pedagogy and curriculum for the program. I'm not quite sure exactly why, but maybe because I was a prior law enforcement practitioner and we shared a professional trust, or it could have been because nobody else was lining up to teach the program, but they gave me the green-light to develop my very own curriculum as long as it was submitted for BOP approval.

Please keep in mind, I always had a very clear understanding of my relationship within FCI McKean as a volunteer educator. I considered our relationship similar to a marriage. Some days it was great and on others, everyone was thinking divorce. However, they had a clear and final say-so on everything that was done within the prison-setting. I not only respected their complete authority and power, I understood it. Contrary to what you might hear from some over-the-top prison reform activists, there is a need for *correctional learning facilities* (CLFs) in this country. There are men, many who are trapped in a counter-culture of crime, who will victimize others simply because it has become a way of life, with an identity-based addiction to the power of violence and money, who need to be housed in a BOP facility. I am very skeptical of theories, concepts, or programs that naively advocate prison reform without thoroughly understanding the holistic nature of the criminal justice system, both from its potential contributions to the social construct of justice and liberty, as well as its systematic complicity in creating and maintaining a culture of hopelessness in black communities. In fact, I firmly believe that prisons play a vital role in what needs to be a multi-layered correctional paradigm within our criminal justice system in America. This was my truth and I never hid it from the BOP prison staff or my incarcerated students.

THE EVIDENCE-BASED INDUSTRY

Since I had several months before the start of another victim impact class, I began an extensive literature review on prison reentry initiatives, concepts, and programs. What I discovered was that all the nationally-based organizations that warehouse prison reentry research, studies, and publications consistently repeated the same bullet-point statements, recommending what they considered as "evidence-based practices" (Aos, Miller, and Drake, 2006; National Institute of Corrections, 2013; Center for Effective Public Policy, 2012; Urban Institute Police Center, 2013; National Reentry Resource Center, 2013). In summary, they all promoted the following:

• Assess offender risk/need levels using actuarial instruments
• Enhance offender motivation
• Target interventions
• Provide skill training for staff and monitor their delivery of services
• Increase positive reinforcement
• Engage ongoing support in natural communities
• Measure relevant processes/practices
• Provide measurement feedback

My argument against using so-called "evidence-based" reentry approaches is that they: (1) inherently define the criminal offender as the problem; (2) intentionally ignore the realities and results of racism, marginalization, and inequality; (3) promote a script or cookbook program mentality, failing to take into account individualized factors such as race, ethnicity, nationality, etc.; (4) perpetuate the myth that the criminal justice system is always looking out for the best interest of those incarcerated; (5) emphasize success through measuring recidivism rates instead of focusing on improving the overall quality of life for those incarcerated; and (6) attempt to use abstract empirical research and data to measure "what works and what does not work" in the human experience.

Additionally concerning is that these "information clearance houses" have convinced the federal government, that they are the sole gatekeepers of the "$500 Million Second Chance Act Powerball ticket," ensuring that their funds should be earmarked solely on prison reentry initiatives deemed as passing their so-called "evidence-based test." Sadly, all the evidence-based hype has done is create a multi-million dollar prisoner reentry cottage industry, with literally hundreds of academic entrepreneurs ready to use their advanced research-based analytical tools to clinically assess the 2.2 million incarcerated and the roughly 700,000 yearly released "laboratory subjects," at least until the money runs out.

It gives me great pause when our criminal justice system, which I respect and openly admire due to its untapped potential in applied social justice, despite its obvious structural flaws, defines success in so-called "reentry" as a concept I term as the *staying out of prison* (SOP) model. More disturbing is the phenomenon that countless black men around the country, incarcerated and not, have adopted the mantra of SOP as their measure of success in America. For some black American men, as long as they're "staying out of prison" they're a black success story. Expectations such as involvement in post-secondary higher education, obtaining professional financial security, traveling abroad, and/or advancing one's legacy through family and community enrichment projects have become pipe dreams for way too many black males. Thus, the cycle of victimization for black males in part is a self-inflicted wound, with fathers passing the SOP psyche down to their sons, generation after generation. There is no better example of the SOP phenomenon than what is occurring for young urban black men today in Chicago, which I examine in much greater detail later in the book. We as a black people can and must do better than this. It's not only a time for serious self-reflection but also immediate action.

SUSTAINABLE WHOLE PERSON BY TRUTH

This book is designed as a pedagogical "blueprint" to lay the foundation for a different paradigm, one that I hope will make many of us re-think what our goal should be in the prison-community transition process, a social justice concept that places its emphasis on making a *sustainable whole person by truth*. The HHP is a common sense approach that emphasizes that, once an "incarcerated black student" has been educated on the *truths* about his history, the *truths* about the criminal justice system, and the *truths* about the real victims of crime, he is now qualified to finally make *choices*. If that choice is to live within the black counter-culture of crime and to pass *his* choice onto his children, family, and community, we must use every legal mechanism available, including the power of the criminal justice system, to ensure there is always an open prison cell waiting for him, because he has truly chosen his own fate.

You see, I believe that once an incarcerated student has been exposed to the truth and ownership of knowledge, the greatest liberating force in the universe, there are no more excuses for abandoning your children, family, and community for a prison cell. Accepting membership into the black counter-culture of crime then becomes a matter of free will and choice: critically assessing and weighing the benefits, risks, and ultimate costs for an action. Let me be very clear, there is no moral penalty levied against an individual, who after analyzing his life choices, decides to engage in criminal behavior solely for the benefit of his children and accepts his fate of imprisonment; however, that has never been the reality I've lived in over two decades as a practitioner in the criminal justice system. I never met a man who was selling drugs solely to feed his children or even fund their college dreams. That's a fairy tale, created by Steven Spielberg on a Hollywood movie set.

In reality, the epic journey from humiliation to humility is not an easy one. The road to redemption and reconciliation for an incarcerated black student returning back to his community is paved with temptations, disappointments, and failures. When he goes home, unemployment will still be high. Our educational system will still be broken. He will still have the greatest opportunity to be victimized by a person within his own community of similar race or ethnic background. There will still be more liquor stores than schools in his neighborhood. Street hustlers will still operate in open drug markets with community-supported impunity at times. In this book, I hope to provide the reader with a pedagogical approach to help inspire the development of the sole critical factor that can ultimately withstand these warped social and psychological barriers to successful prison-community transition, and to make the transformation from humiliation to humility: the indestructible nature of the human spirit.

DEFINING HUMILIATION AND HUMILITY

One of the first challenges to overcome in understanding the *Humiliation to Humility Perspective* (HHP) is that neither humiliation nor humility can be easily or operationally defined. As noted earlier, examining the human experience, especially the black American experience, cannot be measured in variables, statements of hypothesis, or defined as a systematic process that hopefully leads to data that can be generalized for the masses. It can only be understood through the collective lived experience. In any regard, the incredible journey that black men are required to make does not make sense in any rational manner. How can a people be in such a historical position that places them at the origin of mankind and creating one of the greatest civilizations we have ever known, to falling prey to arguably the greatest crime and genocidal humiliation ever perpetrated in the world, the African Holocaust, and to be subjected to the black codes and Jim Crow, surviving and transforming humiliation into humility all the way to the steps of the White House? It is impossible to operationally define when Clarke (1997, p. 106) said, "my revolution starts with me," when Dyson (1996, p. 52) suggested that "race has always been a deep characteristic American problem," when West (2001, xiii) labeled Jim Crow as "American terrorism," and finally, as Barack Obama, our nation's first but not last black President echoed in countless speeches across the world, "change has come to America," without living within the soul of the black American experience. In the black American experience, this journey of humiliation and humility can only be understood in terms of an ongoing narrative, a sort of novel in which the author is unsure of its ending, but its characters seem to be on an almost spiritual manifest destiny. However, I will try to place these concepts in a biographical form, where they can be described through the actions of formerly incarcerated black students who have transcended their pain of humiliation by living their lives through the successful humility of others.

Humiliation is a complex phenomenon. It is one of the most powerful forces in the human experience. It is a weapon of mass destruction on the human body and soul, capable of motivating unthinkable acts of direct and structural violence; however, if transformed and channeled properly, it can be used as an inspirational tool for some of the greatest acts of micro- and macro-level transformation success in mankind. Humiliation is the individually or institutionally enforced "lowering of any person or group by a process of subjugation" that damages or in many cases strips away pride, honor and human dignity (Lindner, 2006). All human beings seek dignity and respect. Without self-worth, self-pride, and self-respect, dignity becomes impossible to realize not only for the individual but the community as a whole. Nihilism, the complete and utter loss of hope, settles into the human psyche and gives birth to a culture of desperation, fear, and rage. Shame, pain, suffering, anger, and violence become the universal language of those who have been humiliated, creating and maintaining a perpetual cycle of victimization. Whom do you victimize first? The people who you see every day: your family, children, and community. You see, humiliation is the "missing link" in the human experience that explains why black men across the country have channeled their anger into murdering other black men, at a rate that would fill Harvard, Yale, and Princeton's yearly student enrollment with educated black men ten-fold (Fox and Zawitz, 2005). It explains the deep-rooted shame associated with black male unemployment and poverty rates that almost triple our national averages, and the indignity of introducing their very own children to the *culturally addicting* Temporary Assistance for Needy Families program (U.S. Census Bureau, 2010). Finally, it explains the hopeless desperation that would allow 1 out of every 3 black males to willingly give up their freedom and voluntarily submit themselves, as well as their children, community, and historic BCP, to the indentured correctional servitude of the criminal justice system. Humiliation has become the primary catalyst that has kept black men in chains mentally and physically, stymying their true human potential and openly accepting their fate as the "other" in this 400-year journey in America. Garvey (1986) explained over eighty years ago:

> The greatest stumbling block in the way of progress in the race has invariably come from within the race itself. The monkey wrench of destruction as thrown into the cog of Negro Progress is not thrown so much by the outsider as by the very fellow who is in our fold, and who should be the first to grease the wheel of progress rather than seeking to impede it . . . the illiterate and shallow-minded Negro who can see no farther than his nose is now the greatest stumbling block in the way of the race. He tells us that we must be satisfied with our condition; that we must not think of building up a nation of our own, that we must not seek to organize ourselves racially, but that we must depend upon the good feeling of the other fellow for the solution of the problem that now confronts us. This is a dangerous policy and it is my duty to warn the four hundred million Negroes of the world against this kind of a leadership—a leadership that will try to make Negroes believe that all will be well without their taking upon themselves the task of bettering their condition politically, industrially, educationally and otherwise. (p. 37)

The humiliation of slavery, the black codes, Jim Crow, and the plethora of other conscious and subconscious acts of institutionally sanctioned racism, white supremacy, white privilege, oppression, and marginalization will always be a part of the black male's journey in America. However, black Americans had an incredible and rich legacy centuries before the "White Lion" hit the banks of Jamestown, Virginia, in 1619. This fact has been erased, however, by the shortcomings of "historic amnesia" largely due to the trappings of self-prescribed standards of total cultural assimilation by black Americans. This book seeks to remind the nearly 840,000 black males who are currently incarcerated in our nations prisons, the 2.5 million who are currently on probation and parole, the 5 million who have completed their term of incarceration or supervised control within this generation, their families, friends, researchers, students, and the millions of people who work within the criminal justice system, that only by transforming and rechanneling humiliation into humility, can one become a whole person. As Maya Angelou (1969) noted countless times:

> Someone was hurt before you, wronged before you, hungry before you, frightened before you, beaten before you, humiliated before you, raped before you . . . yet, someone survived. . . . You can do anything you choose to do.

Humility is often described as a quiet virtue. It does not shout out its characteristics, but you recognize the final project when you see it. At its root, humility is a concept in which one thinks and acts in accordance with the idea that the needs and desires of others are the main priority

(Worthington, 2007). It places an emphasis on having enough self-confidence, inner strength, and universal vision, to create the spiritual freedom to place others, specifically your children, ahead of yourself. You see, self-confidence allows people freedom from fear, even the fear of death, creating an incredible opportunity for transformation, forgiveness, and reconciliation. As Malcolm X added, "If you're not ready to die for it, take the word 'freedom' out of your vocabulary." Humility is something bigger than we as individuals, and we know it. It is always noticed by others more than by oneself. It comes from understanding the many obstacles in life's daily journey are not going away by themselves, but need to be confronted. Humility allows a person to unshackle him or herself from the deep pains of shame, anger, bitterness, structural and direct violence, and the power to channel them for an opportunity at redemption, not for the individual but for the greater benefit of others. In fact, humility is often forged through the human experience of imprisonment, whether it is in the physical barriers of a prison cell or the mental chains of cultural nihilism.

MANDELA AND MALCOLM

One of the greatest examples of the HHP in existence is the life story of the late Rolihlahla Dalibhunga "Madiba" Mandela, or the man who is commonly known to the world as Nelson Mandela. After sitting in a South African prison for twenty-seven years, on April 29, 1994, Nelson Mandela was elected the first black president of the Republic of South Africa in the first democratically held election in the country's history (Adi, 2008). You see, it took over two decades of imprisonment to forge his resolve to serve others above his own needs. Prison hardship taught him patience; wisdom; the importance of having empathy for others less privileged than himself; and compassion:

> There are . . . things that you have to learn as a prisoner. There are walls . . . you can see the walls and forever be a prisoner, or you can break through and have the whole world before you in your mind. The greatest challenge is yourself . . . the enemy within. You have to work with and change yourself. Prison compels a breadth of your vision and understanding. If you wanted something, you had to get on your knees and plead with someone. This compels you to a sense of spirituality . . . of you not being in total control of everything. There is a recognition that sometimes you have to depend on some other force, real or imagined. Anyone who goes to prison and is subject to those conditions learns humility. Prison tempered a lot of the animal instincts in us. Prison and age. You mix with people you never would have if you had not gone to [prison]. You share the same [bathroom] facilities, eat the same food . . . you talk to people and discover that although they are

not from the same social background they have much to offer. (Smith,
2003, pp. 64–65)

Mandela learned in prison that the humblest people sometimes have
the greatest insights. He was remarkably able to set aside his individual
anger, bitterness, and contempt for those who were responsible for his
subjugation and imprisonment for the betterment of the collective legacy
of his people. Mandela did not see non-violent resistance as a life philosophy, such as Ghandi or MLK, but as a political tactic. Instead, "Madiba"
was inspired by the philosophy of Fanon (1952, 1967). Regarding the
"enemy within," Mandela often asked himself while sitting in a prison
cell, "Did I make the right decision in leaving my family and letting my
children grow up without security?" This is the exact same question that
every black male sitting in a prison cell and contemplating the journey
from humiliation to humility should be asking themselves. They must
ask, "Is there ever enough money, power, rage, lust for sex, or even the
quest for street creds [credibility] that will allow me to continue to contribute to the victimizing of my children, family, and community and to
voluntarily hand over my cultural legacy to the criminal justice system?"
The answer must be a loud and unequivocal, "Not while I'm alive!"
Issues of racial oppression, educational marginalization, and economic
inequality become the fuel for transformation, forgiveness, and reconciliation. As a result of his transformation from humiliation to humility,
Mandela insisted:

> True reconciliation does not consist in merely forgetting the past. It
> does not rest with black forgiveness sensitive to white fears and toler-
> ance of an unjust status quo on one hand, and white gratitude and
> appreciation underlined by a tenacious clinging to exclusive privileges
> on the other. It has to be based on the creation of a truly democratic,
> nonracial and nonsexist society. . . . Vengeance is not our goal. . . . We
> seek not just freedom but opportunity, not just legal equity but human
> ability, not just equality as a right and a theory, but equality as a fact
> and as a result. (Smith, 2003, p. 144)

As such, there is clearly no single formerly incarcerated black student
in American history who has embodied the HHP philosophy more than
El Hajj Malik El Shabazz, a/k/a Malcolm X, before his assassination on
February 21, 1965. My fascination with what I define as the "Malcolm X
experience" dates back to my early childhood. I still remember during a
third grade "show and tell" class project in 1973, I instructed my teacher
that I planned on dressing up as Malcolm X and performing one of his
speeches. The only thing I knew of Malcolm X at this point in my life was
that he was being highlighted and discussed by legendary boxing champion Muhammad Ali on a television program that my dad was watching,
and he pointed at the TV screen and commented, "Those men never took
shit from anybody." That's all the encouragement I needed in my very

brief and filtered life experience. When I brought my idea to class, my teacher, who was a white female, responded with a look of utter contempt, indicating that Malcolm X was a "black revolutionary" and that there was no place in our [Catholic] school for him. She suggested that I choose someone like Martin Luther King or even James Augustine Healy, who was the first black American Roman Catholic priest. I received an "F" for that class project, an academic grade I rightfully earned by faking an illness the day of the class presentation, missing school altogether. A couple of years later, based on guidance from several black female school teachers, I was able to secure a copy of the text, *The Autobiography of Malcolm X* from my school library, and read it from cover to cover within a few days. Although I've spent many years of my academic life conducting ethnographic studies, similar to the type of scholarship completed for my doctoral studies where I researched the impact of the USA PATRIOT Act on the lives of Muslim Americans (Gaskew, 2008), whenever I find myself questioning, as a black man in America, my purpose in this life journey, I re-read Malcolm X's autobiography. I would roughly estimate that I've read his autobiography over 100 times, and every single time it takes me down a new path from humiliation to humility.

Malcolm X understood that he was lost as a human being if he could not somehow find his dignity that was surrendered by his transformation from the black counter-culture of crime lived by Malcolm Little. My pedagogical theory does not advocate the use of one religion over the next; in fact, it does not even utilize the concept of formalized religion. However, I clearly understand that one's spiritual faith can serve as a bridge for some black incarcerated students taking this journey. I have been around too long and have seen too many things to become a champion of one religious label over the next. I believe at the core of all of their foundations, without the corrupting economic and political agendas of men, each contributes a connective role within the spiritual dimension of the human experience, one that solidifies the universal moral duty of mutual respect, dignity, compassion, and social justice. In Malcolm X's journey, he also discovered that religion is a manmade social construct, ripe with betrayal, self-profit, envy, and jealously. His steadfast faith was to his spiritual God but his moral duty was to make a better black American experience.

In 1946, as America was enmeshed in the depths of Jim Crow, Malcolm X began what was to be a six-year prison term for weapons-related charges, serving his sentence at Charlestown State Prison, Concord Reformatory, and Norfolk Prison Colony. For Malcolm X the simple act of kneeling, something he had done willingly so many times to facilitate the selling of drugs, armed robbery, and shooting dice, but this time as a humbling ritual of prayer, set him on a path to restore his dignity and opened up the floodgates to an intellectual revolution. He discovered that the truth about his past, present, and future was located inside a prison library, just as my grammar school homeroom teacher, Mrs. Hollister, once told me, "Tony, your runway is the library." With an eighth grade education and starting with the word "aardvark", Malcolm X copied and memorized the definition of every single word in the dictionary. Malcolm X transformed the *humiliation from criminal offender* to the *humility of incarcerated student* and never looked back.

Every single waking moment was spent reading a book and debating its contents to increase his public communication skills. He stated, "I will tell you that, right there, in the prison, debating, speaking to a crowd was as exhilarating to me as the discovery of knowledge through reading had been" (Haley, 1964). In fact, he had chosen to transfer to Norfolk Prison Colony due to its outstanding library, where he studied and debated history, law, philosophy, and religion. He envisioned his prison as a university campus, his cell as a dorm room, and himself as a college student, where he would spend fifteen hours a day dedicated to the craft of owning knowledge and critical thinking, preparing himself to reenter his community and his continued journey from humiliation to humility. He discovered that, only by the truth of what an education can offer, can a person be truly free. Malcolm X offered these words regarding his prison education experience:

> Let me tell you something, from until I left that prison, in every free moment I had, if I was not reading in the library, I was reading on my bunk. You couldn't have gotten me out of books with a wedge . . . my reading of books, months passed without me even thinking about being imprisoned. In fact, up to then, I never had been so truly free in my life.

He added:

> I don't think anybody ever got more out of going to prison than I did. In fact, prison enabled me to study far more intensively than I would have if my life had gone differently and I had attended some college . . . where else but in a prison could I have attacked my ignorance by being able to study intensively sometimes as much as fifteen hours a day? A prisoner has time that he can put to good use. I'd put prison second to college as the best place for a man to go if he needs to do some thinking. If he's motivated, in prison he can change his life.

And finally:

> I have often reflected upon the new vistas that reading has opened to me. I knew right there in prison that reading had changed forever the course of my life. As I see it today, the ability to read awoke inside me some long dormant craving to be mentally alive. (Haley, 1964, pp. 169–190)

This was the man that I honorably traded the *humiliation* of receiving an "F" in a third grade social studies class in 1973, for the *humility* of receiving my PhD in 2006.

THE HUMILIATION TO HUMILITY PERSPECTIVE (HHP) MODEL

The *Humiliation to Humility Perspective* (HHP) was inspired by the time-tested radical pedagogy implemented by "black voices" that have transcended their period of incarceration into the platform of "education as the practice of freedom." The use of the basic principles of truth, knowledge, and the "lived" inclusive nature of critical thinking, served as their foundation for individual transformation and community redemption. As I have shared with every incarcerated man in my path, successful transformation from humiliation to humility is an individual journey with community outcomes. Keep in mind, although in this book, I utilize my pedagogy to address specific issues related to incarcerated black male students preparing to transition back into their respective communities and take ownership of their own lives, in the true spirit of radical pedagogy and multi-culturalism, the "cultural code" can be altered to apply to any race, ethnicity, or gender. The HHP consists of five educational tenets: owning the truth; understanding your history; processing the criminal justice system; knowing the victims; and making tough choices (see fig. 1.1).

Each educational phase is a designed as a building block for the next, exposing the incarcerated student to the truths that will not only take back his life, but the lost lives of his children, family, and community. There is no specific time period to moving from one educational phase to the next because, as I have already noted, the transition from humiliation to humility is an individual journey.

Time is the most valuable resource for an incarcerated student. Going back and forth between phases is not only encouraged, it's recommended. As well, this pedagogy is designed to inspire the discovery and ownership, not the depositing, of knowledge. It's just a foundation and the incarcerated student making the journey must take and expand the process, through application, and engagement. As Karenga (2002) noted, "The one who has become knowledgeable and aware cannot refuse to act and, in acting, must combine talents with the power of the people to act as a force of one" (p. 8).

For much of this first chapter, we have covered the initial educational tenet of the HHP, *owning the truth*, starting with my own. I would encourage prison-based educators to start your program by telling incarcerated black students the truth about who you are and why you are there, and ask that they do the same. No matter how grim or exciting, regardless of whether it will inspire or anger, never lie to someone who is incarcerated.

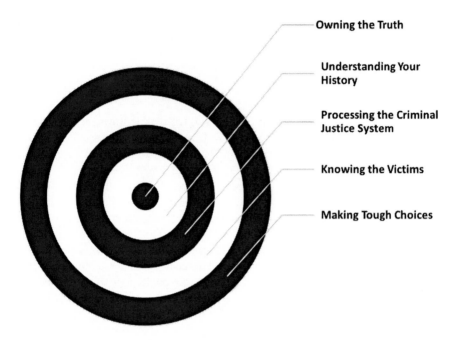

Owning the Truth

Understanding Your History

Processing the Criminal Justice System

Knowing the Victims

Making Tough Choices

Figure 1.1.   Humiliation to Humility Perspective (HHP) Model.

Most incarcerated black students have lived their entire black American experience in a world created and sustained by cultural lies. Lies about themselves, their so-called friends, the money they were supposed to make in the counter-culture of crime, their own cultural history, and about their roles as black fathers. In fact, their blind faith and allegiance to these cultural lies were vital to the creation of our New Jim Crow.

The truth ushers in a new beginning for incarcerated black students trapped in a cycle of transgenerational learned helplessness. The truth doesn't stop time; it allows it to finally start moving forward. Incarcerated black students must own the truth about their history, their role in the criminal justice system, the victims of their involvement in a black counter-culture of crime, and finally their real choices. How do you know if an incarcerated student is ready to hear the truth? I suggest giving them a take-home assignment. Start by asking them at the end of the very first day of the class, that when they return to their confined living area, to find and look into a polished metal mirror, the same one that was made to keep them in a perpetual state of lies of who they really are and what they can really become, and have them answer the following question, "How did I get here?" Near the end of the following class session, ask them for their replies. Then inform them that if they can answer that question without owning the truths about the collective lived black experiences regarding their connective cultural history, the truths about the criminal justice system and their role in a counter-culture of crime, and the truths about their role in the victimization of their children, then they can't make a truthful choice about whether they're coming back or not. Inform them they are almost guaranteed to be a "70 percenter" (an incarcerated student who has made a decision, not a choice, to never leave the lifestyle and humiliations created by a black counter-culture of crime) and destined to further the cruel agenda of mass incarceration, infecting the lives of their family and community alike. Inform them that for an incarcerated student, an education is more than just memorizing and regurgitating material. Inform them that as incarcerated black students they must be able to uncover and channel their humiliations and use these collective lived experiences to push their erudition to new levels of humility.

If you as a prison educator are unable to communicate these basic truths to a room full of incarcerated black students, you are part of the problem and need to reassess why you are involved in prison-based education initiatives. You see, telling the truth is sometimes harder than hearing the truth. As an educator using the HHP pedagogy, you must also be willing to invest yourself to the truths of your very own lived experiences. A painful self-actualization process occurs that will expose the realities of racism, white supremacy, and white privilege in the very lives of the educators and incarcerated students alike, and that will be present every single day of the class. If as an educator you can't begin to confront these realities on the very first day, you will be starting the class on a foundation of "cultural lies" that you will have to sustain the entire time period of the course. Truth sits at the center of this prison-based education pedagogy.

FROM CORRECTIONAL FACILITIES TO CORRECTIONAL LEARNING CENTERS (CLCS)

I am not a prison abolitionist. I know this will not sit well with some of my readers. The ugly truth is, there will be people for whatever explainable reasons, whether it is the result to 400 years of protracted structural violence and institutionalized discrimination smeared with racism, white supremacy, and white privilege, poverty, substance abuse, or mental illness, who will commit crimes and require specialized control, supervision, care, treatment, and housing outside of the general population due to public safety issues. The unequal access to meeting basic human needs and the brutal historic subjugation of people of color since the birth of our nation guarantee the production of crime, the asymmetrical application of the law, and the creation of prisons. Our nation was created on this wicked formula and there is no moral duty encouraging it to change.

Thus, the conversation will always center on the length and type of prison sentences, including the use of solitary confinement or the death penalty. Truth be told, to suggest that there are people, including some black males, who have not earned the right based on their loyalty to a black counter-culture of crime to be confined and separated from their families, children, and communities, is not only irresponsible but harmful to the true essence of the black American experience. Public safety is a right of black Americans as well. The big question becomes *how* we choose to control, supervise, and provide treatment for incarcerated offenders.

Despite the unfair application of the criminal justice system and its horrific impact on the black American experience, specifically for black men, I believe its final component, *Corrections*, can still play an invaluable role in transforming humiliation into humility. Within the pedagogical framework of the *Humiliation to Humility Perspective* (HHP), I advocate that black males must transform the *humiliation of criminal offender* to the *humility of incarcerated student* and, just as important, I hope to inspire prisons and jails across the nation to also transform their paradigms from the *humiliation of correctional facilities* to the *humility of correctional learning centers*. Correctional facilities have systematically failed in the "community transition processes" because their goal has always been to "fix" criminal offenders under the paradigm that they are "problems that need to be corrected." Instead, their goal should be to "teach" incarcerated men under the new paradigm that they are "students that need to be educated." Correctional facilities must take on the mindset of college campuses. The truth of this paradigm shift is a reality because we have already laid the foundation. If we look close enough, today's prisons and jails mirror college campuses in physical appearance, location, populations, costs, employees, and depending on which paradigm you accept, in graduations or inmate releases per year.

One of the best examples is found in Pennsylvania. The locations of Pennsylvania Department of Corrections (PDOC) facilities and Penn State University campuses are in similar geographic locations throughout the state (see figs. 1.2 and 1.3). Comparisons on the number of facilities, population, costs, graduations/releases, and employees are eerily very similar (see table 1.1).

Table 1.1.   Comparative Chart of PDOC and Penn State University

Per Year (2012)	PDOC	Penn. State
Facilities/Campuses	25	24
Population	52,000	64,000
Cost	$37,000	$34,000
Releases/Graduations	20,439	21,020
Employees	15,000	25,000

Figure 1.2. Geographical Map of PDOC Facility Locations.

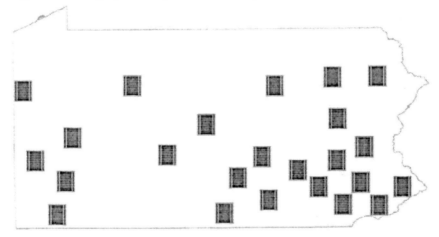

Figure 1.3. Geographic Map of Penn State Campus Locations.

In this example, all the paradigm shift requires is for the correctional facilities in Pennsylvania to institutionally *humble* itself enough to realize that the "old model" that boasts a recidivism rate over 60 percent is not effective; however, a "new model" consisting of post-secondary educational programming is effective. There is no more debate. When the transformation from *"criminal offender"* to *"incarcerated student"* occurs, there is over a 40 percent increased likelihood of that person never seeing the inside of a prison cell again (Davis, Bozick, Steele, Saunders, and Miles, 2013).

How can we as moral human servants, stand before an audience of incarcerated offenders and proclaim that "an education is the key to success and freedom" and then withhold access to post-secondary college programs knowing that these will not only save their lives but the lives of their children? I have personally witnessed the impact of how post-secondary educational opportunities can change the entire culture of a correctional institution, and there is no better example than FCI McKean.

The monetary cost of this endeavor can be offset by the incredible profits generated through asset forfeiture and by restoring Pell Grant eligibility to all state and federal incarcerated offenders, regardless of their crimes. Created in 1972, the Pell Grant awarded federal student aid for postsecondary education based on financial need, a criterion met by most incarcerated offenders. However, the signing of the Violent Crime Control Act of 1994 led to the elimination of Pell Grant eligibility for all prisoners (Gorgol and Sponsler, 2011). HHP advocates building open and honest partnerships between prisons and college campuses across the nation, not in an attempt to undermine the goal of public safety, but to facilitate transforming the "internal culture" of *correctional facilities* into *correctional learning centers*. Even under the ugly and skewed umbrella of racism, white supremacy, and white privilege, at the end of the day, public safety interests are much better served having 840,000 *incarcerated black students* than 840,000 *black criminal offenders*.

TWO

Uncovering Black Cultural Privilege

The most heinous crime ever perpetrated on the black American male has been the successful institutionalized marketing campaign and unquestioned transgenerational acceptance that, for the most part, black Americans are inferior and white Americans are superior (Burrell, 2010). What makes this crime so insidious is that so often today, black men knowingly and voluntarily perpetuate this ugly socially constructed lie, hating and victimizing themselves and anyone who looks, hears, and shares their own racially constructed identity. This four-hundred-year "war on blackness" using the politics of shaming and self-segregation as its primary weapons, has inflicted long-term psychosocial damage to black men, and one of the results has been the creation of a black counterculture of crime and generations of mass incarceration. In order to overcome this structural humiliation, it is essential that black men know, understand, and own the true essence of their blackness. Black men must be able to successfully navigate the rich legacy of an African past with the evolving and indestructible nature of their glorious journey into their black American present. This is the fundamental core of *black cultural privilege* (BCP).

THE SEARCH FOR BLACKNESS IN AN AGE OF MASS INCARCERATION

When Tom Burrell (2010, xi) noted, "Black people are not dark-skinned white people," it was not meant to be a disparaging slight on white America. In fact, the inherent beauty behind his words is that the true essence of American "blackness" and its incredible historic cultural diversity journey is not based on any socially constructed standard of American "whiteness." Blackness stands on its own two feet and defines itself, in whatever limitless shapes, sounds, or shades that are determined by the people who own and occupy its essence. Blackness is not homogenous. It crosses macro- and micro-level social perspectives of religion, politics, class, ethnicity, language, and music, infusing itself into the multi-faceted identities of the lived black American experience. At its roots, the unifying component of blackness in America resonates in the collective pride of a people that is so culturally rich, diverse, and powerful, four hundred years of systematically supported structural violence only served to strengthen its inner core.

However, the reality of black American men today collectively being able to navigate through the political and social campaign of black shame and black humiliation that started in 1619, without leaving them feeling spiritually, physically, emotionally mentally, and culturally "raped," is nearly impossible. This humiliation is part of the lived black American experience, although class differences may sometimes hide its impact, until the psychosocial opportunity presents itself. I've discovered the secret to successfully transforming this humiliation into humility is through educational recognition: knowing and understanding the historical truths behind the who, what, where, when, and how of black humiliation and black shame. This awareness strips humiliation of its negative powers that create self-hate and nihilism among black men, and gives birth to a humility-filled realization where pride, self-worth, and predictable success become part of the black cultural consciousness.

When I discuss the concept of *blackness* with incarcerated black students at FCI McKean, much of our intellectual exchanges start with the prophetic words of Frantz Fanons' classic *Black Skin, White Masks*. Fanon (1952) believed that black men have been conditioned by white colonization to despise the very essence of their blackness, in every shape and form, thus learning to hate everything about themselves and their very human existence: that black men have been taught that their own blackness is an infectious cancer, an evil growth that needs to be surgically cutout and removed in its "cultural whole" from the body, mind, and spirit of those who have become infected, by those who have become infected. Thus, the collective conscious of a black man who identifies his own blackness as a humiliating birth defect dons a "psychological white mask" in an attempt to hide from himself. This "mental costume" allows a black man to willfully exploit his role as the sub-oppressor to his own blackness, where his truth and humility are connected to accepting his own black inferiority and white superiority, resulting in a perpetual state of "learned helplessness."

One of the most painful aspects of being a black male educator involved in any prison-based programming is seeing the growth of *transgenerational learned helplessness*: the aggressive nature that some incarcerated black men have expanded in their accepted role as sub-oppressors. Instead of a white mask, many don an identity-based affiliation to some form of gangsterism connected to the black counter-culture of crime. Perhaps Cureton (2011) makes a valid point regarding his Emergent Gangsterism Perspective (EGP) and its virtual stranglehold on the perpetually lost identities of black males in America today. Transgenerational learned helplessness among incarcerated black men is so powerful that it has become ingrained into the "prison politics" of correctional facilities. Even when I come across incarcerated black students who are scholars of African history, many walk out of the classroom and put on their "gangster masks," re-submerging themselves into a black counter-culture of crime until the next class, where the cycle continues to play itself out. Let me be very clear, this includes some incarcerated black students who self-identify as practicing Muslims or any other religious affiliation. Prison politics sometimes dictate that religious affiliation simply becomes an extension of black gangsterism.

Clearly, many forms of correctional black gangsterism are extensions of their "lives on the outside," and many incarcerated black students argue that they are required for surviving inside some correctional facilities. Notwithstanding, the promotion of oppressive racial stratification and marginalization by some correctional staff and the culture of imprisonment have also contributed to this cycle. However, in the end millions of incarcerated black men return back into their communities and teach other young black men, including their children, the skills of sub-oppressiveness and an identity-based connection to a black counter-culture of crime, continuing the cycle of mass incarceration and transgenerational learned helplessness. Their influence on other young black men and the black culture is immense. Sadly, for many years, men within the black community, the 70 percent who are not directly involved in the criminal justice system, through the humiliation attached with having another black male family member living in the black counter-culture of crime or just plain cultural apathy, have not been willing to confront this issue head-on. Thus, the search for the essence of blackness in an age of mass incarceration presents unique challenges for black Americans. As I've noted earlier, in order to address this cycle of mental servitude for black men, I have directed my attention to the third party in the *triad of culpability*: the incarcerated black counter-culture of crime—to implementing a prison-based educational pedagogy that will inspire the intellectual curiosity of black males trapped in a counter-culture of crime with the opportunity to uncover their black cultural privilege and to free themselves from the socially constructed requirement to mask their own black consciousness.

BLACK CULTURAL PRIVILEGE

Black cultural privilege (BCP) is the physical, mental, and spiritual awareness that connects the rich diverse history of an African past with the ever
evolving journey into the legacy of the collect lived black American experience. It's an unconscious bond that exists among a people whose roots
share an indestructible cultural DNA that has only been strengthened by
four hundred years of direct and structural violence, acts of slavery, the
black codes, and Jim Crow. BCP defines the essence of blackness.

You see, unless a black male is fully aware of his own BCP, the type of
spiritual confidence that connects body, mind, and soul, a "cultural
swag" in his actions, writings, and thoughts, he will never allow himself
to respect his children, family, community, and to enjoy the inherent
diversity of other cultures. Without BCP, a black male will feel uncomfortable working, socializing, or connecting with whites, Hispanics,
Asians, etc., in their own environments because he will place *their* comfort level above his own. Without BCP, a black man might hide his copy
of *Faces at the Bottom of the Well* or *The Isis Papers,* solely because others
would feel more comfortable. Without BCP, a black man will feel
ashamed and uncomfortable to have black friends or family who choose
to use the term "nigga" in front of a white audience because he doesn't
want to be perceived as one of "those people." It has always amazed me,
the fascination that white Americans have with cementing their rights to
say the word *nigga,* solely because black Americans can and do at times,
and if they can't, neither can blacks. Ridiculous. Without BCP, a black
man can change his economic class and social status, or obtain a terminal
degree, yet still feel the shame, anger, and depression of black inferiority
and white superiority. Without BCP, a black man will believe a prison
cell and the counter-culture of crime is a normal part of the black
American experience.

Black cultural privilege is not defined by the social construct of white
privilege, which would encourage the comfortable political excuse labeled as affirmative action to dilute the achievements of the black
American experience. BCP stands as a lone voice that has been forged by
connecting the continued legacy of an African past with a black
American present. It's a narrative that rests on the foundational cultural
pride of unparalleled transformational survival skills. It allows a black
male to know that despite the four hundred years of structural injustices
perpetrated by white supremacy, he will survive and succeed in life because it's in his *cultural DNA* to do so.

After spending almost three decades in the criminal justice field as
both a practitioner and academic, I am convinced that once an incarcerated black student knows, understands, and accepts the truth about his
own rich historical legacy, a cultural narrative that he is morally obligated to pass on to his very own children, and his multi-faceted identity that

connects Africa to his black American experience, he would be hesitant to willingly expose himself or his children to the crimeogenic social death penalty of mass incarceration. Asante (2003) described this phenomenon as "Afrocentricity." Asante (2003) says: "Afrocentricity is a philosophical perspective associated with the discovery, location, and actualizing of African legacy within the context of history and culture" (p. 3).

If he does expose himself or his children to this penalty, the criminal justice system I describe in this book should do everything in its power to keep him separated from his family and community as long as the law legally permits. I am very harsh in this regard, because once an incarcerated black male has successfully transcended his role from "criminal offender" to "incarcerated student" and owns the truth about himself, his culture, the criminal justice system, and the legacy he is obligated to leave his children, and still continues to live within the black counter-culture of crime, he is the worst type of traitor, a sort of modern-day black slave catcher that enjoys enslaving other black men for either social or economic profit. He then has earned the right to sit in a steel cage for the rest of his life.

You see, an incarcerated black man cannot make the transformation from humiliation to humility unless he can educate and share his *blended* African history along with his *lived* black American cultural experiences with his own children, and with others within his own black community. These two worlds, *Africa* and the *collective lived black American experience*, must become one universal narrative, neither more nor less important than the other. This is the essence of black cultural privilege. You see, Africa cannot replace the lived black American experience for black males. This perspective would not only insult the cultural legitimacy of the lived black American experience, but it would also jeopardize the rightful place of Africa as the "centerpiece of human regeneration" (Asante, 2003, p. 2). Africa must be like water: it sits at the core nourishing all human existence, while at the same time, it seeps into any crevice or opening without altering the shape of the object. As Asante (2003, p. 11) notes, "One does not live in the past . . . but one uses the past for advances toward the future." The *Humiliation to Humility Perspective* (HHP) advocates that when both entities work in universal harmony, the true collective consciousness known as the *black cultural privilege* (BCP) will be achieved.

INTRODUCING BCP INTO A CULTURE OF CONFINEMENT

Introducing a prison-based pedagogical formula that involves BCP is a challenging task and you must first be able to overcome three primary cultural hurdles: (1) the defiance of a black counter-culture of crime; (2) the cultural limitations of prison educators; and (3) the resistance of the correctional staff culture. However, what I've discovered in dealing with crisis situations for almost thirty years is that the root causes of many conflicts lie within multi-faceted identities dueling in issues of power and control. Thus, I recommend spending a great deal of time at the correctional facility building trust with all the prison stakeholders. There is no other way to understand the black offender culture, prison politics, or staff culture without investing your time and energy listening and learning from those who have the power and control. It may take a few months or several years to establish institutional trust and build sustainable relationships with these stakeholders in order to create this opportunity; however, without the support of these entities, prison-based educational programs designed to address transgenerational learned helplessness will ultimately fail. I can assure you as a prison educator over the past several years that the outcome will be well worth the effort.

As noted earlier, the black counter-culture of crime is embedded into the core of prison politics for incarcerated black students. However, it is not immovable. I discovered that by initially focusing my efforts on incarcerated black students who are extremely influential both inside and outside the class environment, I could "place my foot in the door" of the black counter-culture of crime. I made a concerted effort to gain not only their individual trust but their collective input on my pedagogical theory. Critical engagement is the key, and it always has been for motivating black students. If incarcerated black students were open to discussing my concept of *black cultural privilege* inside the classroom, they might be willing to debate and critique BCP outside on the prison yard. You see, those are the critical moments when the black counter-culture of crime within a correctional institution has the ability to shift. Incarcerated black students conceiving, generating, and producing intellectual motivation for others trapped within the counter-culture of crime creates other *de facto* incarcerated black students, a process no different than the systemic growth behind the culture of black gangsterism. In the end, the transformation from humiliation to humility through BCP must be owned and controlled by incarcerated black students in order to succeed.

Secondly, one must confront the cultural limitations of prison-based educators. Some of the key components of HHP and vital to the understanding the transformative awareness of *black cultural privilege*, are the deep-rooted discussions that prison educators must have with incarcerated black students on the injustices of racism, white supremacy, and white privilege. Regardless of an educator's academic discipline or course content, if educators are not prepared to engage in discussions surrounding these issues in their own personal lives, it's fair to question their true intentions as prison educators. As I discuss in greater detail later in this book, this becomes a formidable task when the overwhelming majority of prison educators are white Americans and have benefited whether directly or indirectly from these historic injustices. In fact, the willful ignoring of these issues runs much deeper than many prison educators are willing to accept. I've been involved in discussions with prison-based educators, many of whom are some of the most genuine and sincere social justice and anti-racism activists I've ever met, who cringe and become uncomfortable when the topic turns to how their own white privilege is perceived among the black offenders they teach inside correctional facilities. An even greater "taboo" is any discussion examining why there are so many white female prison educators. If these conversations are not taking place in the safe confines of the ivory tower surrounded by like-minded academic colleagues, it is safe to assume they are not occurring inside the walls of a prison setting in front of incarcerated black students. To overcome this cultural limitation, I encourage prison-based educators to engage in a lengthy period of self-reflection and self-awareness on white privilege, and discover how it has shaped their own identity and self-worth before walking into a prison classroom full of black men. Make yourself vulnerable to yourself first. Know your own truths as a prison-based college educator. Preparation before you walk into the classroom is the key.

Finally, and just as challenging, is addressing the resistance of the correctional staff culture. The number one priority in any correctional facility is to ensure that the individuals who have been convicted or pled guilty to a crime are confined in a secure manner due to public safety concerns. In a Federal Bureau of Prisons (BOP) facility, those would be crimes against the United States of America. However, my intent is not to debate the philosophical merits of custodial confinement "as punishment" or "for punishment" but to implement a prison-based educational pedagogy within the lived realities of today's prison settings. Prison educators must understand and accept the reality that it is inherently engrained into the criminal justice cultural mindset to never trust an inmate. This is a criminal justice survival mechanism that crosses racial, ethnic, and gender boundaries. I do not write this to mitigate the impact that racism, white supremacy, and white privilege plays in the correctional staff culture, because it's alive and well. However, black correctional staff do not trust incarcerated black men, which is no different than their white correctional counterparts not trusting incarcerated white men. It's a part of the profession's cultural DNA that will never change. This is their truth. There are countless crimes, ranging from rape, murder, assault, cell phone smuggling, and drug distribution that take place on a daily basis in prisons across the country. Correctional staff is responsible for policing these "cities within cities" and managing inmate behavior. In fact, as discussed above, some incarcerated black men who are trapped within the counter-culture of crime provide the greatest empirical and anecdotal support for the dysfunctional relationship between correctional staff and incarcerated black offenders. Incarcerated black men who are the by-products of transgenerational learned helplessness become the de-facto "voice" of all black incarcerated men in the eyes of correctional staff. This lack of institutional trust extends to all facility visitors, including college educators. Thus, correctional staff resistance to "externally" motivated programming efforts is a natural extension of the culture.

How do you begin to bridge this "cultural trust" gap? Build a partnership that places the goal of custodial security as a mutual number one priority. Strip searches, closed-circuit video camera monitoring, routine inmate population counts, and administrative segregation will always be part of custodial security, and any effort to judge these as unwarranted inhumane tactics will not and should not be tolerated by correctional staff. I share this message with executive staff and ensure they understand that "I'm just a visitor in their house." I do not want any power or desire to make any changes in their policies or procedures. I explain to them that my only goal is to provide a post-secondary educational experience for BOP offenders, and that my pedagogy is specifically designed to critically engage incarcerated black men. I establish trust through full disclosure. I immediately offer them any and all program materials or syllabi for critical review. I encourage correctional staff to attend the programming and to assess the BCP themed curriculum. I want them to see the intellectual prowess of incarcerated black students who struggle with their psychosocial identity constructed within the counter-culture of crime. I want them to hear the schisms between incarcerated black students debating each other regarding the global issues of race, politics, justice, history, religion, and family. I want them to experience the myth of homogeneous blackness. I want them to respect that if so inspired, incarcerated black students could shift the cultural paradigm of their own confinement from the *humiliation of correctional facilities* to the *humility of correctional learning centers* (CLCs). I want them to understand that if they choose to support this cultural transformation, their own work environment would become exponentially safer, increasing the primary goal of custodial security. It's a win-win situation for all stakeholders.

ENDING TRANSGENERATIONAL LEARNED HELPLESSNESS

Although there are countless theories that attempt to explain the results of transgenerational learned helplessness on the black American experience, whether it's the nihilism behind poverty, unemployment, or even the birth of a black counter-culture of crime, the one constant is its historical origin: *slavery*. Slavery was the "starting line" for the American dream for blacks. It set the moral and ethical tone for our entire nation. Its impact on the American legacy is so powerful that to even utter the spoken word immediately polarizes its cultural audience into black descendants and white benefactors. Its by-products of racism, white supremacy, and white privilege continue to operate as modern-day reminders of its influence. Slavery was so brutal that it inspired a four-hundred-year climate of direct and structural violence that serves as the measuring bar for the concepts of forgiveness and humiliation within the black American experience. BCP confronts slavery head-on, emphasizing that this nation's second worst intentional act of genocide failed to destroy the mind, body, and spirit of a culture, and ultimately only served to empower the essence of blackness. BCP exploits the invisible fear of slavery, educationally stripping it of its historic ability to impact the consciousness of the black male identity. BCP seeks to transform the humiliation of slavery into the humility of an indestructible culture that sits at the core of advancing an African heritage that gave birth to mankind.

To end transgenerational learned helplessness, incarcerated black students must allow themselves the opportunity to see themselves as an extension of a greater legacy than anything being offered through gangsterism or a counter-culture of crime. They must have the owned knowledge of Africa to explain that their ancestral homeland is the birthplace of all humanity. Their intellect must be groomed so that they are aware that Africa had a rich economic, religious, and cultural history thousands of years before European colonialism set foot on the continent (Bennett, 1961). They must be thoroughly familiar with the fact that the African Holocaust, also commonly known as the transatlantic slave trade, has triggered a chain of culturally destructive social and psychological events that continue to impact the lives of black Americans today (Anderson, 1999; Dyson, 1996; West, 2001; Wilson, 2009). One need not look any further than to what's occurring in Chicago today to get a clearer picture regarding the cycle of transgenerational learned helplessness trauma facing young black men today (Schwab, 2010). Finally, incarcerated black students must be able to inspire an "intellectual revolution" among themselves (Gaskew, 2009a), one that will resuscitate a counter-culture from the manifest destiny of nihilism long predicted by Du Bois (1994), Frazier (1968), and Garvey (1986).

Arguably, there has never been a greater manmade "planetary shift" than the benefits inherited from evils of the African Holocaust. In fact, it would be hard to imagine what the world would look-like today, economically, culturally, spiritually, politically, and socially, if what many historians estimate were between 50–100 million Africans had not been violently kidnapped, inhumanly enslaved, and transported like animals across the globe to "kick-start" the Dark Ages into what can be viewed today under the holistic definition of globalization (Curtin, 1969; Clarke, 1993; 1998; Karenga, 2002, 2005; Diouf, 2004; Adi, 2003, 2005; Asante, 2005, 2007; Nehusi, 2005; Zuberi, 2005). The Atlantic slave trade was a genocide created, owned, and implemented as part of the European formula for continental re-birth (Osei, 2005). It's synonymous with inhumane savagery, animalistic cruelty, institutionalized dehumanization, and cultural destruction, and it redefined and set the new standard for how we view the phenomenon of mass incarceration. Its stench spread across the Americas like a virus, infecting everything and every person in its path, whereas its remnants continue to negatively impact the black American experience some four hundred years years later.

When I speak to incarcerated black students regarding the topic of slavery, it is clear that although the concept is not foreign to them, the overwhelming majority are "purposefully ignorant" as to the specifics of the Atlantic slave trade. They either don't care or don't have any desire to understand anything about the concept of slavery. In fact, I'm normally the "angriest black man" in the room most of the time when the topic of slavery is breached. Many are uninspired and seem almost embarrassed to discuss slavery, especially in the presence of other incarcerated white students. When I ask if they feel victimized today by the historic act of slavery, the overwhelming majority strongly disagrees. When I suggest to them that their lack of knowledge on this barbaric period in American history allows them to be perpetually victimized by themselves, specifically by other black men, I often receive puzzled or blank stares. When I inform my audience that many of them have never escaped the manifest destiny of slavery, and that in fact, they are "mentally weak but physically strong" living in a "frozen psychological state of dependency," and furthermore, that black men today enjoy being modern-day slaves to a welcoming criminal justice overseer, their blank stares quickly turn to a simmering anger.

I then suggest that if the gates of the federal prison that currently cage them opened up today, allowing them an unanticipated chance at freedom, the overwhelming majority would never run away because their "new master" provides everything for this new culture of black males: free meals, free recreation, a free social agenda, freedom from responsibility in terms of children, wives, or bills. I add that even the human freedoms of love, respect, and trust are provided to them, as long as these are constructed on the terms of their "new masters." Hell, their "new masters" even provide personal entertainment by way of the use of MP3 players and music downloads, for a very profitable surcharge. Soon afterward, their angry stares are quickly vented by the hollow echoes of "bullshit" or "fuck this nigga" that ring throughout the room.

However, I don't stop there, because they are not quite yet ready to hear the truths of slavery and how this applies to their very own black American experiences. Finally, I ask if any of them are familiar with the book, *The Willie Lynch Letter and the Making of a Slave,* and out of a crowd of maybe ninety offenders, one or two recognize the title. After suggesting that they all should be very familiar with this specific literary work, since it serves as the "behavioral modification manifesto" for today's twenty-first century slave, the incarcerated black male, I tell them that the concept that Willie Lynch (2011) created is quite simple, yet horrifically effective and efficient in its modern-day application to black males:

In my bag here, I have a fool proof method for controlling your Black slaves. I guarantee every one of you that if installed correctly, it will control the slaves for at least 300 hundred years. My method is simple. Any member of your family or your overseer can use it. I have outlined a number of differences among the slaves and I take these differences and make them bigger. I use fear, distrust, and envy for control purposes. I shall assure you that distrust is stronger than trust, and that envy is stronger than adulteration, respect, or admiration. The Black slave after receiving this indoctrination shall carry on and will become self-re-fueling and self-generating for hundreds of years, maybe thousands. Don't forget you must pitch the old Black male vs. the young Black male . . . you must use the dark skin slaves vs. the light skin slaves. You must also have your white servants and overseers distrust all Blacks, but it is necessary that your slaves trust and depend on us. They must love, respect, and trust only us. Gentlemen, these kits are your keys to control. Use them. Have your wives and children use them, never miss an opportunity. If used intensely for one year, the slaves themselves will remain perpetually distrustful. Thank you gentlemen. (pp. 6–9)

He added:

For orderly futures, special and particular attention must be paid to the female and the youngest nigger offspring . . . both must be taught to respond to a new language. Psychological and physical instruction of containment must be created for both. . . . Keep the body and take the mind. In other words, break the will to resist . . . pay little attention to the generation of original breaking but concentrate on future generations . . . take the meanest most restless nigger male, strip him of his clothes, in front of the remaining male niggers, the female, and the nigger infant . . . tie each leg to a different horse to pull him apart . . . when in complete submission, the nigger female will train her offspring in the early years to submit to labor when they become of age . . . for fear of the young male's [infant] life she will psychologically train him to be mentally weak and dependent but physically strong . . . you've got the nigger woman out front and the nigger man behind and scared. This is the perfect situation. (pp. 10–18)

Finally, he stated: "We have created an orbiting cycle that turns its own axis forever, unless a phenomenon occurs and re-shifts the positions of the male and female savages" (p. 20).

A silent, yet almost shameful climate of disgust fills the room. Echoed as a continuous theme throughout this book, education and knowledge of one's history are at the cornerstone of the HHP. In fact, my hope is that the HHP inspires this "phenomenon [that] re-shifts the positions" of the black American male experience within the counter-culture of crime. A plethora of emotions are usually vented, ranging from anger, shame, disgust, to even laughter. I ask them to reflect on their lives and personal experiences, contemplating whether the concept of control described in

The Willie Lynch Letter was ever consciously or subconsciously used against them, and if so, who used it. When I ask them if they feel a sense of humiliation yet, the majority often reply positively. When I ask why, most indicate because they are tired of being treated like animals by the criminal justice system. I then suggest to these inmate students that their humiliation should be first directed solely with themselves, for not knowing or not caring enough to know and understand the contents of *The Willie Lynch Letter* and other forms of literary works written about themselves. We then involve ourselves in an open discussion about the emancipating power of education, and how it is the only mechanism that can be used to "re-shift the positions" of black males today, and stressing that only through knowledge can any sense of true freedom be achieved, taking one from humiliation to humility. At this point in our program, the class is now ready to examine the African Holocaust and its continued impact on the transgenerational learned helplessness of the black American experience.

FREEING MENTAL SLAVERY

At the sunset of the Golden Age, the African continent was in an unstable state of social, political, and religious equilibrium. The great Sudanese Empire and its incredible Mecca of erudition, Timbuktu, were in disarray. Critical infrastructure changes were occurring; tribal conflicts and war became more prominent, which triggered a mass migration from the South Sahara region. Africa was extremely vulnerable to the destructive elements of European colonialism (Bennett, 1961). The most tragic result of colonialism is that it created a climate that sought to destroy the last fourteen centuries of rich African culture and history, along with its contributions to humankind. Colonialism would ignore, erase, or rewrite African history, rendering the Golden Ages and the Sudanese civilization invisible to the eyes of the world, and more importantly, to the black American experience. Europeans created their very own version of African history, and it started with the Atlantic slave trade.

According to Clarke (1998) during this time period, Western Europe was just awakening from its very own ugly curse: the Dark Ages. The term "Dark Ages" became a popular designation in the eighteenth century, when many classical historians looked back to the glories of the Roman Empire, a period that covered over eight hundred years of civilization decline from the sixth to the fifteenth century, and despaired over the violence, brutality, and apparent lack of intellectual activity that characterized the post-collapse era. One of the most devastating events of this era was known in Europe as the "black death." It was considered one of the most devastating pandemics in human history, killing between 75 million and 200 million people. The disease is estimated to have killed 30 to 60 percent of Europe's population. All in all, the plague reduced the world population from an estimated 450 million to a number between 350 and 375 million in the fourteenth century (Hays, 2005). The period was thus labeled as "dark" for its lack of the lights of civilization and intellectuals, which had been replaced by feudalism, religious dominance, disease, and death. According to Clarke (1998), the motive and rationale for the African Holocaust started in the minds and hearts of Europeans, who needed to dig themselves out of the economic and cultural plunder of the Dark Ages: "The story of the African slave trade is essentially the story of the consequences of the second rise of Europe . . . who needed to search for new markets, new materials, new manpower, and a new land to exploit. The African slave trade was created to accommodate this expansion" (p. 58).

However, slavery was not a brand new invention to either the world or the African continent. As Bennett (1961) noted, "slavery was old when Moses was young" (p. 30). The concept of slavery had existed in ancient Rome, Athens, Middle Ages Europe, as well as across the western Sudan in Africa. In fact, if it were not for slaves, the magnificent Pyramids of Giza would not be standing today. That being said, there was a critical difference between the aforementioned ancient slavery and the new European model of slavery. First, ancient slavery had absolutely nothing to do with issues of race, which became the foundation for the new European model. Second, slavery usually occurred as a direct by-product of war. Third, slavery was categorized more in the likes of a contractual servitude. Fourth, no continent, including Africa, had ever had a slave economy. Finally, ancient slavery did not seek to destroy the sanctity of the family unit, and religious, cultural, or social bonds of human beings.

One of the greatest weaknesses of the African *cultural spirit*, which continues to invite unique comparisons to today's black American experience, was its naiveté. Although never advocating for pacifism, ancient African societies simply believed that a basic level of humanism and social justice existed among people and nature alike. They governed themselves by a code of "honor and obligation." They trusted the fundamental concept that someone's "word is bond." They never questioned the essential equilibrium of life, as the continent had inherited an incredible abundance of natural resources. As Clarke (1998, p. 58) noted regarding Africa, "Land could nether be bought or sold; there were no fights over the ownership of land. The land belonged to everyone." However, Europeans were just the opposite, as mother-nature was rather stingy regarding their own natural resources, and everyone competed for food, property, and social status. The Africans were completely blind-sided by the destructive nature of European colonialism and hoodwinked into trusting that Europeans would unconditionally accept them as equals, respecting the delicate natural balance that exists between survival and conquest. You see, the first Europeans to visit the West Coast of Africa were treated as guests and did not have to fight their way into the region.

The Europeans came with great big smiles and an open hand, the cornerstones of any true friendship. The Europeans approached them as business partners, where both parties could profit in trade from Africa's rich resources. However, Europeans quickly interjected themselves into the daily family lives of Africans, exploiting protracted tribal disputes, pitting brother against brother. In order to barter for the continent's gold and its most precious natural resource, its people, they used two of the most seductive vices ever created, leaving a permanent aftermath of cultural destruction that continues to plague black communities across America some five centuries later: guns and alcohol. Europeans needed "ready-made slave catchers" and were prepared to trade guns and rum for Africa's "black gold" with people who were very familiar not only with navigating the land but the culture as well. For greed and a few short-term gains in the art of war, some Africans were willing to poison their legacy. In fact, the same truths apply today when black males introduce the lifestyle of guns and drug trafficking into their very own communities. Can you imagine what the black American experience would be like today if it were not for guns and alcohol? Sadly, the two things that so many black males glorify today, which can be found in almost every urban music video or song lyric, are akin to a deadly cancer in our culture. Incarcerated black students must understand that, four hundred years ago, guns and alcohol were the primary catalysts responsible for causing a few Africans to hunt down and enslave millions of their very own brothers, handing them over to ready-made European slave masters, and that today, they have become the "slave-catchers" where alcohol and guns are doing the exact same thing, but on a much more deadly scale. You see, now it's young black American males handing their own brothers and many times, themselves, to a criminal justice slave master. What these young black men don't see is that alcohol and guns are being used to self-medicate and to provide an instant means of self-respect in order to ease the pain for their psychological and social humiliations. I would argue there are more handguns in the possession of our young urban black men today than laptop computers. In fact, July 2013 marked for the first time in our nation's history a "Computer for Guns" event. Residents in urban communities of color across Baltimore were afforded the opportunity to trade in their guns for a brand new Dell laptop computer. Disappointingly, the event took in barely over fifty guns (Rector, 2013).

Some four hundred years later, the scars of this antiquarian betrayal continues to linger in the black American experience, as this initial "social fraud" later morphed into the structurally and institutionalized American creations of the historical *socially constructed lie* that Columbus discovered America, the African Holocaust, the black codes, and Jim

Crow, forever throwing in doubt any level of long-standing trust between black Americans and their collective government, specifically regarding issues of racism, white supremacy, and white privilege within the criminal justice system and matters of law and social control. Clarke (1998) added: "In order to justify the destruction of these African societies, a monster that still haunts our lives was created. This monster was racism. The slave trade and the colonial system that followed are the parents of this catastrophe" (pp. 58–59).

As I already briefly noted, one of the greatest "social frauds" in American history was the institutionally sanctioned historical *socially constructed lie* concerning the European discovery of the so-called "New World." Since the start of my elementary school years in Chicago around 1970, I and every student around me was hoodwinked and taught one of our nation's greatest lies: that Columbus was a hero and that he was the sole discoverer of the Americas. In fact, in 1937 when my father was just five years old, during the depths of Jim Crow and racial segregation, our country legitimized this "grand lie" by recognizing Columbus with his own federal holiday. Unlike many of my classmates, I was reading the classic works of John Henrik Clarke, Lerone Bennett, the likes of Chancellor Williams' *The Destruction of African Civilization*, Eric Williams' *Capitalism and Slavery*, and countless others during my youth, which exposed me to the Columbus myth. By the time I was ten years old, I had a clear picture of what Columbus had "discovered": the concept of racism. There was simply no such thing as a "New World." David Stiddem in his speech, *It's Time We Rethink Our History*, noted:

> When we begin to rethink our history, we understand why history books were wrong. We were all miseducated. Columbus did not discover America. The historical facts: in December 1492, Columbus was totally lost, wandering around the Caribbean islands thinking he was in Asia, when he was discovered by native Arawak Americans who lived in these islands. Columbus didn't discover anything. He was so confused and lost, he thought he was in India, and called the Arawaks "Indians." Christopher Columbus was considered a saint by the European who hailed his great so-called "discovery." We need to rethink our history. Columbus was no saint. And the Arawak were not uncivilized savages. Like the African who came to America before and after Columbus, these were gentle people with a rich culture, who worshipped the one Creator. When we begin to rethink your history, we begin to put into historical perspective the true role of Europeans in our 500-year history. The prosperity, the wealth, the good European lifestyles we enjoy today in America began in 1492, and from an infant's beginnings. This prosperity grew out of slavery. You see slavery did not begin with the importation of African people to America. Slavery in America began with Columbus. The first slaves were not African, but Native Americans. Columbus enslaved the gentle Arawak Haitians, forced them to give up their gold, and their land. After all, he

had "discovered" these riches; they were his for the taking. In a short forty years, the entire race of people in Haiti, a half million native Americans, were wiped off the face of the earth by Columbus and the Spaniards that followed him. No, Columbus was no saint. We need to rethink our history. (pp. 6–8)

It is estimated that when the first Europeans arrived in fifteenth century, there were between 15–20 million American indigenous peoples living in the land referred to as the "New World." In fact, they spoke over 1,000 languages, under the umbrella of a wide variety of diverse indigenous cultures. According to Russell Thornton in *American Indian Holocaust and Survival: A Population History since 1492*, epidemic disease, enslavement, and warfare were by far the leading contributing factors of the population decline of the Native Americans after 1492, each of them related to European contact and colonization. Thornton (1990) added that these "man made" events contributed to the near extinction of the American indigenous peoples, which, similar to the historical black American experience, set into motion the institutionalized exploitation, dehumanization, and cultural destruction of our nation's first people. Over the next few centuries, their population was reduced to a morally reprehensible 250,000. According to U.S. Census Bureau Data (2013a) today, approximately 2.9 million U.S. indigenous peoples identify themselves as solely Native American. Mike Ely, in *The True Story of the Columbus Invasion* (1992), stated:

The U.S. imperialists love Columbus. They have named cities, counties, towns, rivers, colleges, parks, streets, and even their capital after him. And now they are organizing a global celebration. Yet, to the people, the facts are plain: Columbus was a thief, an invader, an organizer of rape of Indian women, a slave trader, a reactionary religious fanatic, and the personal director of a campaign for mass murder of defenseless peoples. The bourgeoisie hides these truths as they insist on celebrating him. They say, "Why can't we celebrate him for his seamanship and his daring?" Columbus was utterly lost when he arrived on the beaches of the Bahamas. Until he died, he swore that he landed in the eastern shore of Asia (which in reality is half a world away!) On his second voyage, he had his crew sign papers that declared that if they told anyone the island of Cuba was not the mainland of China, he would have their tongues cut out. Any reading of his diaries reveals that he was filled, not with a lofty courage or adventurous curiosity, but only the most extreme craving to plunder and enslave unarmed people. They say, "Why can't we judge Columbus by the standards of his time, not ours?" This is a revealing argument. We can ask whose "standards" of 1492 is the measuring rod. The Taino people? The African people? The peasant rebels of Spain? Or the conquistadores themselves?

He added:

The modern imperialists even adopt a sly "multicultural" cover saying, "Why can't we celebrate all the cultures that come together to make America today? Can't we use this celebration to heal the wounds from the past?" And the answer is that this view refuses to distinguish between oppressor and the oppressed—the Spanish conquistador and subjugated Indian are not just two "heritages" to be celebrated. Why should such wounds be "healed" when this celebration glorifies capitalist oppression that continues—when the legacy of the past is stamped on every event and social relationship." (pp. 1–9)

UNDERSTANDING THE JOURNEY TO CULTURAL GENOCIDE

Truth be told, Columbus set into motion an unprecedented era of human genocide, using race and ethnicity as the primary fuel to establish a climate of hate and the cultural demise of the *other*. The structurally perpetuated myth of Columbus as the great "discoverer" of the Americas still persists in many elementary schools across the country, and only adds to the continued lack of credibility that America's legacy as a land of social justice and equality has with people of color (Weatherwax, 1963; Williams, 1942, 1963, 1984). Columbus's one true legacy was that he discovered how to effectively use race as a "force multiplier" against people of color. Clarke (1998, pp. 34–35) added that the "Christopher Columbus Era" laid the psychological blueprint for how Europe colonized not only people and history, but more importantly, information about the people and history. The dehumanization of the African continent started with educating the world on several "myths" concerning its people and culture:

- The myth of a people waiting in darkness for another people to bring them to light.
- The myth of a people without a legitimate God.
- The myth of the primitive and aborigine.
- The myth of the invader and the conqueror as a civilizer.

Each of these myths, if taken at face value, provided a social and spiritual climate where the history of Africa and its rich culture could be completely erased and replaced with a demonizing narrative designed to humiliate its people and remove any historical memory of its rightful place as the birthplace of mankind. Can you imagine a world where every child in the Americas, since its inception, was taught the truths of Africa and its peoples? Slavery, the black codes, and Jim Crow simply became institutionally sanctioned tools used to extend the genocide of structural violence against the descendents of the *African cultural spirit*. Thus, Africa and its "history has been locked into a 500–year room" behind the steel curtain of slavery (Clarke, 1998, p. 36). This is the primary reason today why so many young black men lack the proper

knowledge, are ashamed, or feel absolutely no connection to their ancestral legacy. They, like many Americans today, have accepted these
"myths" as fundamental truths and believe the black American experience started with slavery. How can someone legitimately feel a sense of
pride, dignity, and respect if they were taught that their cultural roots
and subsequent role were those of subservience? Nothing can be further
from the truth.

Africans had been sailing the waters of the Western Hemisphere and
had become familiar with the Americas centuries before the first enslaved
Africans hit the shore of Jamestown, Virginia, in 1619 (Whittaker, 2003).
Africans were already familiar with the territorial lands of Mexico and
South America, and anthropological evidence of an early African culture
is widespread throughout these regions. Numerous large stone head statues, dating back to at least 1500 BC, representing images of kings have
been found in southern Mexico, in locations such as La Venta and Tres
Zapotes (Clegg, 2003). These statues depicted helmeted men with strong
black African physical features: large eyes, broad fleshy noses, and full
lips. Clegg (2003) added:

> The best evidence of the Black presence in America before Columbus
> comes from the pen of the "great discoverer" himself. In his Journal of
> the Second Voyage, Columbus reported that when he reached Haiti the
> Native Americans told him that black-skinned people had come from
> the south and southeast in boats, trading in gold-tipped medal spears.
> At least a dozen other European explorers, including Vasco Nunez de
> Balboa, also reported seeing or hearing of "Negroes" when they
> reached the New World. Nicholas Leon, an eminent Mexican authority,
> recorded the oral traditions of his people. Some of them reported that
> "the oldest inhabitants of Mexico were blacks." The existence of
> blacks . . . is commonly believed by nearly all the races of our sail and
> in their various languages they had words to designate them. (p. 1)

Truth be told, slavery in the Americas went through three "melanin"
stages: white, red, and black. European colonialism first attempted to
enslave their own race, white males and females; however, they did not
have a "tool for demonization" such as the noted myths to legitimize the
process to the masses. Whites were citizens and therefore fell under the
protection of the government. As well, whites could easily escape and
blend into the community, making captivity virtually impossible. Native
Americans were next; however, their ancestral knowledge of territorial
America made them very powerful adversaries and difficult to enslave.
Europeans also perceived Native Americans as somewhat unsuitable for
the incredible physical demands of slavery (Bennett, 1961; Clarke, 1998).

The African peoples did not have any of these disadvantages. Africans
were the epitome of the *other*: (1) They were dark-skinned, spoke a varied
and completely unfamiliar dialect, were often Muslim, and they originated from a continent and culture that few people on the planet had any

specific knowledge of. (2) They did not fall under the protection of any European-controlled government. Thus, they could be labeled as the perfect enemy in war, and dehumanized as such. (3) Due to the continent's warm climate, Africans were very strong laborers and could work in an outdoor environment for long extended hours under the most harsh weather conditions. And (4) there was nowhere to run or hide. The protective and naturally smooth dark pigmentation of Africans was used as a weapon, making assimilation in the Americas after an escape a complete impossibility. As well, there was nowhere for Africans to escape: home was 6500 miles away.

There has never been a definitive number of exactly how many Africans were enslaved in arguably the worse act of cultural genocide in history. At the lowest end of the continuum, Henry Louis Gates Jr. in *Life upon These Shores* estimated that no fewer than 12.5 million Africans were enslaved. However, eminent African historians Kimani Nehusi and Tukufu Zuberi in the documentary *500 Years Later,* John Henrik Clarke in *Christopher Columbus and the Afrikan Holocaust,* and other scholars suggest that based on African population loss estimates, these numbers can easily rise to between 60–100 million people (Adi, 2003, 2005; Asante, 2005, 2007; Karenga, 2002, 2005; Nehusi, 2005; Woodward, 2005). However, what is consistent throughout all of these African historians is that millions of Africans were murdered or died senselessly during what Asante (2005) referred to as the transatlantic "slave economy."

The overwhelming majority of slaves came from a 3,000–mile area bordering the West Coast of Africa. In fact, the first twenty or so Africans on the English ship *White Lion* that found its way to Jamestown, Virginia in 1619 were from Angola (Gates, 2013). For centuries, European nations fought each other for the right to possess Africa's most precious cargo: humans. Whether it was Portugal, which embarked for the African coast first, or its successors Holland, France, and Britain, each used the same barbaric process. Africans were hunted down and kidnapped or captured in traps like animals, from thousands of different tribes and villages across the coast. Some were obtained through African military campaigns or bartered for guns and rum, then later sold to slave-merchants for transport. Others were captured in the interior of the continent and forced to march hundreds of miles to the coast, to be processed in horrific dungeons of death.

DOORS OF NO RETURN

In the summer of 2009, President Barack Obama, along with first lady Michelle and daughters Malia and Sasha, visited Cape Coast Castle, in Ghana. As a social scientist who has personally seen the origin of transgenerational learned helplessness for myself, I despise to even call this and other fortified structures designed for the "deculturalization" of African men, women, and children "castles" because they fall under the same demented category as the Nazi concentration camps in Europe. Thus, I will refer to them in this book as "African holocaust camps." In fact, many of these holocaust camps held religious services directly above the submerged dungeon areas, within full auditory distance from the human indignity and barbarism occurring below (Simmonds, 2009). As sermons were read and hymns were sung, the suffering and torture of enslaved Africans could be overheard nearby. An emotional President Obama said his daughters needed to see the "Gates of No Return" to be reminded of the evil that exists in the world (Tapper, 2009). As well, after visiting Bunce Island, the site of an eighteenth-century, British-owned holocaust camp in the Republic of Sierra Leone in West Africa, former Secretary of State, General Colin Powell (1995) would later say, "I am an American but today, I am something more . . . I am an African too. I feel my roots here in this continent."

During the Trans-Atlantic slave trade, the continent of Africa was divided up among the Portuguese, the Spanish, the Dutch, the French, the Germans, the Italians, and the British. Each of these nations built holocaust camps along the West Coast of Africa, very close to the Atlantic Ocean to facilitate easy access for loading their human cargo onto slave vessels. Along a 2,800-mile span of the coast, from Senegal to Angola, over one hundred holocaust camps crowded the shores of the continent. The average dungeon would account for approximately 30,000 African slaves per year. In fact, no other stretch of the African coastline carries the scars of this human atrocity more than Ghana. In the peak of the trade, more than fifty holocaust camps crowded the shores of Ghana. One of the most infamous of these "doors-of-no-return" was Elmina Castle, which was erected by the Portuguese in 1482. Ghana's Elmina was used as the model from which many of the other dungeons took its lead.

The average stay in a holocaust camp lasted about a month to six weeks and it was not subliminal; it was real and it was very physical (Taylor, 2009). The men, women, and children were "stored" in separate areas of the dungeon. Conditions were horrifically inhuman; the slaves were packed in literally like sardines in a can. One of the primary purposes for the lengthy stay was to mentally and physically torture the African captives, in order to break their "warrior spirit" so by the time the slave ships arrived, they would be docile and ready for the next part of the process. It was only a barbaric prelude to what was to come later, on the other side of the infamous doors-of-no-return, the last sight millions of Africans would ever see of their precious homeland of Africa.

Bennett (1961) suggests that each of these "human factories" was equipped with a dungeon or what was dubbed as the "Negro House" by its creators, where all slaves, African men, women, and children were held captive until shipment abroad. Here, European merchants would trade guns, alcohol, clothing, trinkets, and goods for human beings. The process could be described in five connective parts: (1) Captive slaves would be purchased from brokers at these human factories, and placed in "booths" in an open-market style display near the beach. (2) While completely nude, medical practitioners would examine every crevice of their bodies, similar to purchasing an animal. (3) Those who passed the "inspections" were placed on one side, and those rejected (anyone over the discernible age of thirty; defective in eyes, teeth, limb, or other physical imperfection) were detained in a separate holding area. The "rejected" slaves were later murdered under captive starvation, thirst, or torture. (4) Slaves, regardless of whether man, woman, or child, who passed the inspection, were rewarded with a physical "brand" placed on their breast area with a red-hot iron, signifying the mark of company of purchase. And (5) branded and chained, the slaves were then rowed out to the slave ships to begin the dreaded Middle Passage across the Atlantic.

As unbelievable as it might seem, the torturous conditions became even worse once the slaves were aboard the transport ships. Bennett (1961) stated:

> They were packed like books on shelves into holds, which in some instances were no higher than eighteen inches. "They had not so much room," one [slave] captain said, "as a man in his coffin, either in length or breadth. It was impossible for them to turn or shift with any degree of ease." Here, for six to ten weeks of the voyage, the slaves lived like animals. Under the best conditions, the trip was intolerable. When epidemics of dysentery or smallpox swept the ship, the trip was beyond endurance. (p. 47)

He also added:

> On many of these ships . . . the sense of misery and suffocation was so terrible in the tween-decks—where the height sometimes was only eighteen inches, so that the unfortunate slaves could not turn round, were wedged immovably, in fact, and chained to the deck by the neck and legs—that the slaves not infrequently would go mad before dying or suffocating. In their frenzy some killed others in the hope of procuring more room to breathe. Men strangled those next to them, and women drove nails into each other's brains. It was common . . . to find a dead slave and a living slave chained together. So many dead people were thrown overboard on slavers that it was said that sharks picked up ships off the coast of Africa and followed them to America. (p. 47)

Just imagine the complete and utter inhuman and barbaric nature of this process: each transport ship, containing between 300–500 African slaves chained together by the neck, hands, and feet, crammed in the lower deck areas of the vessel where temperatures exceeded 100 degrees, in complete darkness most of the time, with minimal food and water, and with no means of hygiene other than small wooden buckets to be shared among all the enslaved captives, for a period of two months. Starvation suicide became an option for some Africans, as well as throwing themselves "overboard" in the endless waters of the Atlantic Ocean if any opportunity arose during the journey. Although it is very difficult for scholars to even estimate the number of Africans who died during the transatlantic journey, most historians feel reasonably confident that nearly as many Africans died en route as actually made it to the Americas. By all accounts, from the records that do exist, a successful voyage was one in which only one-quarter of the African captives died.

However, it must be stressed that many captive Africans never succumbed to the "slave economy," often choosing death instead, later inspiring the heroic ideology of Che Guevara's manifesto of freedom, "I would rather die on my feet than live upon my knees." Millions of Africans perished defending their moral right to live as free humans, fighting at each stage of the enslavement process. Active resistance occurred within the African continent, on transport ships, and upon arrival to the Americas. Sylviane Diouf's *Fighting the Slave Trade: West African Strategies* clearly points out that active resistance came in the forms of cumulative offensive, defensive, and protective measures. In fact, one form of resistance that has received little or no attention is that some Africans involved in the aforementioned "gun-slave trade policy" would only do so to obtain weapons to defend themselves and fight against European enslavement. One of the most famous African resistance leaders was Abdel Kader Kane, the Muslim king of northern Senegal. Kane not only fought against the enslavement of his own people, but he also forbid slave caravans from passing through his territory. During a letter to the French Governor dated March 1789, Kane said:

> We are warning you that all those who will come to our land to trade [in slaves] will be killed and massacred if you do not send our children back. Would not somebody who was very hungry abstain from eating if he had to eat something cooked with his blood? We absolutely do not want you to buy Muslims under any circumstances. I repeat that if your intention is to always buy Muslims you should stay home and not come to our country anymore. Because all those who will come can be assured that they will lose their life. (Diouf, 1998, p. 27)

Eric Taylor's *If We Must Die: Shipboard Insurrections in the Era of the Atlantic Slave Trade* illustrates that thousands of enslaved Africans participated in shipboard rebellions, with well over 500 documented incidents. One of the most successful and certainly the most celebrated shipboard revolts occurred in 1839 on the *Amistad,* where fifty-three enslaved Africans seized the ship, killed the captain, and ordered the remaining crew to sail back to Africa. Although the ship was intercepted off Long Island, New York and the rebels were imprisoned in New Haven, Connecticut on charges of murder for over two years, many of the Africans were returned to their homeland after successfully arguing their case in front of the U.S. Supreme Court in 1841. Whether the Stono Rebellion in 1739 in North Carolina, the Haitian Revolution in 1791, or the historic resistance movement led by black American Nate Turner in 1861 in Virginia, slavery and all of its cultural and physical inhumanity was resisted over and over again by all means necessary. The *Humiliation to Humility Perspective* (HHP) seeks to inspire incarcerated black students to fight just as vigorously to protect themselves and their children from the enslavement of transgenerational learned helplessness and mass incarceration.

DISCOVERING THE COLLECTIVE BLACK AMERICAN EXPERIENCE

When twenty or so Angolan Africans landed on the shores of Jamestown, Virginia in late August 1619 and had their very first children in the Americas, a year before the Mayflower landed on Plymouth Rock in Massachusetts, the black American experience had begun. Over the next couple of centuries, over a half a million more African slaves would land on the shores of the United States of America, creating a culture of over four million enslaved black Americans. Over the next four centuries, the journey of the black American experience has never been given its true historical justice. My father once told me, "Life is pretty simple . . . it's just what you accomplish between the two dates on your cemetery headstone." Truth be told, what black Americans as a people have accomplished from 1619 to 2014 while under the umbrella of arguably the most institutionally and structurally supported acts of oppression, marginalization and human genocide in modern times is a testament to courageous willpower, cultural preservation, and the unstoppable human spirit of the people. As I end this chapter, I would like to inspire my readers, especially incarcerated black student, to continue the scholarly *discovery* of the black American experience. Remember, true knowledge is not taught but discovered. If you stop here, you will never discover the true essence of the lived black American experience.

This chapter was designed to inspire intellectual accountability for incarcerated black student to own the collective knowledge of their *black cultural privilege* (BCP). I attempted to dismantle the historical cultural barriers that exist for incarcerated black men making the transition from humiliation into humility, ending transgenerational learned helplessness. I hope it inspires readers to understand the grave importance of seeking the truth of their ancestral history, for whoever knows their own *true* history controls their own *true* destiny. There are no better words I've ever come across in my life to describe this sentiment than of African scholar and historian Runoko Rashidi:

> There was a time when I was ashamed of Africa too; I didn't want to have anything to do with Africa. And now, I'm just the opposite of

that. Malcolm X is an example of that. He's said in his auto-biography that he was a pimp, a burglar and a thief and then he began to find out about who he was and it changed everything. I think the motto is: "What you do for yourself depends on what you think of yourself. What you think of yourself depends on what you know of yourself. And what you know of yourself depends on what you have been told." So if you're told you come from the jungle, if you're told you come from a bunch of savages, barbarians, people who have no civilization, no history, you'll act that out. But if you know you come from the continent that gave birth to humanity and civilization and that slavery did exist but that we fought it and we resisted it, I think that changes everything. You'll have a new found sense of pride and you'll want to identify with Africa. When somebody attacks Africa, you'll fight because you'll know they are attacking your mother, they are attacking your heritage and you won't have that. But if you don't see that connection, then we're just doomed to wander in the wilderness and that can't be our fate. (Balola, 2011, p. 7)

THREE

The Great White Shark

If I had to guess, during my decade-long career as a drug task force agent, I was personally responsible for the arrest of easily over 2,000 people, many for state and federal drug and weapons offenses, the overwhelming majority of whom were black males. I understand in a nation that has arrested more than 45 million people and spent more than one trillion dollars in the *War on Drugs*, this figure sounds somewhat miniscule; however, don't be fooled. My individual "body count" does not include the "collateral psychosocial damage," such as its short- and long-term impact on children, spouses, and caretakers (grandparents, aunts, uncles, cousins), which based on my first-hand experience normally adds an additional five black *offenders* per arrestee. I say *offenders*, because historically, black males who are arrested have an incredible ability to produce "offender clones." This number doesn't include the millions of dollars seized, through civil asset forfeiture, court costs, lost wages, as well as the lost tax-base and the negative impact on consumer spending within the community. It doesn't include the race and class-based shame, anger, and hopelessness that will be imposed on you and everyone around you. Institutionalized racism will be flaunted in your face like a badge of honor until your mental and physical will is completely broken. What will make the issue of racial inequality so unbearable will be the fact that the majority of the nations "drug warriors" will be middle-class white males and their "white privilege" will not even afford them the ability to recognize the incredible damage they will have inflicted upon the black community at the end of the day. So, when these social force multipliers are included, I will have introduced well over 10,000 black males, the size of a small town, to the criminal justice system, where they will either be physically taken into custody and incarcerated or psychologically indoctrinated into a counter-culture of shame, anger, control and domination. Either way, they will all be ready to perpetuate the cycle of criminal justice servitude.

You see, my "invisible" job description in this system, just like the tens of thousands of other local, state, and federal drug agents scattered throughout the nation, was not only to arrest drug or weapons traffickers, but to psychologically humiliate the individuals involved in this underground economy, along with their entire culture. To humiliate their family, friends, and community either by legal fear of arrest and asset forfeiture, or by the most powerful weapon in my arsenal: *planting cultural doubt*. That is, doubt in your ability to trust family and friends and doubt in their ability to trust you. More importantly, doubt in *everyone's* ability to trust *anyone* that shares the same racial or ethnic cultural traits. This can easily be perceived as an updated version of *The Willie Lynch Letters and the Making of a Slave*; however, this time it's urban black males who are the co-authors of the manifesto. The incredibly sad part of this entire scenario is that most of the "drug warriors" at best don't understand or at worst don't care about the impact of these humiliations. Many do not accept the role of "mitigators" within the criminal justice system. To enforce the law with a keen understanding of how the criminal justice system contributes to racial stratification, and to choose enforcement strategies that inflict the least amount of systemic damage possible. They see policing as a "video game" where win or lose, the end result will have no impact on the life of the game player. Again, the "lived" experiences allow me and other officers of color the ability to be the outliers in this tragedy, whether we like it or not. Recognizing the dire impact of these humiliations, as gatekeepers in this system, we must ensure that each person is treated with as much dignity, respect, and "truth" as possible. We must all learn to become *criminal justice mitigators*.

Within the *Humiliation to Humility Perspective* (HHP), the goal is to address the *politics of shaming, self-segregation, and transgenerational learned helplessness* by providing inspiration for incarcerated black students to access their own truths through their own lived experiences. Within this framework, improving one's "criminal justice system IQ" is paramount for allowing incarcerated students to see the justice system as both an institutional process and as a business entity. Someone trapped in the counter-culture of crime must clearly understand that the criminal justice system is a carnivorous "Great White Shark" with an endless appetite and that *everyone* who comes into contact with it is going to be *bitten* and that their wounds will subsequently become infected and will infect others. They will understand that those who come in contact with the system will either unknowingly or intentionally allow others to swim in shark-infested waters, primarily of the same race, ethnicity, and class. More importantly, they will rarely ever again fear the criminal justice system, and will teach the same to their children, family, and community, because they will understand that the only person who has the power to "feed the shark" is themselves.

Most people are somewhat surprised to discover that most of the offenders who are imprisoned do not have a cultural understanding of the criminal justice system. Some people might think that's a good thing and that ultimately people who commit crimes get exactly what they deserve. Although I completely understand those feelings, most of the people who share those sentiments have never been formally introduced into the criminal justice system themselves. Let me clarify. I'm not suggesting providing some type of "pro bono" process where incarcerated students can receive free legal advice for an appeal or to try to "beat" their charges. I have been approached and received letters from federal offenders countless times trying to seek legal advice regarding their respective crimes, and my response has always been the same: *not a chance.*

I fully advocate and support the concept of social justice, which means that if the criminal justice system has not followed the legal limitations dictated within the U.S. Constitution, which does occur, I hope those convicted of crimes are freed, their rights fully restored, and that they are fully compensated for the injustice done to them. What I'm suggesting is to educate incarcerated black students on the *application* of the formal components and the *outcome* of the informal processes of the criminal justice system, so they can make a better informed decision on whether they want to continue to be part of a counter-culture of physical and mental servitude. Reconciliation and redemption are not about winning the legal battle but the cultural war.

AN EATING MACHINE

Not surprisingly, given the very nature of our over-politicized and media-driven culture, with an overabundance of "CSI" and so-called reality-based television shows such as "Cops" on the airwaves, criminal justice programs are one of the most popular college academic disciplines in the country. Although diverse in their academic requirements, specialties, and curriculum, what every program in the nation shares is that all criminal justice majors at some point will complete a basic lower-level course entitled "Introduction to Criminal Justice" or its equivalent. The course content is universal. Students will be exposed to the three fundamental components of the criminal justice system: policing, courts, and corrections. However, I believe the course provides the most important and vital information any post-secondary educational experience can offer. It provides students access to survival skills that will be required for them to navigate through the shark-infested waters known as the criminal justice system.

On my very first day and often during my very first lecture, I provide a quick fifteen minute snap-shot of the entire criminal justice system. I tell the incarcerated students, if they only remember one thing from their post-secondary educational experiences with me, regardless of their race, ethnicity, or religious affiliation, is to be able to recognize, understand, and respect that the criminal justice system is just like a *Great White Shark*. I offer to them, without this specific knowledge, they and their children will continue to be the "main course" on the *justice systems menu*. I then display the following illustration (see fig. 3.1).

I explain to them, the great white shark, also known as "carcharodon carcharias," is an eating machine. Virtually unchanged by evolution, all it does, twenty-four hours a day, seven days a week, is eat, digest its food, and excrete waste. Sometimes after a shark has eaten very well, it travels to the bed of the ocean and undergoes a cognitive activity of "rest" that

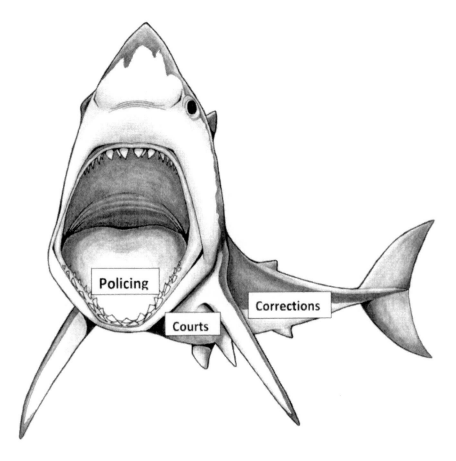

Figure 3.1.   The Great White Shark Model of Justice. Drawing courtesy of Jamie VanAlstine. Concept by author.

means it relaxes only one side of its brain at a time, allowing the other side to remain alert for predators or more food as it continues to move through the water. In fact, even in the womb great white sharks are hunting. During pregnancy, a "cannibalism phenomenon" occurs within the womb, where the larger pups actually kill and feed on the smaller, underdeveloped ones. The shark's distinctive power, size, and fearless nature make it an almost unstoppable force. It has a bite force of over 18,000 newtons, which is about 4,000 lbs. or the equivalent of having a fully loaded Range Rover fall on your head.

I discuss that great white sharks are carnivorous and prey upon almost anything that moves. However, they can be very territorial, and will feed until the entire food supply has been completely consumed. They have also been known to eat objects that they are unable to digest. Even when unsuccessful in the kill, with over 3,000 razor sharp teeth in its mouth at any given time, the great white shark leaves its prey bleeding profusely, drawing the attention of other sharks. If its prey is fortunate enough to escape, the prey is left with unforgettable physical and mental scars.

I inform them that although water-based ambush hunters, great whites are known to regularly lift their heads above the sea surface to gaze at other objects such as prey, known as spy-hopping. In fact, many display a breaching behavior, which is when they go so fast that they can completely leave the water. Their peak burst speed is approximately twenty-five miles per hour. The shark displays countershading, a coloration that makes it difficult for its prey to spot because the coloring breaks up the sharks outline when seen from the side. From above, the darker shade blends with the sea, and from below it exposes a minimal silhouette against the sunlight. Its digestive system is just as impressive. Great whites mostly swallow their food whole or bite it into relatively large pieces. Their stomachs contain very strong acids and enzymes to dissolve almost everything they eat. Indigestible things are vomited up within twenty-four hours. Everything that is not absorbed into the body is then excreted in liquid form through the cloaca, which is located near the anal fin, back into the ocean from whence it came (Tricas and McCasker, 1984; Klimley and Ainley, 1996; Medina, 2007; Wroe et al., 2008).

THE GATEKEEPERS

Exactly like the *great white shark*, the criminal justice system is a machine, largely unchanged by the social evolutionary forces of due process, poverty, civil rights, war, demographics, or even politics. Separated into a connective but distinguishable *three-course meal*, policing, courts, and corrections, it is designed to arrest, process, and confine human beings, twenty-four hours a day, seven days a week (see fig. 3.2).

The general public is often "bamboozled" primarily by police chiefs looking for additional funding for more cops or equipment, policy-making think tanks looking for additional funding for grants, or politicians looking for additional funding for votes, into believing that the criminal justice system was designed to do something other than to arrest, prosecute, and warehouse people.

The truth is, the justice system is a "one trick pony" people, because it's in the institution's social, cultural, and political DNA to "eat." Again, have you ever witnessed a domesticated great white shark? I've been to Sea World in Orlando, Florida, at least fifty times in my life and I have yet to see the great white shark performance. You know, the one where the trainer gets into the water tank for the "Killer Whale Show" and swims, feeds, and rides on the back of *Shamu* to the delight of the audience. I especially enjoy the part where the trainer sits on the tip of the killer whale's mouth, submerged completely under water, and is thrown into the open air only to land safely and unharmed on the tank deck. This is how Sea World makes its money, folks. Now imagine this same show but with a great white shark in the tank, and the majority of the trainers are black males. This is how the criminal justice system makes its money, folks.

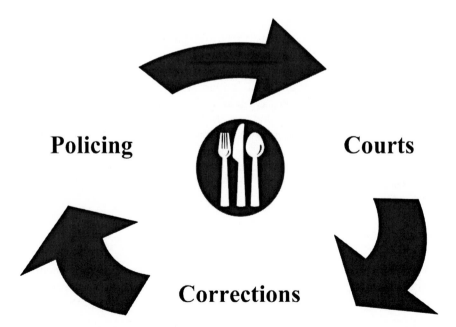

Figure 3.2. The Criminal Justice System Menu.

The two best examples of some absurd policing policies that have been epic failures primarily because they promote a philosophy contrary to the *criminal justice system's DNA*, has been the hugely funded Drug Abuse Resistance Education (D.A.R.E.) and the Community Oriented Policing (C.O.P.) programs. Did any rational person really believe that a drug education program created by former LAPD Chief Daryl Gates was in the best interest of communities of color? Did any rational person really believe that a policing initiative that has added more than 130,000 police officers to our nation's streets, wouldn't place those officers in communities of color to make more arrests?

When questioned by members of the New York City Council's Public Safety Committee on the possibility of hiring additional police officers in 2013, NYPD Commissioner Ray Kelly, who leads the largest police force in the nation with nearly 40,000 officers, responded that he did not want any additional officers. "When you hire more officers, they make more arrests," which Kelly believes would deplete his already taxed resources (Robbins, 2013). Can anyone blame him, with a staggering 422,982 arrests in NYC in 2010 alone, many of them for drug offenses? Think about this for a second. In 2010 NYC police officers in just one borough, Brooklyn, made 40 percent more marijuana arrests, primarily of people of color, than the total number of forty states in this country. Again, besides the obvious racial overtone, this is not a criticism of policing, but a tough reality check on what their role truly is within society (Robbins, 2013).

Similar to the great white shark, the criminal justice system "half-rests" because it has the unique ability to generate new "customers" (via arrests) while simultaneously moving people already in custody through the legal system. Its dietary requirements can be very selective, as the disproportionate number of young black men involved in the criminal justice system clearly indicates. The justice system's entire existence depends on the policing component, the gatekeepers of the entire system, and their ability to make arrests. Over the past three decades, police agencies have kept the system at near obesity levels, arresting well over 250 million people, with approximately 45 million for drug offenses alone (Federal Bureau of Investigation, 2013a, 2013b). Just like its evolutionary cousins and although selectively, the system also practices cannibalism, arresting police, corrections officers, prosecutors, and even judges when hungry enough.

The legislative and judicial branches of the government have provided the executive component with ample resources to make these arrests. In fact, an inventory of the legal and technological tools, specifically available for the *War on Drugs*, makes the "hunt" almost unfair. With over 18,000 local, state, and federal policing agencies nationwide, employing over a million full and part-time sworn police officers, we have approximately three police officers for every 1,000 Americans. The demographic make-up of policing sits at over 80 percent white males, and the social ramifications of this cannot be underestimated (Bureau of Justice Statistics, 2008).

Although macro-level racial biases have been built into the criminal justice structure, the most lethal biases occur in the form of individualized discretion, the ability to pick and choose who gets arrested, prosecuted, and jailed. Discretion falls ultimately on the individual police officer, prosecutor, and judge. Although the discretionary powers of prosecutors and judges are enormous, which we will also discuss in this chapter, policing discretion is the most dangerous because police serve as the gatekeepers of the entire system. Regardless of the nature of the offense, without police serving as the initial point of contact, there is no prosecutorial discretion to charge or judiciary discretion to sentence.

In 2011, adult black males made up over 30 percent of all nationwide arrests, despite representing less than 3 percent of the adult population in America (NAACP, 2013). As well, black males under the age of eighteen were over 32 percent of all juvenile arrests (FBI, 2013a). If we extract the estimated number of Hispanic arrests from the Uniform Crime Report data (which classifies them under the category of "white"), how can we rationally explain how a racial demographic that represent over 72 percent of the U.S. population, makes up less than 35 percent of all police initiated arrests? Over the past twenty-five years, federal agents from the Drug Enforcement Administration (DEA) have arrested 786,770 people on drug charges. Disproportionally, an incredible 75 percent of these arrests were people of color (DEA, 2013, U.S. Sentencing Commission, 2011). In fact, the overwhelming majority of the DEA's cases over the past two decades have been directed at cocaine base (crack cocaine), in which the criminal defendants are overwhelmingly black (83 percent) and only a handful (6 percent) are white Americans (U.S. Sentencing Commission, 2011). How can the United States of America's premier federal agency for drug enforcement, make fewer cocaine hydrochloride (powder cocaine) arrests than cocaine base, when the main ingredient for crack cocaine is powder cocaine? Part of the answer is uncovered when asking "who" is ultimately responsible for selecting federal criminal investigatory targets.

Again, how can this racial disproportionality in arrests be rationally explained? If your answer is that black Americans use or distribute drugs at a higher rate than white Americans, think again. According to the U.S. Sentencing Commission (2011) the number of white drug users in America is six times the number of black Americans, at approximately 14 million; however, blacks are sent to prison for drug offenses at a rate ten times greater than whites. Black males represent over 60 percent of offenders sentenced to prison for drug offenses. In fact, black males serve virtually as much time in prison for a drug offense (fifty-eight months) as white Americans do for a violent offense (sixty-one months).

A 2013 study by researchers from the University of Wisconsin-Milwaukee, on the racial disproportionality of our nation's prisons, made a surprising discovery. The state that confined the greatest percentage of black males in the nation was not one of the ones with the highest concentrations of blacks such as Georgia, North Carolina, Florida, New York, California or Texas, which total over half the entire black American population, but in fact Wisconsin (see figure 3.3). With a demographic population of 88.3 percent white and 6.5 percent black, in Wisconsin, 1 in 8 adult black men (12.8 percent) are incarcerated. The national average is 1 in 15 (6.7 percent). In fact, Wisconsin also leads the nation in the percentage of Native American men behind bars; 1 in 13 is incarcerated. However, its percentage of white men in prison is consistent with the nation's average at 1.2 percent (Pawasarat and Quinn, 2013).

In Milwaukee County alone, over half of the black men in their thirties and forties have been incarcerated in state correctional facilities. The report, *Wisconsin's Mass Incarceration of African American Males: Workforce Challenges for 2013*, goes on to collaborate a consistently ugly theme which I highlight throughout this book regarding the criminal justice system: race pays. In one of the most convincing examples of this phenomena, given the grossly disproportionate representation of black men imprisoned and the $3.88 billion cost to manage the prison system in 2012, the state of Wisconsin was spending over half a million dollars a day to incarcerate 5,631 black men from the Milwaukee County area alone (Pawasarat and Quinn, 2013).

At roughly $32,000 a year, which is the starting salary for a correctional officer with the Wisconsin Department of Corrections (WDOC), every single unemployed and incarcerated black male from Milwaukee County, was responsible for employing sixteen full-time positions, in which the vast majority are white males. Now imagine these employment ratios across the national board within the criminal justice system, policing, courts, and corrections, when we're talking about nearly 3.5 million black Americans in some form of correctional supervision in the nation. The fact is, unemployed, uneducated, and unknowingly, black

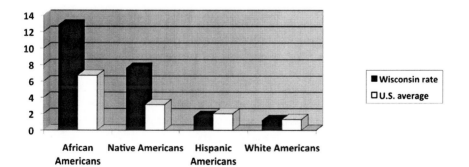

Figure 3.3.   Percent of Incarcerated Men in the WDOC in 2010.

Americans, who make up nearly 30 percent of our nation's arrests, nearly 40 percent of our nation's prisoners, and nearly 50 percent of our nation's probationers, are keeping the nation's criminal justice system "in the black."

Wisconsin should not be the only state morally embarrassed. Oklahoma reflected an incarceration rate for black males at 9.7 percent, and Iowa, a state that only has a black American population at roughly 3 percent, boasted an incarceration rate of 9.4 percent. The state of Pennsylvania ranked fourth in incarcerating black men at a rate of 9.1 percent, although it is similar to Wisconsin with a demographic that is 84 percent white (U.S. Census Bureau, 2013c). The fact is, race pays, and nowhere more than in the *War on Drugs*. As a former Organized Crime Drug Enforcement Task Force (OCDETF) member, a concept I will go into much greater depth later in this chapter, I had the ability to pick and choose from countless drug dealers who would be investigated, and if probable cause existed, who would be arrested. I had full discretionary powers, and not everyone who violated drug offenses was arrested. The choice was all mine. Now, just imagine similar types of discretionary powers dispersed among a million police officers nationwide, all having the ability to pick and choose who will be arrested, each one with the ability to use race as a factor if they so decide. What made me different? Again, my self-actualization and awareness of humiliation and humility. I never tried to make the criminal justice system something that it wasn't: color-blind. There is nothing "accidental" about understanding the relationship between race, crime, and justice.

THE BELLY OF THE BEAST

Once suspects are in the custody of the criminal justice system, the courts, which form the digestive system of this eating machine, take over. This judiciary component of the criminal justice system has the same underlying issues as policing regarding race, crime, and justice. Once the police make the arrest, the court system has the authority to literally pick and choose, without any oversight, what stays in the digestive system of the shark or what gets regurgitated back into the population. It is no surprise that race has always been a variable in prosecutorial filing and court sentencing decisions. How can a judicial system that ruled *Plessy vs. Ferguson*, the government sanctioned legal segregation of black Americans, to be the law of the land, not fall under the national spell of white supremacism? How can we begin to explain a judicial system that ensures that over 840,000 black men are housed in our prisons, with another 2.5 million more on probation or parole, and over 5 million more who have previously been sentenced to jail, prison, probation or parole, despite only accounting for roughly 3 percent of the adult population? How can we begin to explain how black Americans nationwide represent 44 percent of youth who are detained, 46 percent of the youth who are judicially waived to criminal court, and 58 percent of the youth admitted to state prisons? How can we begin to explain how 1 in 3 black males can be trapped in the belly of our judicial system without racism being a significant factor (NAACP, 2013; National Urban League, 2013)?

In 2013, Texas elected its first ever black district attorney, Craig Watkins. In one of his first public speaking appearances at Wake Forest University School of Law, he was asked about issues of race, crime, and justice. Watkins replied, "Traditionally, people of color have had a negative view of law-enforcement, and it's warranted." He added, "Anyone who believes that race doesn't play a role in the criminal justice system is naïve" (Hewlett, 2013). DA Watkins is not alone in his assessment and was simply sharing a *truth* that countless other black professionals on the "inside" of the criminal justice system have known for years: race matters. As noted by black American scholar and Harvard University law professor Charles Ogletree (2012), the judicial system has from its roots always had "the presumption of guilt" for black Americans. He added:

> The presumption of guilt can have an insidious presence beyond an individual's interaction with the police. We can imagine how this bias can affect juries, judges, the strength of a defense, and the outcome of the trial as well as a prescribed sentence. We can imagine that well-meaning, well-regarded individuals perform their daily roles unaware of their preconceived biases and their eventual effects. (p. 116)

However, similar to policing, significant barriers are created for these professional "voices of color" to be heard, in part due to the demographics of prosecutors and judges around the nation. According to the National Black Prosecutors Association (2013), there are under 1,000 black American prosecutors representing just 3.3 percent of the estimated 35,000 criminal prosecutors in America. These numbers include the chief federal law enforcement officers, ninety-three United States Attorneys (USAs), who supervise an additional 5,600 Assistant United States Attorneys (AUSAs) throughout the country and the U.S. territories (National Association of Assistant United States Attorneys, 2013). Again, the overwhelming majority are white males. Chicago has never had a black American U.S. Attorney in the city's history. According to the U.S. Sentencing Commission (2011), the federal government processed 86,361 federal criminal cases in 2011 with a judiciary budget of $6.97 billion.

Since judges are lawyers first, the dearth of black criminal persecutors has a direct correlation to the number of black judges in America. As a nation with 12,149 judges, fewer than 6 percent are black Americans. In fact, less than 5 percent of all U.S. federal judges, hearing over 85,000 criminal cases each year, are black Americans (Chew and Kelley, 2012). Is it any surprise that over 70 percent of offenders sentenced to federal prison are people of color?

ASSISTANT U.S. ATTORNEYS SPEAK OUT

Robert Smith and Justin Levinson, in their article *The Impact of Implicit Racial Bias on the Exercise of Prosecutorial Discretion* (2012), pointed out that racial biases impact prosecutorial decisions regarding three important phases:

> (1) charging decisions, including both the decision of whether to charge and the decision of what crime to charge; (2) pretrial strategy, such as the decisions to oppose bail, offer a plea bargain, or disclose potentially exculpatory evidence to the defense; and (3) trial strategy, such as the decision to strike potential jurors or to analogize the defendant to an animal during closing arguments. (p. 805)

Daniel Medwed's *Prosecution Complex: America's Race to Convict and Its Impact on the Innocent* (2012) adds:

> American prosecutors are asked to play two roles within the criminal justice system: they are supposed to be ministers of justice whose only goals are to ensure fair trials—and they are also advocates of the government whose success rates are measured by how many convictions they get. Because of this second role, sometimes prosecutors suppress evidence in order to establish a defendant's guilt and safeguard that conviction over time. (pp. 1–3)

Although widespread racial disparities occur across the country from local and state jurisdictions within *lady justice*, I try to focus my attention on the federal criminal justice system throughout this book because when someone falls under the prosecutorial criminal scope of the federal government, they will receive a document clearly stating the *United States of America v. "fill in the blank."* Let me be very clear. There is no greater or more sacred legal war within the halls of American justice than the war that forces you to defend yourself against criminal charges from your very own country, the United States of America. No person, country, or civilization who has ever gone to war with the United States of America has ever been the same in mind, body and spirit. Thus, if one cannot find truth and justice within the protections of a federal courtroom, there is absolutely no hope in any of the remaining local and state jurisdictions around the country.

A report by the Brennan Center for Justice at New York University School of Law, *Racial Disparities in Federal Prosecutions*, expressed the narratives of twelve former prosecutors, most of whom had served as United States Attorneys, to take a critical look at the racial and ethnic disparities within the federal criminal justice system. Their findings were not surprising:

> Racial disparities have been documented at every stage of the criminal justice system. African Americans and other racial and ethnic minorities are more likely to be arrested than white citizens, more likely to be charged once arrested, and more likely to be convicted and imprisoned once charged. . . . The federal criminal justice system is often viewed with great distrust because of the disproportionate numbers of African Americans, Hispanics, American Indians, and other racial or ethnic minorities in our jails and prisons—and especially because of the disproportionate severity in their sentences. (Johnson et al., 2010, pp. ii–2)

The report notes that federal prosecutors and law enforcement agents alike wield enormous power to shift this axis, and although their intentions regarding the delicate balance between justice and public safety are in the right place, their efforts are unwillingly "compromised" by the reality of racial and ethnic disparities. As such, these former federal prosecutors drafted a set of six guidelines (Prosecutorial Decision-Making; Law Enforcement and Task Forces; Training; Management and Accountability; Community; and Influencing Legislation and Policy) to serve as a foundation to address race-based biases within the federal criminal justice system:

1. Prosecutorial Decision-Making:

   - The U.S. Attorney should be conscious of potential racially disparate impacts when setting district prosecution priorities, and should consider statistical evidence of community crime indicators and qualitative evidence of community concerns in setting prosecution priorities and initiatives.
   - They should be proactive in his/her leadership and partnership with law enforcement agencies to prevent racial and ethnic bias and ensure that similarly situated defendants receive similar charges and sentences, and should consider the racial effects of his/her charging and disposition policies and ensure that racially disparate effects are tolerated only where strongly justified by legitimate law enforcement needs.

2. Law Enforcement and Task Forces:

   - The U.S. Attorney should provide oversight of all law enforcement task forces operating under his/her jurisdiction and encourage diversity of membership, leadership, policy makers, and decision-makers in each task force enterprise.
   - They should charge task forces with the obligation to consciously review their rationales for conducting or declining

to conduct investigations in order to eliminate racially disparate treatment and effects.

3. Training:

   - All training of federal prosecutors should incorporate education about the role of racism in our history and criminal justice system. This includes providing training to all supervisors, attorneys, and other staff that is specifically directed toward eliminating racial bias and racial stereotyping in recruitment, hiring, retention, promotion, supervision, and prosecutorial decision-making.
   - They should provide or advocate for racial disparity/profiling training for law enforcement agencies and advocate conditioning the receipt of federal funding for law enforcement efforts on agents' participation in such training.

4. Management and Accountability:

   - The U.S. Attorney should support office policies that ensure diversity among his/her professional and support staff, including the active recruitment, hiring, retention, and promotion of African Americans, Hispanics, American Indians, and other racial and ethnic minorities.
   - Every prosecutor should review his/her own personal beliefs and biases, including use of racial and ethnic stereotypes or use of proxies for race and ethnicity (such as class/socio-economic status or geography), and take affirmative steps to eliminate racial/ethnic bias or stereotyping that is within his/her control and supervision.
   - This process should include collecting and analyzing quantitative and qualitative data on the race and ethnicity of the defendant and victim at each stage of prosecution.

5. Community:

   - The U.S. Attorney should meet with community members, including members of the bar and criminal justice professionals, to obtain their input on crime problems and effective solutions.
   - They should adopt measures that allow lay community members to voice their concerns about real or perceived disparate treatment in prosecutorial policies and disparities in their final results.

6. Influencing Legislation and Policy:

- Each U.S. Attorney has the affirmative obligation to raise the racially disparate effects of legislation and policy with the Department of Justice.
- They should advocate sentencing alternatives and reforms that lessen the impact on those adversely affected by racial disparities in the federal criminal justice system. (pp. 3–8)

THE LEFT-OVERS

After passing through the mouth and digestive system of the criminal justice system, very little is left of a person in mind, body, and spirit, if the shark's internal organs are working properly. If anyone on this planet doubts the efficiency of the criminal justice system's racially dysfunctional structure, they need to look no further than the correctional component of the criminal justice system. Over 5 million black men have been excreted out of the anal cavity of the system as convicted felons over the past decade. Currently, over 4 million are either housed in prisons, jails, or under the community-based supervision of a probation officer. Black males have become the "leftovers" of a financially rewarding but socially costly *three-course meal*.

The financial rewards for incarcerating black males are enormous. I've already highlighted some of the monetary incentives within the Wisconsin Department of Corrections; however, this is a national epidemic. Just imagine how many jobs are created by placing millions of young black men into the correctional component of the criminal justice system. Just do the math. According to the Sourcebook of Criminal Justice Statistics (2013) and the American Correctional Association (2013), there are 4,575 correctional facilities in operation in America, employing just under 300,000 people. There are an additional 125,000 probation and parole officers employed across the country. We're talking about almost a half a million jobs in corrections alone!

EVERYBODY'S GETTING PAID

According to Bureau of Justice Statistics (2010), states spent $48.5 billion on corrections in 2010. By comparison, states spent $571.3 billion on education and $462.7 billion on public welfare. The mean state corrections expenditure per inmate was $28,323, although a quarter of states spent $40,175 or more. According to the Vera Institute of Justice 2012 report, *The Price of Prisons: What Incarceration Costs Taxpayers,* a noticeable portion, almost $6 billion a year of what taxpayers are paying to incarcerate the nation's 1.4 million state prison inmates, goes toward employee compensatory packages, not including salaries:

- Underfunded contributions to retiree health care for corrections employees ($1.9 billion);
- States' contributions to retiree health care on behalf of their corrections departments ($837 million);
- Employee benefits, such as health insurance ($613 million);
- States' contributions to pensions on behalf of their corrections departments ($598 million);
- Capital costs ($485 million); and
- Underfunded pension contributions for corrections employees ($304 million). (p. 4)

Imagine if you added the annual Department of Correction (DOC) salaries for each of the fifty states, which is approximately $40,000 per year, to this equation. In the Connecticut Department of Corrections (CDOC) alone, over 34 percent of their annual budget is dedicated to employee benefits. These figures do not include the multi-billion-dollar enterprise of the private prison industry. Byron Price and John Morris provide some insight in *Prison Privatization: The Many Facets of a Controversial Industry.* Corrections Corporation of America (CCA) and The Geo Group, Inc., are the two largest private prison companies in the nation, reporting revenues exceeding $3.7 billion annually. They provide bed space for over 150,000 state inmates, spread out over 120 facilities across the country. CCA CEO Damon Hininger received an executive compensatory package of $3.8 million alone in 2011. Over the decade, these companies have spent over $20 million in lobbying efforts and political contributions to secure their billion-dollar revenue earning contracts.

When you add in the price tag to incarcerate federal offenders, it is impossible to not recognize the financial rewards of having a racially disproportionate number of black males feeding the shark. With a 2013 budget request of $8.6 billion, the Federal Bureau of Prisons (BOP) manages and confines over 218,000 offenders, at a cost just under $29,000 a year per offender (BOP, 2012). The average annual cost per inmate housed in community corrections (residential reentry centers and home confinement) is $25,838. By contrast, the annual cost of supervision by probation officers in the community is about $3,433 per offender (BOP, 2012). Approximately 180,000 of those offenders are located in 117 facilities, and the remaining 18 percent are housed in privately operated prisons, residential reentry centers, and local jails around America. The BOP makes up less than 10 percent of the overall 2.2 million prison population in the nation; however, they have consistently operated over capacity (i.e., institutions house more than the maximum number prisoners they are designed to handle) for the last several years. Over 40 percent of their occupants are black males (BOP, 2013).

According to the U.S. Sentencing Commission (2011), almost half of all sentenced federal offenders (48 percent) were held for drug-related crimes, while only 8 percent were held for violent offenses. However, this statistic is very deceiving, and does not take into account the overall criminal history of the offenders. Over half of all incarcerated federal offenders have a documented history of criminal violence, with some being designated as leaders or supervisors within criminal organizations. For example, of the 7,858 firearms cases in 2011, 25 percent (1,911) involved the possession or use of a firearm in connection with a crime of violence or drug trafficking crime. Half of the cases (3,992) involved a convicted felon who illegally possessed a firearm. In 2011, over 80 percent of 25,813 offenders were convicted of drug crimes, involving the manufacture, sale, or transportation of drugs. In fact, in 6 percent of drug cases, the court determined that the applicable guideline range should be increased because of the offender's role in the offense as an organizer, leader, manager, or supervisor (U.S. Sentencing Commission, 2011).

Estimates place the BOP as operating at around 42 percent over total capacity today; thus overcrowding is an effective reality, a situation that presents significant safety concerns for staff and reentry programming issues for offenders. Overcrowding is of special concern at higher security facilities, with 50 percent crowding at high-security facilities and 39 percent at medium-security facilities. Admissions to federal prisons increased 12 percent (up by 6,513 inmates) in 2011. Although 55,239 federal offenders were released back into their communities in 2011, 86,361 federal criminal cases were prosecuted, resulting in 60,634 offenders receiving prison sentences and subsequent incarceration at federal correctional facilities.

With over 97 percent of all federal offenders being released back into their communities at some point, and with a 40 percent recidivism rate within three years of release, prisoner reentry has become a top priority for the Federal Bureau of Prisons. As well, the BOP estimates that 40 percent of federal inmates have diagnosable, moderate-to-severe substance abuse problems, that over half (52.0 percent) of the offenders sentenced in 2011 had not completed high school, and that (93.8 percent) of immigration offenses are committed by non-citizens; with a staggering 80 percent of these same offenders with less than a high school education, the BOP is facing unprecedented reentry programming challenges (BOP, 2012).

Prison reentry is also a big money business. Douglas Thompkins article, "The Expanding Prisoner Reentry Industry," provides a critical eye into the prisoner reentry industry (PRI) and its "for-profit" ideology at an unprecedented social cost to the black American experience. Thompkins (2010) suggests that, the PRI has become a significant part of our nation's social control industrial complex, adding:

> It [PRI] is not just a collection of institutions, organizations, and interest groups (both public and private); it is also a state of mind. Developing

and facilitating programs and services for the formerly incarcerated have become a huge "cash-cow," producing profits for the PRI at the expense of the taxpayer, while doing little to link the formerly incarcerated person to the social capital and human skills necessary to become a 'citizen.' (pp. 589–604)

The cornerstone of this financial windfall comes in the form of what is known as the Second Chance Act. Signed into law on April 9, 2008, the Second Chance Act (P.L. 110–199) was designed to improve outcomes for people returning to communities after a period of incarceration. This first-of-its-kind legislation authorizes federal grants to government agencies and nonprofit organizations to provide "evidence-based" program strategies and services designed to reduce recidivism in both a pre- and post-release setting. Since its inception, the federal government has authorized the release of over $450 million in grant monies for these so-called evidence-based reentry initiatives (Justice Center, 2013a).

Whether these millions of dollars are going into the pockets of countless faith-based organizations, halfway houses managed by former correctional employees, programs for hand-picked former inmates who have a statistically higher rate of success, or into the coffer of some ivory tower academic researcher promising to develop an evaluative tool for measuring evidence-based success, the Second Chance Act does not live up to its name and has become just another political tool used to exploit and "cash in" on the flesh of predominantly disenfranchised former black male inmates.

As already noted, my fundamental argument against using so-called "evidence-based" reentry approaches is that they (1) inherently define the offender as the problem; (2) intentionally ignore the realities and results of racism, marginalization, and inequality; (3) promote a script or cookbook program mentality, failing to take into account individualized factors such as race, ethnicity, nationality, etc.; (4) perpetuate the myth that the criminal justice system is always looking out for the best interest of the offender; (5) emphasize success through measuring recidivism rates instead of focusing on improving the overall quality of life for the offender; and (6) attempt to use abstract empirical research and data to measure "what works and what does not work" in the human experience.

A successful prison-community transition can never be measured under the *staying out of prison* paradigm. Recidivism is a concept of quantitative abstracts, which does not calculate the systematic historical havoc that the institution of white supremacy has wreaked on the black American experience. The *Humiliation to Humility Perspective* (HHP) is designed as a pedagogical "blueprint" to lay the foundation paradigm shift both for offenders and the correctional facilities that house them, one that I hope will make everyone re-think what our goal should be in the prison-community transition process: a social justice concept that places its emphasis on creating *correctional learning centers* that educate incarcerated students on becoming a *sustainable whole person by truth.*

IF YOU DON'T WANT TO BE BITTEN, STAY OUT OF THE WATER

I must admit, the discussions centered on relationship building between incarcerated black students and the police are among the most contempt-filled in my entire post-secondary educational experience. The complete lack of trust that so many incarcerated black students have for the criminal justice system almost blinds them from making any objective decisions regarding their future interactions with the police. As I've noted throughout this chapter, the criminal justice system has created a well-deserved reputation of "untrustworthiness" from black Americans across the nation. Institutionalized racism within the justice system cuts deep into the soul of the black American experience and can never be minimized. The problem is that, to make the transformation from humiliation to humility, as an incarcerated black student, you must come to terms with the fact that the criminal justice system will never completely disappear from your life. A former federal offender will always be on the radar of the police. In fact, the overwhelming majority of the U.S. population, which includes black Americans, do not involve themselves in the type of behavior that would result in intervention from the criminal justice system, regardless of the motives, demands this type of "policing" for ex-felons. The criminal justice system is "cynical by design" when it comes to dealing with ex-felons, and based on the behavior of some ex-offenders, their cynicism is well founded. Regardless of the length of your sentence, whether it's 36 or 360 months, the criminal justice system only remembers you by your past criminal history, regardless of any new aspirations you may have, and will always treat you accordingly.

I know that's a very bitter pill to swallow for those trying to genuinely change their lives, but as I tell them as *formerly incarcerated students,* they do not automatically qualify as a "trustworthy" person simply because the federal government has given them a release date. I tell them that, just like the criminal justice system, black communities don't forget and only remember them based on their criminal reputations, as they rightfully should. Why should two-thirds of the black communities forgive one-third of the incarcerated black males who helped establish the *cultural legitimacy* of racial profiling, for which 100 percent of the black community must suffer the social cost? Trust has to be earned and, unfair or not, the burden to reestablish trust falls on the formerly incarcerated students, not the criminal justice system or their respective black communities. I tell them that "real citizens" don't hesitate to dial 911 when their neighbor's house is being burglarized, and that they need to remove the concept of "snitches get stitches" from their vocabulary for life. That being said, I tell them that they must keep moving forward in their lives, and to be prepared to do everything necessary to rebuild societal trust. The first step in this journey starts with losing their "culturally learned fear of the police." Most incarcerated students vehemently deny this "fear the police" accusation; however, nothing is further from the truth than that denial. This "fear" has been passed on for generations, where fathers tell their sons, "fuck the police," while at the same time running at the sight of a patrol car. Those involved in the black counter-culture of crime are enablers of a system that many vocally despise, however, are unable or unwilling to accept this truth. I suggest to my incarcerated students that *black men* do not run from the police. That *black men* may not respect a police officer's decisions, their application of the law, and may openly question their authority at times, but they don't run from the police. That *black men* ultimately control their own destiny, and by placing themselves in a position where they must run from the police, they are actually running away from their parental responsibilities as fathers.

Incarcerated black students must understand that once you get past all the technological advances of electronic surveillance, data mining, biological, and impression evidence, the *great white shark* uses three primary methods to eat: (1) consent; (2) reasonable suspicion; and (3) probable cause. In other words, under the constitutional jurisprudence of the Fourth Amendment, police officers may lawfully conduct searches/seizures of a person if (a) a person voluntarily and freely provides police consent; (b) police can articulate facts that support reasonable suspicion that a person has committed or is committing a crime, or if a brief investigative detention is permitted, and police may also conduct a "frisk" of the person if they can articulate that a weapon may be involved; or (c) police can articulate facts that support probable cause that a person has committed or is committing a crime, in which case an arrest is permitted, which includes a *search incident to arrest* of the person and a search of their surrounding area.

Although I spend time discussing these three types of police-citizen contacts as they relate to racial profiling, I cannot stress enough to incarcerated black students that the bottom line is that, if you're not "dirty," you have nothing to worry about. I explain that I've been racially profiled for "driving while black" numerous times in my life, and although I always questioned the credibility of the officers conducting the traffic stops, I never feared the eventual outcome because I was never "dirty." *Dirty*, not simply by choice but by lifestyle and culture. It has never crossed my mind to put myself in an intentional situation *that would allow the criminal justice system to decide my fate as a black man.* Thus, it's not about blind faith in the criminal justice system, but about an unwavering confidence in my ability to understand and apply the truth that governs my behavior. My *black cultural privilege* (BCP).

Now, occasionally I get a few comments regarding how police officers "plant evidence" and although I let incarcerated students know this is unethical criminal behavior on the part of law enforcement and in no way do I condone it, I ask them what they did in the first place to place themselves in this situation. I will admit, this is where I hear comments from incarcerated students about me being "a fucking cop." I instruct them that there is a distinct difference between an *ethical code of fairness* and a *moral code of fairness*. Police ethics is governed by department policy or criminal statute; however, morality is governed by internal discretion. I ask them, "Do you have a *moral code of fairness* that everyone abides by in the black counter-culture of crime and the underground economy?" I then ask them, "Do you call the police every time someone robs you or one of your friends of drugs, guns, or money?" I then ask them, "Can you show me the rule book that states that the police have a *moral code of fairness* when dealing with a black male who lies, cheats, and uses violence when he commits crimes against the United States of America?" It's ridiculous to expect to be treated morally fair by the police, if you are actively committing crimes. Ethical treatment yes, but moral treatment, not a chance. This bizarre mindset is simply part of the "hubris of the criminality" possessed by those in the black counter-culture of crime.

The fact is, nobody involved in the "underground game" commits a single crime. The black counter-culture of crime is a lifestyle, not a single criminal choice. Thus, incarcerated black students are in no position to use morality to defend their criminal conduct and unfair or unequal treatment by the criminal justice system. There is no doubt that police misconduct does occur, and such officers should be punished under the full weight of the law; however, what does that have to do with black men selling drugs to other black men, robbing other black men, or murdering other black men? I explain to incarcerated black students, this is the counter-culture of crime mindset, where they try to declare their "legal criminal innocence" instead of focusing their energies on taking themselves out of the cultural criminal lifestyle. I tell them, if you don't want the police to use their questionable discretion or be less than truthful on an incident report, as some incarcerated black students routinely allege, then don't voluntarily place them in a position of power to do so, because ultimately, there are no moral rules of engagement. In fact, I inform them, "If you don't want to be bitten, stay out of the fucking water."

Unfortunately, the result of being a black male by birth virtually guarantees you contact with the *Great White Shark* in one form or another. This is largely due to both the cultural corruption of the uneducated police and cultural corruption of the uneducated black male. Incarcerated black males and their counter-culture of crime are just as responsible for racial profiling as the police. Unfortunately, all black American men, past, present, and future, will pay the price.

According to the U.S. Department of Justice Special Report, *Contacts between Police and the Public*(2011b), it is estimated that police come into contact with adult citizens over 40 million times each year. Since black Americans are more likely to have multiple contacts with the police, the overall number of total police-citizen contacts increases to over 67 million per year. The most common reason for contact with the police was being a driver in a traffic stop (44 percent). Although black drivers were stopped at a slightly higher rate (8.8 percent) than white drivers (8.4 percent), black drivers were over three times as likely as white drivers to be searched. Over 60 percent of these searches were conducted with the driver's consent.

According to the John Jay College of Criminal Justice report, *Stop, Question and Frisk Policing Practices in New York City: A Primer* (2010), "stop and frisk" is a national phenomenon. The Philadelphia Police Department stopped over 200,000, and the LAPD stopped over 250,000 people. The Chicago Police Department, the Boston Police Department, the New Orleans Police Department, and many other agencies across the country refuse to provide statistical data regarding *Terry Stops*. In the United States over the last decade alone, adult black Americans have been stopped, arrested and searched subsequent to their arrests by police over 30 million times (Center for Constitutional Rights, 2009).

DOES RACE REALLY MATTER?

In any critical discussion you will ever entertain as an educator facilitating a program or course in a correctional setting, the question of "Is the criminal justice system racist?" inherently comes up. In fact, if it's not brought up by my incarcerated black students, I bring it up myself. It is impossible to run from discussions on the "invisible three-dimensional elephants in the room" racism, white supremacy, or white privilege in a setting of mass incarceration, because prisons and jails house its by-products. Early in my young adult life when I struggled to answer this question, Derrick Bell's *Faces at the Bottom of the Well* provided me with a powerful dose of reality to ease my spiritual equilibrium that was filled with unchanneled anger at times, as well as later providing me with the foundation of "defiance" that helped shape not only my life but the *Humiliation to Humility Perspective* (HHP) introduced in this book. Bell (1992) stated:

> Black people will never gain full equality in this country. Even those herculean efforts we hail as successful will produce no more than temporary "peaks of progress," short-lived victories that slide into irrelevance as racial patterns adapt in ways that maintain white dominance. This is a hard-to-accept fact that all history verifies. We must acknowl-

edge it, not as a sign of submission, but as an act of ultimate defiance. (p. 12)

I ask incarcerated students a series of questions regarding racism and suggest that they come to their own conclusions: (1) How can a system that was directly plagiarized from Europe, the creator of the African Holocaust, not be racist? (2) How can a system, the legal foundational roots of which lie within the U.S. Constitution that originally described black Americans as three-fifths of a person, not be racist? (3) How can a system in which United States of America Presidents George Washington, Thomas Jefferson, James Madison, James Monroe, Andrew Jackson, Martin Van Buren, William Henry Harrison, John Tyler, James K. Polk, Zachary Taylor, Andrew Johnson, and Ulysses S. Grant, all of whom owned black Americans as slaves, not be racist? (4) How can a system that appointed a United States Supreme Court that ruled on *Plessy v. Ferguson*, making the segregation of black Americans the legal "law of the land" and opening the flood gates for Jim Crow, along with the social and physical lynching of black Americans, not be racist? (5) How could a system that produced and sanctioned the "Nation's Chief of Police" J. Edgar Hoover's COINTELPRO (a topic I will discuss in much greater depth later in this chapter), a program and policing philosophy that allowed the criminal justice system to use its incredible executive powers for over fifty years to systematically target black Americans for unlawful and abusive criminal investigations and prosecutions, not be racist? And finally I ask them to consider, (6) How can a criminal justice system fail those it was never built to protect?

What you see today in America is the result of historical and long-term structural violence perpetrated and supported at every level of our executive, legislative, and judicial branch of the criminal justice system. In fact, no conversation on racism is complete without reading from cover-to-cover Frances Welsing's *The Isis Papers* and Neely Fuller's *The United Independent Compensatory Code/System Concept for Victims of Racism*. Welsing (1991) defines racism as follows:

> The local and global power system structured and maintained by persons who classify themselves as white, whether consciously or subconsciously determined; this system consists of patterns of perception, logic, symbol formation, thought, speech, action and emotional response, as conducted simultaneously in all areas of people activity . . . economics, education, entertainment, labor, law, politics, religion, sex, and war. (p. ii)

Fuller (1969) added that this racist "power system" fell under the umbrella of white supremacy. For many people, the term *white supremacy* is over-the-top and way too harsh to accurately describe incidents such as "driving while black" or "walking while black," but I disagree. That is the impact of having the only social structure in the nation designed to support the premise of law, justice, and equity become the instrument of oppression, marginalization, and discrimination. It produces a nihilistic feeling akin to being raped as a child and then being forced to sit and eat dinner with the rapist every night of your life. It clouds the part of the black American psyche that would otherwise recognize the truth and allow one to experience self-respect, dignity, and belonging. It inspires humiliation to manifest itself as shame, anger, and violence in the black American experience. It inspires a young black male to quit his job rather than to be "pulled over" and harassed by the police. It inspires a young black male to quit attending school rather than be "jacked up" against the wall and searched by the police on his way to school. It inspires a young black male to abandon his connective black cultural privilege and adopt a counter-culture of crime and hyped gangsterism. It inspires a young black male to trade the freedom of himself, his family, and his community for the security of a prison cell and a life of enslavement. It inspires a young black male to enjoy spreading a life of transgenerational learned helplessness. No, white supremacy accurately describes the type of racism that manifests itself within the criminal justice system. What Welsing (1991) and Fuller (1969) both understood, and what I hope to illuminate by writing this book, is that only through the willingness of incarcerated black students to recognize, understand, and educate themselves on the dynamics of racism, white supremacy, and white privilege, and its origins in slavery, can they navigate them as powerless social constructs in their lives.

IMPLICIT ASSOCIATION TEST

Racism is so imbedded at every level of the criminal justice system today that professionals who work within the system, many of whom are white and may not have any *individual intention* of using race as a variable, are at the mercy of the *systemic intention*. I can't tell you how many of my former colleagues in the criminal justice field would never dream of committing an overt act of racism; however, they have nonetheless fallen victim to perpetrating covert acts of racism by simply not recognizing the systemic intentions, which by and large are embedded biases against black males.

In the 1990s, researchers Tony Greenwald (University of Washington), Mahzarin Banaji (Harvard University), and Brian Nosek (University of Virginia) created what is known as the Implicit Association Test (IAT). The IAT is a questionnaire designed to examine which words and concepts are strongly paired in people's minds, by measuring implicit attitudes: "introspectively unidentified (or inaccurately identified) traces of past experience that mediate favorable or unfavorable feeling, thought, or action toward social objects" (Greenwald and Banaji, 1995). In other words, it attempts to measure, with some degree of accuracy, individual subconscious biases.

As of today, more than two million people, over 90 percent American, have anonymously participated in the IAT questionnaire on the Harvard Website. The results have been used in countless research studies across the country, which many social scientists believe has revolutionized the study of prejudice in the United States. According to researchers, although people may wish to act in egalitarian ways, implicit biases are a powerful predictor of how they actually behave. Some of the unsettling truths:

- 88 percent of white Americans had a pro-white or anti-black implicit bias;
- 75 percent of white Americans show robust association of white = good and black = bad;
- 48 percent of black Americans indicated a pro-white or anti-black bias;
- Political conservatives (majority being white Americans) showed higher levels of bias against black Americans;
- 65 percent choose to work with a white partner in an employment setting;
- 70 percent of white Americans show an implicit racial bias in choosing their politically elected officials; and
- Regarding employment hiring practices résumés with white-sounding names resulted in 50 percent more callbacks than résumés with black-sounding names. More disturbing, findings indicated that "high-quality black résumés drew no more calls than the average black résumés. However, highly skilled candidates with white names got more calls than average white candidates, but lower-skilled candidates with white names got many more callbacks than even highly skilled black applicants" (Vedantam, 2005; Project Implicit, 2013).

If we take this data and apply it "ideologically" to the criminal justice system, in which the overwhelming majority employed are white Americans, just imagine the negative impact that subconscious individual biases against black Americans has had not only on the decision-making of police officers, prosecutors, judges, probation and parole officers, and on those who work in correctional settings, but on the policy preferences of their respective executive leaders. Issues such as racial profiling, prosecutorial filing, sentencing disparity, and even the low numbers of people of color employed within the criminal justice system can thus be somewhat explained. According to Banaji, the IAT "measures the thumbprint of the culture on our minds . . . if [white] Europeans had been carted to Africa as slaves, blacks would have the same beliefs about whites that whites now have about blacks." Could you imagine what the results would be if the millions employed within our nation's criminal justice system participated in an Implicit Association Test questionnaire? Could you imagine what the results would be if the nearly 840,000 incarcerated black males housed within our nation's criminal justice system participated in an Implicit Association Test questionnaire?

THE NATION'S CHIEF OF POLICE

On June 7, 2013, I sent a Freedom of Information/Privacy Acts (FOIPA) request to the Federal Bureau of Investigation asking for information on COINTELPRO, specifically for documents related to Malcolm X. I'm not really sure why I did it because surely others have done so before me. I've conducted research on and have read about the FBI's counterintelligence programs for over two decades. I've seen many of the declassified documents on-line and inside at least a half a dozen books on the subject. I don't question the authenticity of these documents. However, for some reason I needed to see them for myself. I wanted to make them part of my *own truths* as part of *my own* black American experience.

When I received my written response from the FBI a couple of weeks later in the mail, which contained my FOIPA request number officially acknowledging my request and the commencement of a search in their Central Records System for the information, I felt a wave of both anger and depression. Angry that there was clear evidence that my own government was an active party in the attempted cultural destruction of the black American experience, and depressed that my own government continues to *socially construct lies* about their role in this cultural destruction, as the majority of the documents I obtained have been partly, or entirely, redacted. The fundamental principal to reconciliation, whether personal or professional, starts with the truth. The entire theme of the *Humiliation to Humility Perspective* (HHP) I describe in this book begins and ends with the quest for the truth. Incarcerated black Americans deserve the complete truth, and without it, their relationship with the criminal justice system will always be void and empty of basic trust. The fact remains that the most powerful law enforcement agency in the executive branch of the United States of America actively used the tools of "justice and the rule of law" to criminalize the black American experience and to discredit, neutralize, and destroy black American leaders. The criminal justice system became a co-conspirator in the *politics of shaming, self-segregation,* and *transgenerational learned helplessness* for black men in America.

COINTELPRO

I'm not naïve or gullible by any means regarding the historic abuses faced by black Americans from any number of oppressive forces; however, just like seeing in-person the slave castles in Ghana to remind us of the realities of the African Holocaust, it's just as important to see up-close and personal COINTELPRO documents and the realities of the horrific policing abuses directed specifically at black American males at the hands of the criminal justice system.

On June 25, 2013, I was invited to participate as a panelist along with an attorney from the ACLU, various media, and the filmmakers of *We Steal Secrets: The Story of Wikileaks* at the Harris Theater in Pittsburgh. The idea was to view the film and discuss the latest round of perceived surveillance abuses of the federal government, specifically the information being leaked by former National Security Administration (NSA) contract worker Edward Snowden. Based on my professional and academic credentials, I was assuming the sponsors of the panel, PublicSource, believed that I could maybe somehow explain why the government is using its powers to conduct electronic domestic surveillance programs. I was honored to participate and hopefully add some clarity to the issue; however, the entire concept that "now" people are collectively outraged by the fact the federal government is spying on its own citizens without just cause is somewhat sickening. As a black American male I asked where in the hell have people been, specifically middle-class, white Americans who were the overwhelming majority of the outraged members of the audience, as the United States of America used its incredible law enforcement and national security investigatory powers to "shit" on the civil rights of black Americans over the past century or so? In fact, I question whether we would even be having a panel if the sole targets of these new domestic spying programs were black Americans. During my opening remarks, I very politely voiced these issues to the audience, and further expressed that as a black man, news of any abusive domestic spying or discriminative policing programs are part of my black American experience, past, present, and future. I instructed them that no other criminal justice programs have damaged the legacy of black America more than the FBI's COINTELPRO and the Uniform Crime Report.

For a thorough understanding of the damage assessment of counterintelligence programs on the black American experience, I recommend to my incarcerated students Kenneth O'Reilly's *Racial Matters: The FBI's Secret File on Black America, 1960–1972*, James Davis's *Spying on America: The FBI's Domestic Counter-Intelligence Program*, and Nelson Blackstock's *COINTELPRO: The FBI's Secret War on Political Freedom*.

Incarcerated students should understand that J. Edgar Hoover was the "United States of America's Chief of Police" from 1924 until his death in 1972. From 1919 to 1924, in the five years before his forty-eight–year reign as director of the FBI, he served as the head of the United States Department of Justice's General Intelligence Division (GID). In these federal government positions, over a span of fifty-two years, he institutionalized covert and abusive surveillance programs on black Americans. Let me be very clear. J. Edgar Hoover was a racist his entire life, once referring to Martin Luther King, Jr. as a "burr head," and he used the powers of his office to advance his social and political agenda of white supremacy (O'Reilly, 1991, p. 355). He viewed the civil rights movement as "a threat to his way of life, his bureaucracy, and his vision of a white, Christian, and harmonious America" (p. 357). He ensured that "second-class citizens would have second class loyalty" by making racism a national policing policy (p. 12). He created a culture of racial segregation within the FBI from which the criminal justice system has yet to recover. J. Edgar Hoover did not work alone. Ten presidential administrations were aware and complicit as Hoover criminalized the black American experience (see table 3.1).

In fact, the heads of the sacred "Camelot political machine," John Fitzgerald and his attorney general brother Bobby, both approved J. Edgar's request to wiretap the telephone of Martin Luther King. My apologies for not mentioning the contributions of Lyndon B. Johnson, the presidential architect of the landmark Civil Rights Act of 1964 and the Voting Rights Act of 1965, who gave J. Edgar a complete free hand to implement the FBI's destructive COINTELPRO aimed directly at the black community and its leadership, and who received intelligence briefings on the covert operations of so-called Black Nationalist and Black Hate Groups. Finally, Nixon, not letting a good thing pass on his watch, used J. Edgar's counterintelligence programs to declare war on the Black Panther Party for Self-Defense and also used the results in his own political platform for re-election. Due to Nixon's Watergate fiasco, the Foreign Intelligence Surveillance Act (FISA) and Foreign Intelligence Surveillance Court (FISC) were created.

Despite an intense rivalry between the FBI and the Central Intelligence Agency (CIA), Hoover solicited covert information on "racial mat-

Table 3.1.   American Presidents under the Reign of J. Edgar Hoover

Woodrow Wilson (1913–1921)

Warren G. Harding (1921–1923)

Calvin Coolidge (1923–1929)

Herbert Hoover (1929–1933)

Franklin D. Roosevelt (1933–1945)

Harry S. Truman (1945–1953)

Dwight D. Eisenhower (1953–1961)

John F. Kennedy (1961–1963)

Lyndon B. Johnson (1963–1969)

Richard M. Nixon (1969–1974)

ters intelligence" from the CIA under operations "Project Hunter," "CHAOS," and "RESISTANCE." In Project Hunter, the CIA along with the FBI opened, read, and photographed over 100,000 letters from American citizens, including those of Martin Luther King's wife Coretta. CHAOS focused on the foreign relationship between black social movements and the Nation of Islam. RESISTANCE placed an emphasis on the relationship between communism and black social movements.

J. Edgar masterfully created specialized programs to recruit and retain black Americans as informants to spy on their own black communities within his counterintelligence programs. With BLACPRO (Black Informant Program) and the Ghetto Informant Program (GIP), the FBI maintained over 5,000 active black American informants. Hoover had informants on various HBCUs (historically black colleges and universities), specifically faculty, staff, and students at Florida A&M and Tennessee A&I. He had informants in every black organization, including the NAACP, the Nation of Islam, the Black Panther Party, the Student Nonviolent Coordinating Committee, as well as within Martin Luther King's and Malcolm X's inner circles. In fact, the black community has never recovered from the effects of the FBI's informant counterintelligence programs. Loyalty, trust, connectivity, synergy, safety, cultural and spiritual heritage, all attributes of a healthy community, were taken and replaced with disloyalty, untruth, dependence, selfishness, crime, counter-culture, and historical amnesia.

The Uniform Crime Report Fraud

The second weapon, which was in many regards even more culturally destructive of the black American male's experience than *COINTELPRO*, was the creation of the FBI's Uniform Crime Report (UCR). The best illustration of this is contained in Khalil Muhammad's *The Condemnation of Blackness: Race, Crime, and the Making of Modern Urban America*. Considered our nation's primary tool for measuring the crime rate over the past eighty-three years, the UCR was created in the heart of Jim Crow in 1930 and used by J. Edgar Hoover to solidify the criminalization of black males.

You see, prior to its creation, the only instrument available to measure the impact of "post-slavery" black Americans was the publication of the 1890 U.S. Census. Under the umbrella of twenty-five years of the discriminatory black codes, the report suggested that although black Americans made up 12 percent of the total population, 30 percent of America's prison population consisted of black men (Muhammad, 2010). Taking this data as unquestionable fact and overlooking the biased motivations of a national climate of white supremacy, initially led by academia, this information was used to demonize black males in the hearts and minds of white America. Charles Henderson, a sociologist from the nationally respected and pioneering "Chicago School" of criminological thought, in 1901 published arguably the first academic textbook on crime in America, *An Introduction to the Study of the Dependent, Defective, and Delinquent Classes*, apologizing for the crimes of white immigrants and exasperating the fear of the black male. Henderson (1901) wrote: "The Negro factor . . . racial inheritance, physical and mental inferiority, barbarian and slave ancestry and culture . . . were the most serious factors in crime statistics" (pp. 246–247).

White social scientists around the nation agreed, creating an "imagined community" (Anderson, 1991) of crime, inferiority, and deviant behavior within the black American community, while simultaneously explaining the massive crime wave of organized crime by white immigrants during prohibition as assimilating into the "American Process" (Muhammad, 2010). Have you ever wondered why the likes of the horrific immigrant-based gangsters such as Carlo Gambino, Lucky Luciano, Frank Costello, Al Capone, Charles Dean O'Banion, and such, were created into romanticized figures of Robin Hood–like mythology? The social structure of the United States of America formed a wall of exclusion and alienation for black American males. During the reconstruction and post-slavery era in the very infancy stages of black American emancipation from enslavement, when the nation could have begun to repair the moral, spiritual, physical, and social damage of the African Holocaust, it turned its back and used the powers of the criminal justice system to perpetuate the myths of inferiority, criminality, and to exacerbate the fear of the black male.

Capitalizing on "black fear" under the guidance of these same social scientists, along with the Social Science Research Council (SSRC) and the International Association of Chiefs of Police (IACP) in Chicago, J. Edgar Hoover published the nation's very first government authorized crime statistics, the Uniform Crime Report. Since 1930, the FBI has served as a data clearinghouse, organizing, collecting, and disseminating information voluntarily submitted by local, state, federal and tribal law enforcement agencies on crimes, and the statistics are routinely used by politicians, police chiefs, and policy makers to gauge their "success" in fighting crime around the nation. What J. Edgar did at the height of Jim Crow and white supremacy was to separate crimes into race-based categories, making his agency the sole "authoritative statistical measure of race and crime" in America (Muhammad, 2010).

Initially, the UCR had a category table labeled "Foreign Born White" to represent the crimes committed by Italian, Irish, and other immigrant European Americans; however, this disappeared quickly as Hoover blended their crimes into the "White" category. The other categories were "Negro," "Indian," "Chinese," "Japanese," "Mexican," and all others (U.S. Department of Justice-UCR, 1930–1959). Thus, the FBI presented a "numbers speak for themselves" rationale, pitting white Americans against black Americans, where the outcome was predetermined in J. Edgar Hoover's perception of America. The FBI was able to separate crimes by racial categories because the system was reflective of the annotated race listed on the fingerprint cards sent to their Identification Division by police agencies around the country, the same police agencies that were active systematic provocateurs of white supremacy for decades. Muhammad (2010) noted: "Police misconduct, corruption, and brutality . . . helped to produce disproportionately high black arrest rates, the starting point for high juvenile delinquency commitments and adult prison rates" (p. 12).

The FBI's motivation for documenting crimes by race and/or ethnicity, as well as the credibility and reliability of the information they received and the statistics they disseminated, were never questioned by the executive, legislative, or judicial branches of the federal government because these gave them what they needed to replace the incredible financial capital lost by the free labor of slavery: an enemy of the state. The black race soon became synonymous with crime and a victim of the corrupt legacy of black criminalization, a label that black men have yet to shed, and which today has created a black counter-culture of crime prepared to carry out the type of destruction Hoover could only imagine in his wildest dreams. If only these black males knew it all started out as a lie.

I suggest that if you want to minimize the social construct of race in the criminal justice system, simply remove it as a UCR offender categorical label and replace it with social determinants. Today, "race" very similar to 1930 is constructed within four UCR offender categories: (1) White; (2) Black; (3) American Indian or Alaskan Native; and (4) Asian or Pacific Islander. In fact, the UCR does not even designate a category for Hispanics, deceptively lumping them into the "White" category, a "smoke and mirrors" tactic used to make the "White" category seem larger. There has never been one single positive contribution to understanding the problem of crime by placing offenders into racial categories, other than to entice racial profiling. I would suggest a common sense approach to replace these race-based criminal offender categories with ones that reflect the results of the politics of shaming, self-segregation, and transgenerational learned helplessness: (1) Poverty; (2) Employment; (3) Education; (4) Substance Abuse; and (4) Mental Health. Once these categories are populated, the true essence of criminality is revealed.

In the end, J. Edgar Hoover succeeded in criminalizing the black American experience within the parameters of racism, white supremacy, and white privilege, using the black male as his boogeyman. He used human and electronic surveillance, not to gather intelligence on criminal behavior but to own personal and private information regarding the personality traits, weaknesses, and strengths of his black American targets, including any behavior he deemed immoral, dishonest, or hypocritical. He would then use this information to harass, discredit, and neutralize his targets. The true and accurate level of J. Edgar Hoover and his governmental co-conspirators' criminal activities will never be known, as the overwhelming majority of documents obtained regarding COINTEL-PRO have been partly, or entirely, redacted. Did the FBI play a role in the deaths of black civil rights leaders, members of the Black Panther Party, or anyone else associated with the advancement of social justice for the black American experience? What we do know is that J. Edgar Hoover created a criminal justice system that would become an *economic force* and a *political tool of fear* for generations to come.

AN ECONOMIC FORCE

Although there are no clear national statistics regarding the operating cost of the entire criminal justice system; however, just to give you a generic idea, when you include the victim costs, criminal justice system costs, asset forfeiture seizures, the lost productivity estimates for both the victim and the offender, and estimates on the public's resulting willingness to pay to prevent future violence (more cops, prosecutors, prions, etc.), a single murder costs an incredible $17.25 million (DeLisi et al., 2010). Supporting this calculation, a report from the Pacific Institute for Research and Evaluation (2010) indicated that, when factoring in health care and incarceration alone, one single homicide involving a gun costs $5 million. According to researchers at Iowa State University, each rape costs $448,532, each robbery $335,733, each aggravated assault $145,379 and each burglary $41,288.

If you do the math, the cumulative monetary figures become almost incomprehensible. Given that the United States has averaged over 16,000 homicides, 90,000 rapes, 450,000 robberies, 850,000 aggravated assaults, and over 10,000 burglaries each year since 1992 (FBI, 2013a) the cumulative social cost is over $1 trillion annually. That's more than the federal budget has ever been for the Department of Education, Department of Justice, Department of Housing and Urban Development, Department of Health and Human Services, Department of Labor, and Department of Homeland Security in their cumulative history. In fact, since 1972, the increase in government spending on the criminal justice system has only been surpassed by spending on our dysfunctional health care system.

To put these monetary figures into perspective, the criminal justice system is becoming a growing and important part of the Gross Domestic Product (GDP). According to professor of economics Abbas Grammy's report, *The Underground Economy*, the illicit economy that is created by the criminal justice system is estimated at about 10 percent of the total $15 trillion GDP. At approximately $1.1 trillion annually, the black market for illicit drugs ($327 billion), licit drugs ($148 billion), technology ($253.5 billion), illegal gambling ($110 billion), and prostitution and pornography ($122 billion) is creating a substantial underground economy (see table 3.2).

Grammy (2011) added that expenditures on various components of the criminal justice system (i.e., policing, courts, and corrections) add to the GDP and make the U.S. economy grow even larger. The trillions of dollars generated through millions of jobs, services, and product purchases each year makes the criminal justice system an economic force that has taken on a life of its own.

A POLITICAL TOOL OF FEAR

What started off as an intentional and systematic process to use racism as a tool to murder, dehumanize, oppress, marginalize, and exploit first enslaved Africans and then black Americans, in order to create the perfect "other" for economic greed, has had an outcome today that neither the oppressed or the oppressor could have ever imagined. To structurally deny a people, over a period of four centuries, equal employment, equal education, equal housing, and equal fundamental human rights under the law caused criminal behavior to become a viable career option for young black men. You see, the solution to young urban black men trapped in a counter-culture of crime, to use the "vision" of Du Bois (1903b), was too easy. Just lock them up. Hire more police and prosecutors. Build more prisons. Implement race-based draconian drug laws. Create a *War on Drugs* and place the majority of your "soldiers" in urban black communities to fight street battles. Who cared if there was collateral damage in this war? They were only going to be black men, women, and children, right?

The only problem was that the "forty-year mass incarceration plan" didn't work. It merely ensured that one-third of all black men will fall prey to the criminal justice system at some point in their life. After ensuring that over 30 percent of all black men have lost their right to vote, basically denying them political citizenship. After ensuring that over 7

Table 3.2. Market Estimated Value of the Largest Illegal Black Markets in the United States

Illicit Drugs	$327,000,000,000
Licit Drugs	$148,000,000,000
Technology	$253,000,000,000
Prostitution & Pornography	$122,000,000,000
Illegal Gambling	$110,000,000,000
All Others	$140,000,000,000
Total	$1,100,000,000,000

million children have grown up fatherless, where many have fallen into this cycle of transgenerational learned helplessness and community destruction. After ensuring that over 5 million black men now wear the permanent label of *felon,* scarring them for life regarding access to fair employment, education, and housing opportunities (National Urban League, 2013).

What has been created in the aftermath is an *urban black American counter-culture of crime.* One built on four-hundred years of time-tested humiliation. A counter-culture that cannibalizes its own black American experiences and adopts the very same nihilistic social tools used by its original oppressors, becoming an even more brutal version. A counter-culture that perceives "gangsterism" as a legitimate career path. A counter-culture that does not fear in the very least any repercussions from the criminal justice system. In fact, a counter-culture whose members have not only accepted their fate as "professional slaves" within the criminal justice system, but who have willingly formed their central identity on the premise of the "incarceration experience." A counter-culture that does not acknowledge the rich historical, cultural, and anti-hegemonic ideology that embodies the very essence of blackness. A counter-culture that is readily spread and purchased through music, art, and film. A counter-culture that is socially not only accepted by black communities, but by young mainstream white America as well. A counter-culture that does not respect any form of social control or legal authority. The criminal justice system does not have the ability to stop this counter-culture of young black males alone, because it's now become an ideological social movement built on the structural humiliations of racism, white supremacy, and white privilege. These black males are proud to be part of the underground economy. They are not afraid of "death by incarceration" or even physical death, because for many, either type of death is glorified within their counter-culture. At the end of the day, the black males in this counter-culture of crime do not see the point in investing in their very own citizenship, because they don't see themselves as citizens.

Malcolm X recognized this *black counter-culture of crime* some forty-five years ago, because he first saw it when he looked into the mirror inside his own prison cell:

> And because I had been a hustler, I knew better than all whites knew and better than nearly all of the black "leaders" knew that actually the most dangerous black man in America was the ghetto hustler. Why do I say this? The hustler, out there in the ghetto jungles, has less respect for the white power structure than any other Negro in North America. The ghetto hustler is internally restrained by nothing. He has no religion, no concept of morality, no civic responsibility, no fear — nothing. To survive, he is out there constantly preying upon others, probing for any human weakness like a ferret. The ghetto hustler is forever frustrated, restless, and anxious for some "action." Whatever he under-

takes, he commits himself to it fully, absolutely. What makes the ghetto hustler yet more dangerous is his "glamour" image to the school-drop-out youth in the ghetto. These ghetto teen-agers see the hell caught by their parents struggling to get somewhere, or see that they have given up struggling in the prejudiced, intolerant white man's world. The ghetto teen-agers make up their own minds they would rather be like the hustlers whom they see dressed "sharp" and flashing money and displaying no respect for anybody or anything. So the ghetto youth become attracted to the hustler worlds of dope, thievery, prostitution, and general crime and immorality. (Haley, 1964, p. 311)

The "social experiment" we know today as the mass incarceration movement within the criminal justice system is completely aware of these social facts. The problem is, there isn't a "Plan B." The proverbial white flag went up years ago. Maybe they thought the millions of young black men who have traded their names for prison ID numbers in this *war*, and then returned back to their communities, were going to forgive and forget. You see, fear has begun to set into the collective consciousness of the justice system. A fear that the general public will come to the same conclusion that those on the "inside" of the criminal justice machine have known for years. You cannot arrest your way out of four-hundred years of racially oppressive history. Creating more specialized drug, gang, and fugitive task forces, supplying police with state-of-the-art equipment, zero-tolerance initiatives, gun buy-back programs, tougher criminal penalties, DNA databases, city-wide video surveillance cameras, instituting CompStat, school resource officers, police athletic leagues, putting a police officer on every single street corner, or any other "policing gimmick" that will be implemented, will not change the impact of centuries of transgenerational humiliation.

In this regard, today, the mass incarceration movement of black men in America will continue to occur, not because it has any chance of addressing this black counter-culture of crime, but only because it serves as a convenient *political tool for fear*. Fear is an emotion that has the unique ability to allow the most irrational and destructive behaviors to surface. The fear of young black men is as "American as apple pie"; the image of "a scary black man" has been ingrained into the subconscious of this nation since 1619. It's worked so well that, this same counter-culture of young black men wear *fear* as a badge of honor. Elected officials at every level of local, state, and federal governments, D.C.-based think tanks, the Ivory Tower of academics, black faith-based organizations, and top law enforcement executives alike, do not have the slightest clue on how to deal with this black counter-culture of crime. But don't worry, the system will do its best to hide this counter-culture from public consumption, in the only way it knows how: by locking it up and placing it inside of a prison cell. In fact, you do not have to look any further than the *killing fields of Chicago* to witness first-hand this black counter-culture of crime, and the horrific results it has had on the black American experience. Our only hope is to confront the politics of shaming, self-segregation, and transgenerational learned helplessness that breed black-on-black crime and cultural nihilism.

FACES AT THE BOTTOM OF THE WELL

In June 2011, the recently hired Chicago Police Department (CPD) superintendent Garry McCarthy, the leader of the second largest police department in America, told a large black church congregation at St. Sabina's on the Southside of Chicago some amazing things. He told them that he was not afraid to talk about the infamous "r-word" . . . race. McCarthy suggested that slavery, segregation, the black codes, and Jim Crow had one very important common denominator: "government-sponsored racism." After some thunderous applause, McCarthy then said there was another component to this government-sponsored racism, "Federal gun laws that facilitate the flow of illegal firearms into our urban centers across this country that are killing our black and brown children" (Esposito, 2011). After an even louder series of thunderous applause, McCarthy finally added that after recognizing these facts, he was "changing the face" of how policing would take place in Chicago because he had a "plan to address it."

Roll forward to June 14, 2013. Almost two years to the date of his speech and 1,000 homicides later, please allow me to share his plan for new "police reform" in Chicago: the initiation of *Operation Impact*. As it turned out, his plan was just another "zero tolerance approach," where police officers are saturated into "high crime areas," which has always been code for communities of color, to make as many arrests as financially possible. Spending over $21 million in overtime to pay his police officers the first three months alone for this initiative, it was described as a success by CPD because the city's homicide numbers, whose victims are primarily young black men, dropped from a body count of one hundred to ninety per month. Based on these bargain prices, the cost to save one black male's life in Chicago from a violent death sits at about $2 million each. Just imagine if Chicago Mayor Rahm Emanuel were to increase McCarthy's $1.5 billion annual police department budget, which already accounts for 32 percent of the city's total and where public safety is already the largest expenditure, by another, let's say, $300 million, based on this rationale, we could reduce our murder rate to maybe one or two young black men a month (Chicago Police Department Annual Report, 2010).

The saddest part of this analogy is that, I guarantee you, there is a budget proposal sitting on McCarthy's desk for exactly such a monetary request, using the exact same skewed logic as far as the estimated drops in murder. You see, we cannot be too upset with Superintendent McCarthy. In fact, I give him a great deal of credit. He began his helm by sharing the ugly *truths* regarding the historic connections between race, crime, and systematic injustice within the black American experience. He just didn't know how deep the "faces at the bottom of the well" were in the Windy City (Bell, 1992).

Although McCarthy has seen similar black male counter-cultures of crime with career stops in New York City and Newark, he had never seen one on "cultural steroids" before:

- An Illinois Department of Corrections, whose population is primarily from the Chicago area and still growing, that's cycling back home approximately 35,000 black males each year;
- A city population where an estimated 40–45 percent of the young black males are convicted felons;
- An environment that is home to over 68,000 active gang members, and over 70 different gangs;
- A Chicago-based criminal justice system that, in 2010 alone, ran off the racial fuel of 103,228 arrests of black males, over 72 percent of the total number of the 144,175 males arrested that year, despite making up less than 15 percent of the total adult male population;
- A climate where more black children in Chicago died from gunfire in 2010 than Chicago soldiers died in Iraq;
- An overall unemployment rate of over 22 percent, which is doubled for black males at around 45 percent, and tripled at a staggering 65–70 percent for black males who are convicted felons;
- A city that has the third highest rate of extreme poverty of the nation's ten largest cities, at 21.6 percent; for children, it rises to over 50 percent;
- A dilapidated public school system that is running on a billion dollar deficit in which almost 90 percent of its students are from communities of color, although whites make up over one third of the city's population;
- A city in which only 3 out of every 100 black young men earn a college degree by age twenty-five; and
- A city that due to the social climate of crime has lost the tax base revenue of over 200,000 people the last decade, many of whom were educated and employed black residents. "Black flight" has dropped the city's population down to levels dating back a century to 1910 (Chicago Crime Commission, 2013; Chicago Police Department Annual Report, 2010; Chicago Police Department, 2013; City of Chicago Website, 2013; National Urban League, 2013; Safer Foundation, 2013; U.S. Census Bureau, 2010).

In all fairness, McCarthy doesn't have a chance. Even if his strategy meets some short-term objective in reducing homicides, it will not have any impact on the plight of black males in Chicago. You see, there have always been two cities in Chicago, one black and one white, where the politics of shaming, self-segregation, and transgenerational learned helplessness is alive and well. Similar to his sixty predecessors as Chicago Police Department superintendents, many of whom took part in the creation of this black counter-culture of crime, he has about a four-year life expectancy as the top cop. In my beloved city today, this black counter-culture of crime shoots other black males for sport. Since its incorporation in 1837, the City of Chicago has infused a type of man-made racial nihilism in black neighborhoods across the city that I'm afraid might have caused permanent damage to the psyche of its young black urban men. There is a reason to fear the young black men that have accepted this counter-culture as their own. This counter-culture has now become embedded into the holistic black American experience in Chicago. In fact, it's so dire in the black community that it's sometimes difficult to tell which black men are not impaled in this counter-culture of crime.

In the end, McCarthy simply did what he and every other police chief around the country who has ever attended an executive-level leadership school, such as the National FBI Academy, would have done to fight the black counter-culture of crime: *when in doubt, arrest*. Giving him the benefit of the doubt, what started out as possibly a genuine plan to reform policing in Chicago will eventually crash under the incredible weight of the *economic* and *political fears* created by the 506 murders in 2012. In the end, McCarthy will simply give his constituency, 2.7 million people, which includes a black community of over 880,000, what they want: a body count of black men.

OCDETF AND THE CREATION OF INFORMANTHOOD

During my many classroom discussions with incarcerated students at FCI McKean, one of the most exhilarating conversations takes place regarding the whole "why" question. Not why black males or why poor people, but the rhetorical "Why am I here?" "Why did the Feds pick me?" I know it sounds rather narcissistic or jejune for those who have never been "touched" by the federal criminal justice system; however, this question often serves as a psychological barrier for many incarcerated students trying to break from the counter-culture of crime and move forward in their lives. The reality of experiencing the "United States of America" and the incredible sense of power, intimidation, and structural injustice that is synonymous with that title, versus "you, aka the defendant," regardless of your social, class, or racial status, places an adult male in a perpetual state of post-traumatic stress disorder (PTSD).

I've discovered that incarcerated students who have been charged with drug crimes against the United States of America are very forthcoming, and usually display a remarkable understanding of the tangible financial impact of drug trafficking at both the micro- and macro-levels. The majority are pretty well versed on the legal ramifications of their crimes as well. Thus, many do not see themselves as "victims" in the *War on Drugs*, but as "caught" due to their greed.

However, I'm always amazed by the attitudes of black incarcerated students who are not serving prison sentences for drug offenses. Those incarcerated for murder, robbery, extortion, white collar, weapons, or other crimes against the United States of America, will always make it very clear to me that they are not drug dealers, and quite often have a somewhat contemptuous attitude toward those who are arrested for drug offenses, who statistically make up the majority of offenders in federal prison. Their contempt does not seem to be personalized or based on the ambiguous community-based nature of drug trafficking, because many of them have either used drugs or have family and friends involved in the drug trafficking business.

Based on numerous discussions with these black incarcerated students, their contempt is more of a gut feeling, just an unexplainable instinct that tells them that drug dealers are somehow responsible for their "being arrested" and placed into federal custody, although the incarcerated students who are drug offenders always vehemently deny these accusations. Actually, some of these "non-drug" offenders are not too far off, because again, it really does go back to the *War on Drugs*. Specifically, all roads lead to the Organized Crime Drug Enforcement Task Forces, also known as the OCDETF Program.

America's drug addiction and its title as the number one consumer of illegal drugs on the planet works in perfect synchronicity with the *Great White Sharks* primary mission: to eat. In other words, the more drugs, the more police, the more money, the more arrests, and more informants, from a three-dimensional local, state, and federal perspective. If a federal offender is caught, regardless of the type of crime they committed against the United States of America, there is an incredible likelihood they appeared on the federal radar screen from the work of a multi-jurisdictional drug task force.

The Organized Crime Drug Enforcement Task Forces (OCDETF) Program was established in 1982 to mount a comprehensive attack against organized drug trafficking, and is described by Attorney General Eric Holder "as the centerpiece of the Justice Department's intra- and interagency drug enforcement strategy." OCDETF is based upon a model of pursuing comprehensive, prosecutor-led, multi-agency, intelligence-driven, multi-jurisdictional investigations of major transnational, national, and regional violent and insidious drug trafficking and money laundering organizations. These include the international supply sources, their international and domestic transportation organizations, the regional and local distribution networks, and violent enforcers. At the same time, OCDETF attacks the money flow and firearms trafficking that support the drug trade—depriving drug traffickers of their criminal proceeds needed to finance future criminal activity (U.S. Department of Justice, 2013a, 2013b).

With an annual budget of over a half a billion dollars, OCDETF operates nationwide and combines the resources and unique expertise of numerous federal, state, and local law enforcement agencies in a coordinated attack against major drug trafficking and money laundering organizations. OCDETF has maintained an active caseload of nearly 5,200 cases, resulting in over 40,000 arrests since its inception. In fact, state and local law enforcement agencies participate in approximately 90 percent of all OCDETF investigations nationwide. The participants involved include all ninety-four U.S. Attorneys' Offices, including 588 OCDETF federal prosecutors, the Bureau of Alcohol, Tobacco, Firearms and Explosives, the Drug Enforcement Administration, the Federal Bureau of Investigation, the Internal Revenue Service, the U.S. Immigration and Customs Enforcement, the U.S. Marshals Service, the Criminal and Tax Divisions of the U.S. Department of Justice, and the U.S. Coast Guard (U.S. Department of Justice, 2013a, 2013b).

What does all this mean to a federally incarcerated black student asking "why me"? OCDETF is the single greatest *force multiplier* of all federal law enforcement. If you are involved in the black counter-culture of crime, the chances of you ending up on the intelligence radar of OCDETF is extremely high. For example, as of the fiscal year 2013 there were a total of only 5,250 special agents assigned to the DEA, armed with a miniscule $2.7 million annual budget and an estimated 4000 informants, in order to fight the nation's *War on Drugs*. OCDETF brings in a respectable $525 million annual budget, tens of thousands of informants, and "deputized" local and state drug agents as *federal drug task force agents*, adding tens of thousands of additional officers to investigate crimes. It is estimated that over 30,000 local/state police officers and sheriff's deputies are assigned to these multi-jurisdictional task forces across the nation. Additionally, over 90 percent of the 18,000 police agencies in the nation reported having their own agency drug unit (U.S. Department of Justice, 2007a, 2007b). All of this local and state manpower and their "boots on the ground" resources now become available to OCDETF.

Of even greater significance, these federal drug task force agents bring with them the most valuable resource in any criminal investigation: informants, and tens of thousands of them. There are no measurable statistics on the exact number of police informants that exist in the nation; however, there is no doubt based on my professional experience (I personally cultivated hundreds of informants) that human intelligence, a/k/a informants, are involved directly or indirectly in at least 90 percent of all federal criminal investigations. I am not exaggerating in my belief that there must be at least one hundred thousand police informants nationwide, many brought to the table via the OCDETF Program. To give you an example of how important informants are today, the FBI requested an additional $12.7 million to improve its informant program.

So what's the financial reward and the inevitable social cost of the OCDETF Program? Currently, OCDETF reimburses state and local agencies with funds allocated by the Department of Justice Assets Forfeiture Fund. In 2012 alone, OCDETF reimbursed state and local agencies $29 million for their participation in OCDETF investigations and cases. Much of this money is documented as "overtime dollars" for the local and state drug agents involved in these operations. Keep in mind, almost 80 percent of all OCDETF investigations result in forfeited assets. In 2012, OCDETF seized approximately $476 million in cash and property. Since 2009, OCDETF investigations have been responsible for the seizure of approximately $1.9 billion, with the greatest portion going back into the coffers of local and state police departments due to asset forfeiture statutes (U.S. Department of Justice, 2007a, 2007b, 2013a, 2013b).

The social cost of the OCDETF Program comes in terms of target selection and human intelligence. As already noted throughout this chapter, the *economic incentives* for the criminal justice system to continue to try to "arrest" its way out of crime forces many agencies simply create a "bounty hunter's mentality" of getting paid for every person taken into custody. Since a significant amount of OCDETF intelligence, investigations, and subsequent arrests are generated by "locally deputized" drug agents, resulting in federal drug and weapons charges and with little or no oversight, the case selection process is ripe for abuse based on racial and ethnic biases.

Target Selection

Again, I turn my attention to the Brennan Center for Justice report, *Racial Disparities in Federal Prosecutions,* specifically regarding the concerns of federal drug task forces. Numerous former U.S. Attorneys (USAs) participating in this report described the complicated relationship between federal prosecutors and local law enforcement, as well as how the incredible economic incentives can be a corrupting force, and how the lack of oversight regarding federal drug task force target selection contributes to the massive racial disparity within the federal criminal justice system. One USA noted:

> Where [law enforcement] . . . wants to get a quick statistic is often where . . . the racial disparity occurs. It's a lot easier to go out to the 'hood, so to speak, and pick somebody than to put your resources in an undercover [operation in a] community where there are potentially politically powerful people . . . local law enforcement makes those decisions to put all their cars in the black community and not the suburbs. . . . At the end of the day, if you are getting a disproportionate

> number of [people of color] brought to you, then what can you do?
> (Johnson et al., 2010, p. 15)

Another stated:

> The [state-federal] task forces . . . are the best and worst thing that
> could happen [to you]. There is so much money given to these task
> forces. . . . They generate so many cases, it's like a self-perpetuating
> thing. For [state law enforcement] to get money, they have to bring
> cases to [federal prosecutors]. The more cases you bring, the more
> money they have. (p. 16)

A third added:

> It was our belief that local [law] enforcement was focused on making a
> lot of very small drug-related arrests with the hope of [seizing some
> forfeited assets] and . . . funneling the money back into their coffers.
> Forfeiture [of assets is] a great tool, but it can be abused, and we were
> of the opinion that it was very much prone to abuse. (p. 16)

Finally:

> We . . . said to [the grant administrators] . . . we think the forfeiture
> laws [permitting state law enforcement to retain assets during state-
> federal task force investigations] are being used in a manner that leads
> to disproportionate impacts and are not being used in a manner consis-
> tent with what was intended. What we want to do is . . . take on the
> responsibility of doing training for everybody, but . . . we want you to
> require . . . that anybody who gets money has to be subject to the
> training, and they did. . . . So you couldn't get [grant] money without
> the training . . . we focused on value-based training, that is, teaching
> law enforcement to recognize . . . that to pursue arrests in a racially
> based manner was inconsistent with all . . . the things they had been
> taught and, for most of them, with why they got into law enforcement
> in the first place. That it was unconstitutional, unethical, and all sorts of
> other things . . . we recognized that there were some who weren't going
> to care one way or another. (p. 17)

BLACPRO II

The other significant social cost of the OCDETF Program is the massive cultivation of "informanthood." Look, the fact is not every person
arrested on federal charges cooperates with the government; however,
the overwhelming majority does. They do not cooperate out of personal
spite, but do so in order to receive leniency from an often draconian
prison sentence. This can be done by (1) acceptance of responsibility; (2)
substantial assistance or what is known as a 5K1.1; or (3) section 5K2.0,
which permits the court departures based on factors specifically listed in
the guidelines or "unmentioned" factors which are not adequately considered by the sentencing guidelines. However, much of the criminal

intelligence gathered by law enforcement agencies is obtained via the Rule 11 plea discussions. In the overwhelming majority of plea bargain agreements, there is a written provision requiring the offender's cooperation, that is, the offender will consent to interviews with law enforcement agents in which the offender will be providing criminal intelligence on past, present, and sometimes future crimes. This could be a single interview or entail months, or sometimes, years, of interviews.

Let me make this very clear. Over 95 percent of all offenders charged with a federal offense plead guilty (U.S. Department of Justice, 2011a). Of those who opt for a criminal trial, over 98 percent are convicted. Thus, the majority of the incarcerated students sitting in my classes whether they like to admit it or not, become informants for the government, describing their criminal activities along with the criminal activities of their family members, friends, as well as their enemies to federal law enforcement agents. Law enforcement agents then use this intelligence to open new or further ongoing criminal investigations, which lead to more arrests, convictions, and offenders in federal custody. *Informanthood* is a cycle that takes place twenty-four hours a day, seven days a week. For urban black communities, the social cost for this ongoing "culture of informanthood" has been devastating. The formula is very simple. Urban black males in federal custody will more often than not provide criminal intelligence that will lead to the arrests and convictions of more urban black males, whether it's of their brothers, sisters, cousins, associates, or co-defendants.

In an ironic twist of fate, many convicted black offenders will target members of their very own black community for potential federal investigation in order to secure their own freedom from incarceration. This cycle epitomizes the true essence of "black on black crime." In fact, I'm not aware of any single greater motivator to maintain the status quo of transgenerational learned helplessness for incarcerated black male students than induction into *informanthood*. Remember, it's not that incarcerated white students do not cooperate with the government; they just do it at a lesser rate because there are fewer in custody and because they have less incentive. Again, most cooperate due to draconian sentencing guidelines, which simply impact white incarcerated students less. On average, black males receive almost longer sentences than comparable whites males arrested for the same crimes. In federal courts, the average sentence during 2008 and 2009 was fifty-five months for white offenders and ninety months for black offenders (U.S. Sentencing Commission, 2011). Thus, white males are less likely to go into "informanthood" because it is not necessary.

The majority of the law enforcement agents sitting in these interviews are the "federally deputized" task force agents from municipal and state police departments, who are intimately familiar with both the cooperating black male offenders and the black male suspects the offenders are cooperating against due to their local ties, and who in turn go right back into the same urban black communities to fill their body count. Informanthood creates a climate of self-hate, bitterness, shame, anger, and spite, and "black doubt" permeates the black community. For generations due to the informanthood, black men have been psychosocially conditioned almost at birth to simply never trust another black man, with no exceptions, regardless of whether criminal behavior is present or not.

Whatever community cohesion remained that was not destroyed in black communities across the country during COINTELPRO has been officially killed off by Americans' asymmetrical *War on Drugs*. Black communities that function in political, economic, educational, and moral chaos feed right into the hands of a very hungry shark. Let me be very clear. There is nothing more humiliating "to the soul" of an urban black male than to sit across a table from a law enforcement agent and federal prosecutor, who more often than not are white males, and to become a "snitch" for the government. I have looked directly into the eyes of many young black men who have cooperated on federal criminal cases, and they clearly lost part of themselves, during the interview process. I have looked directly into the eyes of many incarcerated black male students who have cooperated with the government, and they clearly have a void in their "collective soul" which they fill by holding onto a black counter-culture of crime. *Informanthood* is a social and psychological depression that is passed from a father to his children. These same black men then return to their respective urban communities in search of their lost manhood, where they are compelled to either reenter their respective underground criminal activities and the counter-culture of crime to prove they are not "snitches" or to arm themselves with tools of violence to protect themselves from the "code of the street."

I am not advocating, nor will I ever advocate, that black men should not cooperate with the government. At the end of the day, everyone just wants to go home. Anyone who feels they've won a "moral battle" by taking the United States of America to trial, where the conviction rate exceeds 98 percent, and is later sentenced to a draconian prison term of 360 months or greater, also loses their "collective soul." For the next thirty years, they can tell "war stories" to other federal offenders on how they bravely fought the government on "principle" and how, although they lost, they still have their dignity, as they: (1) Make twenty-three cents an hour sweeping the floors of the United States of America. (2) Get served with a divorce petition in the visiting room. (3) Observe their very own son walking off the new federal inmate bus. (4) Miss the funeral services of all their family members. And (5) wake up one morning with gray hair and arthritis, and realize they have wasted their lives and the lives of their children, and are going to die in federal prison.

There are no right or wrong answers for my incarcerated black students, other than to tell them to do everything in their power to *never again* place themselves or the real victims, their children, in the position of the humiliating cycle of informanthood. The first step starts with telling incarcerated black students the truth. I tell them that they must be engaged in a daily struggle to free themselves from the hold of the black counter-culture of crime. I tell them the only way to protect themselves from the *Great White Shark* is to never get in the water. I tell them they are the only ones remaining who have the "collective lived experiences" to save their own children from the politics of shaming, self-segregation, and transgenerational learned helplessness. As William Julius Wilson stated in the film *The House I Live In*: "You should not be able to enter a hospital ward in an inner-city hospital of new-born babies and predict with near certainty, on the basis of their class, background, and race, where these kids . . . where these healthy new-born babies are going to end up in life."

FOUR

Jim Crow Jr.

During post-secondary programming at FCI McKean, usually on the very first day toward the end of our allocated two-hour time period, I normally give the incarcerated students several "take-home" assignments. I ask them, when they return back to their living area, to write down on a piece of paper exactly how much money their lives are worth. When they return the following class, I ask them to write down the monetary figure they either earned or were attempting to earn when they committed their crimes, next to it. Almost 100 percent of the time, the second monetary figure was significantly lower than what they estimated their lives to be worth. A little laughter follows the discussion because for the first time many of the incarcerated students realize one thing: how little they value their own lives.

I then request that they complete one more assignment. I ask them to write down the monetary value of their children. I tell them that I want to see an actual figure, and not some bullshit that "my kids are priceless." I tell them we're way past this lie in our life experiences, and to compare their estimated children's value to the monetary value they gave themselves, and to the monetary figure that resulted in their incarceration. There is very little laughter, because for the very first time, these incarcerate students realize something more important: (1) how little they value the lives of their children; and (2) the cost of their real "addiction to money." You see, while not every incarcerated student has a drug or alcohol addiction, although many create one as a mitigating factor in an attempt to receive a lower sentence, all of them have an addiction to money. There is not one single prison-community transition program in the nation that is attempting to address this issue, because it's an addiction that we all share and it makes us very uncomfortable to discuss publically, whether you're inside or outside of a prison facility. That's right, an urban black male who sells drugs or commits armed robberies shares the exact same addiction to money as do white males who work on Wall Street or the criminal justice system. I wonder what the results would be if criminal justice practitioners participated in the same "value of life" exercise I requested of the incarcerated students in my class?

Finally, I tell them that whatever monetary figure they wrote down for their children doesn't even come close to what the market value of their children is to the criminal justice system. I tell them that their children are truly "priceless" to the justice system because it could not sustain itself without them. I tell them "they" as current "incarcerated students" are worth much less to the criminal justice system than their children, because just like purchasing a new car, its value begins to depreciate within twenty-four hours after bringing it home. I tell them the criminal justice system is always investing in the futures of their children, when no one else seems to care. In the summer of 2013, the City of Philadelphia decided to close twenty-three public schools, almost 10 percent of the city's total, which of course will be in areas that disproportionately affect black communities, while approving the construction of the second most expensive state project ever in Pennsylvania, a new 5,000 bed state-of-the-art $400 million prison. With a state prison population that is filled with over 61 percent black males, although young black male adults only represent less than 5 percent of the state population, it will not be too difficult predicting who will be filling the majority of the new bed space (Hurdle, 2013; Pennsylvania Department of Corrections, 2013).

I tell them they aren't selling their children to the criminal justice system, they are practically giving them away. I tell them that in the end, they are no different than the black Africans who helped the Europeans capture their human cargo in the African Holocaust four hundred years ago, but with one exception. Those black Africans at least had the business savvy to receive some sort of compensation for enslaving their very own children. I tell my incarcerated black students the next time they want to blame the person responsible for the plight of their children, they need look no further than the metal mirror inside of their own cell. The room is usually very quiet for a bit, because the most difficult conversations to have with incarcerated students often pertain to the impact their own lifestyles have had on their children. The negative consequences for their children, the only innocent party in this ugly social construction of lies, are substantial, including financial instability, changes in family structure, an incredible social stigma, and a continuation of the politics of shaming, self-segregation, and transgenerational learned helplessness.

THE LEGACY OF THE BLACK COUNTER-CULTURE OF CRIME

Today, nearly 3 million children have parents that are currently incarcerated, and over 10 million have had a parent incarcerated in their lifetime (Bernstein, 2005; The Pew Charitable Trusts, 2010). This means that 1 out of every 33 children in the U.S. currently has a parent in prison or jail (The Sentencing Project, 2009, 2013b). Additionally, over 5 million children have a parent on probation or parole. Not surprisingly, black children are disproportionally represented in each of these categories. One in every 9 black children has a parent behind bars. This is eerily comparable to the racial demographics of their fathers, where 1 in every 12 working age adult black men is incarcerated. For white children, that ratio grows exponentially to 1 in every 57, and 1 in every 87 white working adults. Over half (58 percent) of the minor children of incarcerated parents are less than ten years old and the vast majority (93 percent) of incarcerated parents are male (Urban Institute, 2005). Over 53 percent of parents who are incarcerated reported never having had a personal visit from their children (The Sentencing Project, 2009). There are so many children being impacted by parental incarceration that, later in 2013, *Sesame Street* will release a new campaign aimed at helping children cope with a parent living behind bars (*Sesame Street*, 2013).

According to the reports, *Collateral Costs: Incarceration's Effect on Economic Mobility*, and *Child Poverty and Intergenerational Mobility*, black children are more likely to live in poverty, and black children who have an incarcerated parent live in such a chronic state of poverty, that it becomes a debilitating transgenerational phenomena. The poverty rate among black children is nearly 40 percent, more than twice as high as the rate among white children. In the fourth grade, 85 percent of black children cannot read or do math at grade level and later almost half drop out of school (Children's Defense Fund, 2011). If a father of a black child is incarcerated, the family average income over the period of his incarceration is 22 percent lower than the family income the year before he was incarcerated. According to these reports, even in the year after the father is released, family income remains 15 percent lower than it was the year before incarceration (The National Center for Children in Poverty, 2009; The Pew Charitable Trusts, 2010). That would take the poverty rate of black children in America who have a black adult male parent in the custody of the criminal justice system to well over 60 percent. This is almost a social death sentence for black male children. Black male children will forever be forced to run "the 100 yard dash of life" six seconds after the horn starts, as their fathers are listening to their favorite music on MP3 players inside of a BOP facility.

SOCIAL WEALTH AND SOCIAL DEBT

Several national studies report that children of incarcerated parents are five to seven times more likely to be incarcerated themselves (Center for Children of Incarcerated Parents, 2004; Congressional Record, 2007; Administration for Children, Youth, and Families, 2004). For black children with an incarcerated father, who comprise nearly half of all the children with an incarcerated adult male, these numbers are almost three-fold. Children inherit the *social wealth* and/or *social debt* of their parents. Black children have been inheriting the politics of shaming, self-segregation, and transgenerational learned helplessness of their parents for over four centuries. I am blessed to have reaped the benefits of a formal education and a professional lifestyle, despite the ugly realities of childhood poverty, structural and direct violence; however, could you imagine what my early family life would have been like if my father, grandfather, and great grandfather had been college educated? If they had simply been given a fair opportunity to obtain employment, education, and equal protection under the law?

You see, the greatest gift that my son could have ever inherited from me was the reality that choosing whether to pursue a college education was never going to be an option in his life. For him, higher education would be just another of life's formalities, which I promise he will pass on to his children three-fold. This, all because the cultural cycle of incarceration had been confronted and broken by my father, who, despite the scars of Jim Crow on his back, provided safe passage for my brothers and me to start the legacy of *cultural wealth* instead of *cultural debt*. Incarcerated black male students must know and accept that their actions or inactions will not only have a direct impact on the social and psychological debt they will leave their children, but will also impact the much broader generational debt they will leave on the black American culture.

The psychosocial debt left to black children by their incarcerated black fathers is nothing short of staggering. Incredible numbers of children who are raised in fatherless black neighborhoods ravaged by crime, poverty, poor healthcare, hunger, unemployment and the constant "hunt" of the *Great White Shark* are experiencing the psychological equivalent of modern-day battlefield conditions. Post-traumatic stress disorder (PTSD) has been immobilizing black children in communities over the past two generations. It is estimated that 1 out of every 3 black children living under these conditions is suffering from PTSD (U.S. Department of Health, 2013). Research on PTSD indicates that children, who have been subjected to the types of trauma experienced in black urban neighborhoods, are vulnerable to serious long-term emotional problems, such as debilitating fear, depression, memory and attention problems, anxiety, irritability, insomnia, withdrawal, anger, and violence.

According to the National Urban League's report, *Youth Violence: Implications for Post-traumatic Stress Disorder in Urban Youth:*

> Violence has a harmful effect on the mental health of youth because they have not developed the cognitive and coping abilities necessary to adapt to certain stressors, such as violence. This makes them more susceptible to the development of mental distress and other emotional problems. Without treatments, these mental health issues will become more severe and last through adulthood. (p. 5)

Studies published in the *Journal of Pediatric Psychology* and the *Journal of Adolescent Health* found that children with symptoms of post-traumatic stress had poor function of the hippocampus, a part of the brain that stores and retrieves memories (Carrion et al., 2009; Carrion and Wong, 2011). Dr. Victor Carrion, one of the research project's principal investigators, stated, "The brain doesn't divide between biology and psychology."

MAKING PERFECT SENSE YET?

If we can agree that an education is the "great equalizer" and the only emancipating factor of a life of structural and institutionalized social inequities, then all of this devastating news regarding the impact of incarceration on black children should be starting to make perfect sense. According to the Children's Defense Fund (2011), 85 percent of black children in the fourth grade cannot read or do math at their appropriate grade level. Unfortunately, academically black children never catch up to their peers. The U.S. Department of Education (2013) reports that black Americans have the lowest high school graduation rates in the country at 66.1 percent (see figure 4.1) and one of the highest dropout rates at 5.5 percent (see figure 4.2).

As well, the U.S. Department of Education's Civil Rights Data Collection survey (2012) paints a very disturbing picture of the plight of black children's educational experience. Black students, specifically males, face much harder and stricter forms of discipline, as well as unequal access to scholastic resources and academic support in the nation's public school system:

- Public school educators unfairly punished children of color. Although black children represent only 18 percent of the sample, they represent 35 percent of the number of students suspended once, 46 percent of those suspended more than once, and 39 percent of all students expelled.
- Black children were less likely to be exposed to high-level curriculums and experienced teachers. On average, teachers in schools with high black and Hispanic student enrollments were paid $2,251

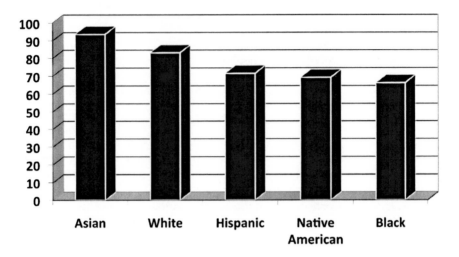

Figure 4.1.   High School Graduation Rates 2012.

less per year than their colleagues working in schools with a majority enrollment of white students.

- In Chicago, black students made up 45 percent of the student body, however, 76 percent of the suspensions.
- More than 70 percent of students involved in school-related arrests or had their cases referred to the police were black or Hispanic.
- Across all public school districts, black students were more than 3 1/2 times more likely than their white peers to be suspended or expelled.
- One in 5 black male students and 1 in 10 black female students received an out-of-school suspension.
- In districts that reported expulsions under zero-tolerance policies, black and Hispanic students represented 45 percent of the student body but 56 percent of the students expelled under such policies.
- Black students represented 21 percent of students with disabilities but 44 percent of students with disabilities who were subject to mechanical restraint.
- Over 55 percent of the high schools with low black and Hispanic enrollment offered calculus; however, only 29 percent of the schools with high black and Hispanic enrollments did so.
- Black and Hispanic students made up 44 percent of the students in the survey, but they were only 26 percent of the students in the gifted and talented programs.

You see, if incarcerated black students were at home with their black children and actively involved in their black communities, instead of making twenty-three cents an hour working inside one of the United

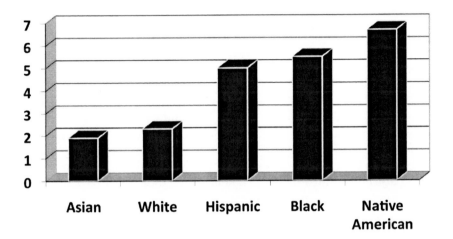

Figure 4.2. High School Dropout Rates 2012.

States of America's one hundred or so BOP facilities across the country, an overwhelming majority of these educational disparities would be addressed. Mothers, regardless of their enormous inner strength and perseverance, cannot alone raise "black boys to become black men." Without my father, there is no doubt I would have been just another one of the faceless and voiceless 2.2 million incarcerated masses or just dead. The truth is, 60 percent of black Americans who drop out before completing high school have spent time in prison and over 75 percent of crimes committed in the United States of America are committed by someone who has never graduated from high school.

According to the Sentencing Projects (2013b) report, *Children in Harm's Way: Criminal Justice, Immigration Enforcement, and Child Welfare*:

> Some children experience adversity before their parents are sent to jail or prison, but arresting and incarcerating parents introduces trauma and hardship of its own into children's lives. Sending parents to jail or prison can disrupt bonds between children and their parents, lead to children being separated from their siblings, trigger residential instability, and cause children to be alienated from friends and ostracized by peers. The arrest and incarceration of parents also takes an emotional toll on children, leaving some psychologically traumatized, fearful, anxious, withdrawn, socially isolated, grieving, or possibly acting out their feelings in disruptive ways. It can result in enduring social and economic hardships for the family members who care for incarcerated parents' children. Accounting for other factors, it can also significantly increase the odds of children living in chronic poverty, which is associated with a wide range of adverse outcomes for youth. (p. 3)

CHILDREN WHO'VE WITNESSED A SHARK ATTACK

When I ask incarcerated students if their children had ever witnessed them being arrested or were present during the execution of a police search warrant, a solid majority affirm an acknowledgment. Today, there is a dearth of information regarding the exact number of how many children are present during the time of their parent's arrest, because nobody tracks those numbers. However, a recent survey by the New York State Division of Criminal Justice Services (DCJS) found that 90 percent of those arrested had also been handcuffed in front of their child, while 9 percent said their child had witnessed police draw their guns. According to the Rutherford Institute (2011) the militarization of police, specifically the rise of Special Weapons and Tactics Teams (SWAT) inherently brings violence in police-citizen contacts. Radley Balko's *Rise of the Warrior Cop: The Militarization of America's Police Forces* and criminologist Peter Kraska, a professor of criminal justice at Eastern Kentucky University, estimate that between 70,000 and 80,000 SWAT-related search warrants are executed each year by police departments around the nation (Barnett and Alongi, 2011). Balko (2013) notes:

> These raids bring unnecessary violence and provocation to nonviolent drug offenders, many of whom were guilty of only misdemeanors. The raids terrorize innocents when police mistakenly target the wrong residence. And they have resulted in dozens of needless deaths and injuries, not only of drug offenders, but also of police officers, children, bystanders, and innocent suspects. (p. 1)

Any person who has been alive and has owned a television set the last three decades clearly understands the incredible military grade hardware that SWAT police operations bring to the "fight" during the execution of a search warrant at a residence. From protective steel face-masks, stun grenades, automatic weapons, armored vehicles, and some of the best tactical training in the nation, black males invested in the counter-culture of crime have a clear understanding of what they're going up against, yet the thought of their children becoming "collateral damage" does not even create a speed-bump in their criminal behavior. I have assisted in the execution of hundreds of residential search warrants and easily over 95 percent had small children present, although an enormous amount of energy was spent trying to avoid this type of contact. After the flash grenade smoke cleared the house, children would be found screaming at the top of their lungs inside bedroom closets or in a forced prone position while being held at gunpoint by police, as their adult father, uncle, brother, or cousin attempts to fight or flee the residence. You ask, "What type of person would leave their children behind to suffer as the police are breaking down their front door?" For black males, my answer will always involve someone involved in the *counter-culture of crime*.

According to Rachel Blustain's (2013) report, *Pushing Cops to Consider Kids When Arresting Parents*, children who witness a family member's arrest and subsequent incarceration experience in many ways the same level of trauma that occurs during the death of a parent. Children often feel "very angry, scared and guilty for being unable to protect their parents." In the SHINE for Kids (2011) report, *The Impact on a Child When Witnessing an Arrest,* child psychologists identify the following in children who have experienced trauma such as an arrest:

- Emotional changes: anger, fear, confusion, helplessness, shame, guilt, rejection;
- Behaviors: aggression, destructiveness, defiance, reversion to childish behaviors, disrupted sleep;
- Learning: dropoff in school performance or attendance, resistance to or suspicion of authority figures; and
- Socializing: withdrawal and isolation, bullying. (p. 1)

Let us not forget another and probably the most destructive consequence of black male children having their father or another adult male family living in the cycle of incarceration: complacency. This phenomenon occurs every single time a black child walks into a correctional facility for scheduled visitation and looks into the eyes of his father or other incarcerated black males. A black male child is conditioned to believe that incarceration is not only a normal part of the black American experience, but that a prison setting can become his "comfort zone," allowing him to escape the reality of life. My comfort zone has always been inside a library, even today, because this is where as a child my father explained to me I would discover the truth. Black children visiting their fathers in a prison setting are permitted to psychologically bond with what many urban children view as "ghetto celebrities," whom they see as role models; these children are taught at the earliest of ages that prison is simply part of the package deal that comes with the black American experience. If you can't see a life beyond the walls of an urban neighborhood, there is no better university than a prison.

I challenge anyone to go to a prison and take a close look at the children visitation rooms. They are equipped with books, toys, and all the physical trappings that would make any child feel right at home. In fact, for some children, the visitation rooms are better than their home environment, because they represent one of complete safety. Although children visitation rooms are located in almost every correctional facility across the country, I will highlight one that is privately owned by the Nashville-based Corrections Corporation of America: the Ohio Department of Rehabilitation and Correction North Central Correctional Complex. On its website, the facility describes its children's reading room as follows:

The reading rooms encourage family literacy by providing a pleasant and comfortable setting for both child and incarcerated parent. Each room is stocked with a wide variety of children's books and has an inmate narrator who reads to the visiting children twice a day. The role of the inmate narrator is to read picture books to the children in much the same manner that children's hour would be done at a public library. A variety of arts and craft supplies for the children are also available in most of the rooms. Many of the supplies and books are donated by employees and service organizations.

Here lies the inherent nightmare scenario for black children. Education will always be at the forefront of liberating black men from the cycle of incarceration and the counter-culture of crime; however, where do we sit morally as a nation when we turn to correctional facilities to provide an educational experience for black children? I'm sorry but to me this is akin to "a fox feeding the chickens." Even with the best intentions, these "comfort zones" provided by correctional facilities across the nation subconsciously implant an "incarceration chip" into the psyche of every black male child who enters a prison setting. The true injustice is that family visitations are part of a positive climate that encourages a healthy transition for incarcerated students reentering back into their communities, while at the same time serving as one of the psychological enablers for continuing the politics of shaming, self-segregation, and transgenerational learned helplessness.

BLACK CHILDREN CAN REFORM THE CRIMINAL JUSTICE SYSTEM

Two of the most frequently asked questions I address are "Given the dire social realities we live in, how can we break the cycle of black-on-black crime?" and "What needs to be done to reform the criminal justice system?" I tell them the only truth that I've discovered in my three-decade-long career in this business comes down to one answer: black American children. That is, those walking the streets today along with those yet to be born. There is only one true method to "neuter" the criminal justice system, besides the common sense but socially difficult approach of "just stop feeding it," and that is by ensuring that black children, specifically black males, become black adults who will serve as jurors in criminal trials.

It's not that Hispanic males will not play an extremely important part in criminal justice reform; however, America has some unfinished business regarding its relationship with black Americans, and until the issues of racism, white supremacy, and white privilege can be adequately addressed within the black American experience, equality will never be able to successfully transfer to other diverse populations in the nation. White Americans will never be able to comprehend the critical role the social construct of race plays in the relationship between black men and the criminal justice system, and black Americans will never be able to stop police officers from arresting, persecutors from filing charges, judges from sentencing, or correctional facilities from housing black men, because the criminal justice system: (1) Was never created to be an inclusive part of the black American experience; (2) Was never created to "police" the social institution of white supremacy within itself; and (3) Will never turn away so much easy money to be made off the flesh of black males.

However, what can be done is to make the criminal justice system pay a "severe financial and an embarrassing social cost" by forcing the system to go to trial for each and every arrest made on a black male. With black men, the only demographic that has been used to define the concept of justice in our nation since 1619, sitting on juries across the country, black male defendants will opt for jury trials instead of succumbing to plea bargains, which will (1) Bottleneck the criminal justice system, literally forcing it to come to a stand-still; (2) Financially cripple the justice system, due to the enormous monetary cost of criminal trials; and (3) Humiliate the criminal justice system, as state and federal conviction rates would plummet, on the understanding that for the very first time in the history of our country, black defendants would have their cases heard before a few jury members who understand the lived black American experience.

Of course black jurors would still convict black defendants. One of the greatest myths ever conspired against a people is that black communities are soft on crime. This stereotype is as ridiculous as any levied against black Americans. It's just difficult for black communities to turn to a justice system that has never provided justice within the context of the collective lived black American experience. However, black American jurors would never allow the court, neither judge, defense nor prosecutorial counsel, the ability to conveniently remove the "invisible three-dimensional elephant in the jury room" racism, white supremacy, and white privilege from the outcome, after the criminal justice system has benefited from the exploitation of this entity in every other facet of the process. Why do you think the criminal justice system becomes so "squeamish" regarding the concept of race when it's inside of a jury deliberation room? Do you think the justice system understands the power shift that black jurors would cause regarding the legal application of the law for black men? You bet, because this would expose the central weakness of the criminal justice system: a lack of accountability to black Americans.

According to the Equal Justice Initiative (2010) report, *Illegal Racial Discrimination in Jury Selection: A Continuing Legacy,* racially discriminatory and oppressive practices regarding jury selection across the country are as strong as ever. Examining the criminal jury selection practices of Alabama, Arkansas, Florida, Georgia, Louisiana, Mississippi, South Carolina, and Tennessee, the research revealed numerous practices that cannot be described in any other fashion other than as white supremacy:

- Majority black counties where prosecutors have excluded nearly 80 percent of black Americans qualified for jury service.
- Prosecutors trained to exclude people on the basis of race and instructed on how to conceal their racial bias.
- Black Americans have been excluded from jury duty (1) because they appeared to have "low intelligence"; (2) wore eyeglasses; (3) were single, married, or separated; (4) were too old for jury service at age forty-three or too young at twenty-eight; (5) for having relatives who attended historically black colleges; (6) for the way they walk; (7) for chewing gum; and frequently (8) for living in predominantly black neighborhoods. (p. 4)

The Duke Population Research Institute (2011) study, *The Impact of Jury Race in Criminal Trials*, analyzed felony trials in Florida between 2000 and 2010 and discovered that (1) juries formed from all-white jury pools convict black defendants significantly more often than they convict white defendants; and (2) this gap in conviction rates is entirely eliminated when the jury pool includes at least one black American. When an all-white jury is hearing a criminal case involving a black defendant, there is an 8 out of 10 chance for a conviction. When at least one black juror is included, the conviction rate for black and white defendants is virtually identical (p. 2).

As well, when a black male is charged with crimes against the United States of America, the probability of obtaining a black juror in a federal trial is even worse. In federal cases, the trial's prospective jury pool expands from the residents within the county where the crime was committed in state trials, to the residents of the considerably larger federal judicial district encompassing it, where there are considerably greater populations of white Americans (Cohen and Smith, 2010) (see fig. 4.3).

However, incarcerated black students, populating the jury pools across this nation with your presence will probably not be your contribution to criminal justice reform. The fact is, the 30 percent of black males who are convicted felons in this country, as many of the current state and federal laws prohibit, will never be permitted to sit on a jury in a criminal trial. Your legacy will be one of redemption and reconciliation, as it will be *your* journey to ensure *your* children will become the "voices" of the invisible black Americans lost within the intersection of race, crime, and justice. Every time someone looks into the eyes of your black children sitting in a jury box, they will be reminded of the humiliations that existed in over 3,500 lynchings, the forty-year, CDC-sanctioned Tuskegee experiments on untreated syphilis, and the disfigured face of fourteen–year-old child Emmett Till, as the justice system stood by in silence. Every time there is an acquittal or a hung jury in a criminal trial because

Figure 4.3.   Geographical Boundaries of U.S. Federal District Courts.

one or two black male jurors do not accept the "truths" of the criminal justice system, humiliation is transformed into humility.

You see, the criminal justice system needs to be humiliated into reform, and only black children will have the ability to do so. Only by being compelled to deal with the survivors of the multi-generational grandchildren of the Atlantic slave trade, the black codes, Jim Crow, the *War on Drugs*, and the countless other humiliations endured through the social construction of race, as well as being the proud cultural inheritors of the cradle of humanity, with a legacy of educational, political, and social brilliance grounded in *black cultural privilege* (BCP), will forge the humility required for criminal justice reform to take hold. In fact, it may take two or three generations of black children sitting on jury's to humiliate the system into humility. The only people who can set this plan of action into effect are the incarcerated black students who currently serve the needs of the criminal justice system instead of their own black children.

This is the essence of transforming humiliation into humility. Black Americans have the extraordinary ability to draw on the historic legacy of their BCP to not only to survive the worst set of transgenerational crimes and structural violence ever perpetuated on human beings, but to transform the shame, anger, and hopelessness that have attached themselves onto these ongoing series of institutionalized humiliations, into the transcendent humility required to make a better world for black children. What my journey within the black American experience has taught me, which was passed down to me by my own dad, is that ultimately, our *cultural DNA* only serves one fundamental purpose: sustaining the legacy for black children. In the end, nothing else really matters.

As incarcerated black students find themselves getting closer in their own private journey toward humility, there are few things more important than the empowering concepts of redemption and reconciliation in their relationship with their own children, and to address the negative impact that their own lifestyle entrenched in the black counter-culture of crime has had on their children. Incarcerated black students must know that it is their sole "cross to bear" to rid their children of the burden and pain caused by their own humiliations. To break the politics of shaming, self-segregation, and transgenerational learned helplessness passed on to them from, most likely, another black male in their own life. To make it "right" for their children. As Marian Wright Edelman has stated, "You didn't have a choice about the parents you inherited, but you do have a choice about the kind of parent you will be."

FIVE

Are You a 30 Percenter or a 70 Percenter?

The absolute worst environment for an incarcerated black student to find himself in, specifically one who is nearing an end to his sentence, is a prison environment where the black counter-culture of crime goes unchallenged. Whether it's the prison politics of racial segregation, the laissez-faire attitude of prison staff, or even the ability to download and listen to your favorite music on an MP3 player, each provides a dangerous mental "cultural safety cushion" for incarcerated black students, where they begin to subconsciously feel more comfortable and free in a prison setting than in their own respective communities.

Cultural safety cushions are present in all prison settings from low to high, and normally consist of the following: free meals, free recreation, free medical/health services, no bill collectors, no parenting or family responsibilities, and the continued ability to use violence, intimidation, and gangsterism to foster their black counter-culture of crime. All of these are examples of cultural safety cushions that are built into the prison environment, and every single incarcerated black student has to fight off the addiction to them before being released, an impossible task if you don't stay mentally sharp. In fact, these cultural safety cushions are the greatest reward the criminal justice system can bestow on its most loyal and dedicated customer base: black men.

For an incarcerated black student who is already entrenched in the counter-culture of crime, whether his prison sentence is 36 or 360 months, the correctional setting then becomes an extension of the "collective delusion" he has already been living outside of the prison walls. Cultural safety cushions are *structurally inspired delusions* that allow incarcerated black students to embrace their prison setting as an extension of their identities, instead of inspiring them to transform into correctional learning centers (CLCs), designed to exploit the truths behind the politics of shaming, self-segregation, and transgenerational learned helplessness.

There is no better example for understanding the powers of the "collective delusion" of cultural safety cushions than the words of David Fathi, Director of the American Civil Liberties Union's National Prison Project. When commenting on the approval of MP3 players in federal prisons, Fathi stated: "It's a positive step toward improving prison security and providing inmates a needed link to the outside world . . . music allows for an important connection [with life on the outside] that assists with their [offender] eventual re-entry to society" (ACLU, 2013, p. 1).

First, I respect, understand, and applaud the central mission of the National Prison Project, which is to ensure that American prisons "comply with the Constitution, domestic law, and international human rights principles" (ACLU, 2013). However, they cannot be blinded by the fact that they are potentially hurting incarcerated students in their transition back into their respective communities through this type of activism. Just ask yourself, who is paying the social cost for the $69.20 MP3 player and the downloaded music? The last thing an incarcerated black student who has been exposed to the trappings of a counter-culture of crime needs is to become more "distracted" by finding a "connection" between music, which can inspire an incredible level of emotional comfort, and his prison environment. Many are simply unable to separate the two, creating just another *cultural safety cushion* to lean on when faced with the choice of either confronting the many challenges of life on the outside, or returning back to controlled comforts on the inside. For too many years, black men have been making decisions without understanding all of their choices. Because at the end of the day, he has to decide whether he is going to be a *30 percenter or a 70 percenter.*

INSIDE-OUT PRISON EXCHANGE PROGRAM

If there were ever a doubt that post-secondary prison-based education programming can serve as a "point of intervention" for impacting the cycle of the politics of shaming, self-segregation, and transgenerational learned helplessness, when Attorney General Eric Holder recently announced the results of the study, *Evaluating the Effectiveness of Correctional Education: A Meta-Analysis of Programs That Provide Education to Incarcerated Adults,* many have been put to rest. The research findings indicate that, on average, *criminal offenders* who transform into *incarcerated students,* who participated in correctional education programs, had 43 percent lower odds of returning to prison; as well, post-release employment was 13 percent higher than inmates who did not participate in prison-based educational programs (Davis et al., 2013). Recognizing the fundamental correlation between education and prison post-release success, the Vera

Institute of Justice also initiated its *Pathways from Prison to Postsecondary Education Project* (2013). Over the next five years, Pathways is investing in the concept of post-secondary college programming in prisons by covering the financial costs for incarcerated offenders to enroll in either two- or four-year degree programs, pre- and post-release.

In February 2012, I was introduced to a new and committed advocate for post-secondary programming at FCI McKean. This executive administrator sang the praises of her personal experiences working with West Virginia University Professor Jeri Kirby and her participation in the prison educational initiative, *The Inside-Out Prison Exchange Program*. Professor Kirby, who was a former federal inmate herself, had introduced "Inside-Out" to Secure Female Facility (SFF) Hazelton, a women's federal facility.

Inspired by "Paul" who is serving a life prison sentence at the State Correctional Institution at Graterford in Philadelphia, the Inside-Out Prison Exchange Program was founded in 1997 by Temple University faculty member Lori Pompa. It is described via its website as an internationally recognized organization that promotes the active partnership between institutions of higher learning and correctional systems, using an educational platform that brings traditional college students together with incarcerated men and women to study as peers in an academic seminar within the confines of prisons (The Inside-Out Center, 2013).

The core of the program is a semester-long academic course, through which fifteen to eighteen "outside" (i.e., traditional university) students and the same number of "inside" (i.e., incarcerated) students attend class together inside a prison or jail setting. All participants read a variety of texts and write several papers. During class sessions, students discuss issues in small and large groups. In the final month, students work together on a class project (The Inside-Out Center, 2013). The Inside-Out Prison Exchange Program offers one-week "intensive" training sessions for anyone interested in becoming a nationally certified Inside-Out instructor. As of 2013, 465 instructors from more than 180 colleges and universities in 38 states and Canada have taken part in an Inside-Out Instructor Training Institute (The Inside-Out Center, 2013).

I must admit, although I had obviously been aware of the Inside-Out Program and its value at bridging the gap between universities and correctional facilities, it did not appeal to me. I felt the program has several barriers as it relates to ensuring that the multiple narratives of the collective lived black American experience are "authentically voiced." First, the program had a reputation as an "academic sounding board" for prison abolitionists. I have never been an apologist for the justice system; however, calls for the shutting down of prisons are not my thing. In fact, there really are people, including some incarcerated black students who are trapped in a lifestyle of a counter-culture of crime, who need to be confined for the safety of their children, families and communities. Although

I highly respect the opinions of many criminal justice reformists and prison abolition activists, as many are personal friends and colleagues, I did not see the upside of debating the merits of such an argument for a week-long retreat in a room full of other educators from whereabouts unknown. Second, I felt the program's pedagogical application promoted the discourse of critical pedagogy, which has questionable applications to a black male audience in a prison educational setting. As well, the program was a bit too "touchy-feely" for me, which directly clashed with my own "confrontational" philosophy. The thought of having a white female Pitt criminal justice student sitting "face-to-face" with an incarcerated black male student in an "ice-breaking exercise" discussing their favorite poem or whatever was never going to occur in one of my classes. To me, this was a programmatic mindset that was not centered on the realities of being an incarcerated BOP black student who was either convicted of or had pled guilty to crimes against the United States of America. In fact, I would argue that these types of "ice breaking" exercises serve as an *intimate distraction* for incarcerated black students, whether implied or not.

Third, and almost a deal-breaker, I must admit that I'm somewhat skeptical of any "externally created prison-based program" where the core membership and leadership does not reflect a significant representation of black male scholars. The "outside" student participants, the program's leadership, and the overwhelming majority of the program's nationally certified instructors are white and primarily female, and with very little representation from black male academicians. As I've mentioned earlier, the overwhelming majority (70 percent) of the educators who completed the National Inside-Out training since 2003 were white females (Van Gundy, Bryant, and Starks, 2013; The Inside-Out Center). Similar to the powerful critiques mentioned on critical pedagogy, "where is the authentic scholarly black American male voice" in one of the largest post-secondary prison college programs in the nation, that advocates social justice in correctional institutions across the country, that are housed by incarcerated offenders who are nearly 40 percent black men? This was a huge red flag for me. Not taking anything away from the program's positive message on post-secondary education, I've discovered that from personal experience in and conversations with incarcerated black students, whether real or perceived, there are many times when white male and female prison program educators subconsciously bring with them the pedagogical baggage of white privilege, playing the role of a social "messiah" for everything that is wrong regarding incarcerated black men, the criminal justice system, and their relationship with the black American experience. Contributing to a modern-day "white man's burden"—the urge of white Americans to "educate and civilize" incarcerated black students became an unwavering perceptual reality and one that I did not want to perpetuate. The quagmire becomes, "How can a white scholar who has never lived the collective black American experience become the *pedagogical authentic voice* of a post-secondary education experience or offer any advice of critical substance directed to any incarcerated black student, without bringing with them the *socially constructed lie* of four hundred years of white privilege?" I cannot envision any post-secondary academic course in existence being offered under the umbrella of a prison-based program where racism, along with the nuances of white supremacy and white privilege, would not impact the critical engagement of incarcerated black male students. To ignore the prison-based educator's role in "culturally responsive teaching" (Gay, 2010) solidifies the hubris of white privilege among academicians that has long existed and is commonplace in classrooms across the nation, to the detriment of black male students. Addressing this pedagogical issue sits at the core of the *Humiliation to Humility Perspective* (HHP).

One of the very few white males who has successfully attempted to bridge the white privilege gap to white audiences is anti-racism activist Tim Wise. Several of his books, *Dear White America: Letter to a New Minority, White Like Me: Reflections on Race from a Privileged Son,* and *Colorblind: The Rise of Post-Racial Politics and the Retreat from Racial Equity,* offer great insight into this debate from a privileged white male's perspective. I recommend these readings to all of my students, especially white criminal justice majors in my Senior Seminar Capstone course, and encourage them to engage in critical discourse of Wise's narrative on the social institution of white supremacy.

Finally, I simply could not see what the program could contribute to what I had already been doing over the past several years at FCI McKean. I had already established a complementary working relationship and a pretty solid reputation with the executive staff at the facility. In my opinion, FCI McKean is the best-kept secret in the BOP regarding progressive prison-based educational programming, a true credit to the executive staff and talented incarcerated students. In fact, I was already fine-tuning my own pedagogical framework with HHP, and I was already bringing University of Pittsburgh students to the correctional facility to assist in facilitating programming. I was already working with the staff and incarcerated students serving on the Inmate Reentry Council and other reentry initiatives. However, after several months, I trusted the personal and professional encouragement of an executive administrator at FCI McKean and attended the Inside-Out Training Institute in Philadelphia during the summer of 2012.

FINDING MOTIVATION IN THE TRUTH

Although the Inside-Out Training Institute offered insight into its pedagogical approach of transformative education, methods of building relationships with correctional facilities, some basic ground rules for prison settings, and "ice-breaking" activities to build rapport between "inside" and "outside" students, I seriously contemplated leaving after the first day of training. As previously noted, I was already "doing my own thing" and I had left the days of "academic ideological indoctrination" far behind me after my grammar school's exposure to *The Autobiography of Malcolm X*. In fact, all of my initial concerns regarding the programmatic barriers and white privilege were confirmed. Suggesting that it was a daily struggle was an understatement, because once you've been exposed to the stench of academicians hiding behind their white privilege, similar to that of a dead corpse, you can immediately recognize the pungent odor any time, any place, or any situation. Besides several somewhat heated conversations with a radical "Occupy Movement anti-government activist," the only things that kept my interest were my dialogues with a couple of likeminded academicians who shared similar "white privilege" concerns with the program, an opportunity to hear the truths of "Paul" and the other "lifers" at Graterford Prison in Philadelphia, and my conversations with Inside-Out staff member and Soros Justice Fellow, Tyrone Werts.

Needless to say, I stayed and completed the entire Inside-Out Instructor Training Academy. Although the program had some glaring weaknesses in my opinion, which I hope they make a strategic priority to address, if tweaked, their platform can be part of a valuable tool for providing a post-secondary college experience to incarcerated students. I left with a much clearer understanding and a more committed focus that, as a black man in higher education, (1) I must learn to apply my very own authentic voice and prison-based pedagogical framework; (2) I must learn to embrace my obligation to go inside *correctional facilities* and help transform the culture into *correctional learning centers*; and (3) I must learn to use every available resource to inspire *incarcerated black offenders* to transform into *incarcerated black students*.

BRINGING INSIDE-OUT TO FCI MCKEAN

In September 2013, *ADMJ 1360: Reentry and the Offender* had become the very first Inside-Out Prison Exchange Program course offered at a male Federal Correctional Institute (FCI) and only the third course in the history of the Federal Bureau of Prisons (BOP) at the time. The previous courses were offered at men's and women's camp facilities. I had chosen fifteen "outside" undergraduate students from the Criminal Justice Program at the University of Pittsburgh (Bradford) and the correctional staff at FCI McKean had chosen fifteen "inside" incarcerated students from their prison population. I was somewhat disappointed at first that of the "outside" students, only one black student wanted to participate in the program, because I understood the importance of what a black undergraduate criminal justice student can contribute to the ongoing dialogue of race, crime, and justice within the context of the lived experience. I had received hundreds of inquiries from students from a cross-section of academic disciplines; however, due to the security and background requirements of the BOP, the immense pressure of ensuring that the "first course" was completed without any internal or external complications, and my ready-made interpersonal knowledge of criminal justice majors, the decision became a foregone conclusion regarding the demographics of my student-body pool. The "outside" student demographics were as follows: seven white males, seven white females, and one black female; ten seniors, four juniors, and one sophomore.

At predominately white higher education institutions around the country similar to the University of Pittsburgh, the dearth of black students in the academic discipline of criminal justice is commonplace. The reality of "black skin, white justice" resonates throughout all segments of life, pushing outstanding black candidates away from either the academic discipline or a professional career in the field of criminal justice, as far as the eye can see. The "inside" student racial and ethnic demographics were as follows: ten black males, three Hispanic males, and one white male. Although I was familiar with at least half of these men due to their participation in my other post-secondary programming activities, I requested that staff select a few younger, aggressive, "70 percenters" that would not normally qualify for this type of program due to their anti-social demeanor.

For this very first men's BOP course, as a matter of critical discourse and to push the concept of racism, white supremacy, and white privilege within the criminal justice system, I chose Michelle Alexander's text, *The New Jim Crow: Mass Incarceration in the Age of Colorblindness*. Without a doubt, the mutual trust that I had established with executive staff at FCI McKean played a significant role in their approval of this text. Alexander's book, whether you're on the *inside* or *outside*, is a powerful description of the multi-dimensional criminal justice social forces that have been levied against collective lived black American male experience in the history of the nation. However, how can anyone predict with any certainty, the type of "empowering" impact it would have on incarcerated black male students? Could its theme be used to manifest disruptive behavior? Hell, I'm a seasoned criminal justice professional and academic who's "been there and done that"; however, as a black man, reading the *New Jim Crow* for the first time made me angry. I could only imagine how it would make an incarcerated black male student feel. I clearly understood that given my "inside" and "outside" student demographic characteristics, if I did not carefully manage the interaction between the two parties, this could easily blow up in my face. Incarcerated students confined within the BOP are not intimidated spiritually, culturally, intellectually, or physically by anyone. By nature of their personalities, incarcerated students are leaders, and by the very nature of their street survival skills, they cannot only sense fear but are conditioned to exploit it. "Outside" students do not get a pass in this environment.

I've discovered during my tenure of allowing Pitt students to assist in facilitating with prison-based programming at FCI McKean over the last several years, white male students often become the "psychological toys" of black and Hispanic male incarcerated students. They receive the brunt of the long emotionless stares and are often challenged verbally by incarcerated students in regards to their values, morals, and academic prowess, clearly stemming from the perceived advantage from the incarcerated black student's standpoint at least, gained by the social construct of their white privilege. It can get psychologically and verbally ugly very quickly.

White females are intellectually challenged by incarcerated students as well; however, I find that the social construction of their "perceived" sexuality, from an incarcerated student's perspective, sometimes allows them more psychological latitude to engage in "personalized" debate-style discussions with incarcerated black students. In fact, I'm antidotally convinced that the psychosexual fascination is enabling this "openness" on the part of incarcerated students. In fact, I've witnessed white female students inquire directly about an incarcerated black student's criminal behavior that led to their imprisonment, sometimes receiving an almost instantaneous response; however, if a white male student had inquired about the same, they would have been immediately verbally challenged. However, these interpersonal dynamics have never been studied and require additional academic inquiry before any empirical conclusions should be drawn.

Not so surprising, black students who are criminal justice majors are treated with the same level of critical inquiry that I normally receive, and must be prepared for incarcerated black students to psychologically "Uncle Tom" them into submission with statements such as "I can't believe you would arrest your own father" or "You wanna be part of the New Jim Crow instead of fixing it." In fact, if any student is under the assumption that their white privilege, class privilege, gender privilege, or black cultural privilege, etc., can protect them from the *cultural hurdle* of the counter-culture of crime, that will determine their psychosocial ability to survive the prison politics of a BOP setting composed of primarily black males, they are in for a very rude awakening. In fact, the dearth of black students who attend prison-based programming is often a topic of great inquiry by incarcerated black male students.

EXPLOITING THE TRUTH

Although I was not surprised in the least bit, the incarcerated students were better academically across the board than the traditional Pitt students. In fact, it was not even close. My incarcerated students were better writers, debaters, communicators, critical thinkers, and simply more dedicated to the art of acquiring knowledge. I believe my application of the pedagogical themes outlined within the HHP helped to inspire a greater sense of intellectual motivation and critical engagement in many of the incarcerated students. Part of the course curriculum required written reflection papers from each student on a weekly basis. These reflection papers allowed me open access into the "invisible voices" of all the students, both incarcerated and traditional. Issues and topics that they might be uncomfortable bringing up in an open classroom discussion were encouraged in this academic format. However, I had to stress to my incarcerated students that reflection papers were not journals used to "vent" personal injustices associated with their specific criminal offenses, which is a routine mechanism used in prison programs, but an academic exercise designed to critically assess and if possible, disprove the concepts presented by Alexander's (2010) work. I encouraged them to apply, compare, and contrast their collective lived experiences with the criminal justice system with Alexander's (2010) and their "outside" academic counterparts.

As I've noted throughout this book, federally incarcerated students, regardless of their crime, are leaders. They are targeted by the *Great White Shark* because of their leadership capabilities, which include the power to influence others within the black counter-culture of crime. They carry with them "competitive characteristics" that have been honed to place them at the top of their respective underground "hustles." The incarcerated students wanted to, needed to, and demanded to discuss matters of racism, white supremacy, and white privilege with their "outside" student counterparts within the context of the criminal justice system; however, my traditional criminal justice students were for the most part outmatched. This gave me great pause, considering many of these same "outside" students will be employed in policing, courts, or corrections professions within months of graduating, with little or no ability to engage effectively in a conversation surrounding the most controversial aspect of their profession. Again, during my Senior Seminar Capstone course, the topics of racism, white supremacy, white privilege, and their by-products, the politics of shaming, self-segregation, and transgenerational learned helplessness, are all confronted. In fact, I have reassessed my program's commitment to engage University of Pittsburgh (Bradford) criminal justice majors in the discourse of racism in every course in the curriculum. It is no wonder the cycle of racial insensitivity and the dysfunctional relationship between black American communities and the justice system continue generation after generation.

The "outsiders," with the exception of a couple of white females and the sole black female student, were intimidated by any discussion that would place race and white privilege in the front and center of any conversation. In fact, some students voiced their frustrations and discomfort both during the course and in their written course evaluations, with being thrust into conversations about racism by incarcerated black students each week. I would be approached by several criminal justice students on campus, and they would sometimes inform me of their difficulty with the topic of racism with the incarcerated students. One criminal justice student stated:

> I was not responsible for slavery so I don't see why I should have to answer for it . . . can't they just get over it. They made the choice of committing a crime . . . what does that have to do with slavery . . . just like I made the choice of going to college. Nobody forced them to be drug dealers . . . but they're so smart . . . it doesn't make sense. But don't blame me.

Another student voiced:

> I'm sick and tired of talking about race. I'm not black and don't know anything about black history. Racism is something that I'm not interested or comfortable in discussing with blacks . . . I don't see it . . . just sounds like an excuse to me. All I hear is excuses and no acceptance of responsibility from those guys. I've never heard white supremacy used so much in my life . . . let it go.

A third criminal justice student described:

> Let me be honest . . . I'm not comfortable discussing race around black guys. I never thought about white privilege until TJ [inside student pseudonym] brought it up in class. Those guys are really smart . . . smarter than I thought and its intimidating. Do you know what it's like to be a senior [at Pitt] and having an incarcerated guy, probably a crack dealer who got his GED in prison, know more about philosophy, law, art, writing poetry, or whatever . . . than me? They win every debate and it's not because we're [outsiders] scared . . . they're just smarter . . . they are the smartest guys I've ever met.

However, one of the greatest benefits of this schism was that CJ students were forced into an uncomfortable state of *self-actualization*, where they were forced to live in the socially constructed world of race and injustice amplified by many of the incarcerated students of color. I explained to CJ students that the process of *self-actualization*, specifically regarding the institution of racism, white supremacy, and white privilege, will pay unimaginable dividends later in their respective professional careers in the criminal justice field. It will provide them a level of civic empowerment, reminding them of their moral duty as guardians of the justice system. It will remind them of their enormous collective power as criminal justice professionals, with a fundamental understanding that the relationship between race, crime, and justice is defined by their individual choices and collective actions.

These "racial fault lines" were also very evident among the incarcerated students. Some confided in me their desire to understand "what the other students really felt about their blackness." I attempted to inspire academic conversations which many times transformed into scholarly debates, that would allow both the incarcerated students and traditional criminal justice students reflective moments that highlighted just how very little they knew about the people underneath the socially constructed labels of "good guys and bad guys." The intellectual curiosity of this dynamic environment resulted in some of the most memorable discussions I've ever had the privilege of participating in.

One of these discussions centered on the topic of how some of the incarcerated students' words and actions differed when they corresponded with fellow CJ students within the class compared to when they communicated with other offenders "on the yard." For example, an incarcerated black student would offer a brilliant reflection paper on the destructive nature of gang activity and fatherless homes in black families, skillfully defending his position within a classroom group discussion debate; however, simultaneously, as soon as the class was over, he would enter the *prison yard* and openly display a gang affiliation tied to the black counter-culture of crime. I would capitalize on the hypocritical nature of this phenomenon by asking the incarcerated black students for an answer. Many were slow to answer, fearing they would lose their credibility among their "outside" student peers, falling prey to the pressure of white privilege. I had to explain to my incarcerated students that the only way they would lose their credibility is if they did not address this issue under the standard of *black cultural privilege* (BCP). In the presence of the entire class, we engaged in a critical dialogue explaining that the powerful counter-culture of crime and white privilege has an enduring historical hold on the black male identity. We determined that some black males who are involved in this counter-culture of crime "love it" more than they do their very own families, and that ultimately, once an incarcerated black student has "owned the knowledge" behind his truths, his history, the criminal justice system, and victimhood of his children, he has the ability to make a choice. An incarcerated black student's first real choice is whether to be a *30 percenter* or *70 percenter*. For too many years, incarcerated black students have been making decisions without understanding all of their choices.

I then explain the fundamental formula of the *30 percenter* and *70 percenter paradigm*: (1) A "70 percenter" is an incarcerated student who has made a *decision* to never leave the lifestyle and humiliations created by a counter-culture of crime; (2) As well, a "30 percenter" is an incarcerated student who has made the *choice* of redemption, reconciliation, and humility in order to take back his legacy within the black American experience. Incarcerated students must make a decision or a choice and be committed to it physically, mentally, and spiritually. I explain to my CJ students as future criminal justice professionals that they will either be passive observers in an institution that encourages 70 percenters, racism, and structural violence or active participants in making choices that compel the fair application of the law. I then explain to my incarcerated students that they will either be passive observers in a counter-culture of crime that encourages excuses and nihilism or active participants in making choices as 30 percenters, enriching the lives of their children. As noted by incarcerated black students, my words offended and embarrassed many of them because they took place in the presence of "white students." This is the power behind the pride of transgenerational learned helplessness. They suggested I should direct my criticism of their behavior away from the youthful ears of the white outsider students. I would laugh, explaining that you should not be embarrassed because it was said in their presence, but humiliated because there is no rational excuse for some incarcerated black students to enjoy being 70 percenters, and investing into the *collective delusion* of gangsterism and the black counter-culture of crime, rather than in the wellbeing of their own children. I suggested that they must learn to humble themselves to the reality that transforming from "criminal offenders" to "incarcerated students" is more than engaging themselves in academic scholarship. Instead, they should focus on discovering their "cultural erudition." They must begin to acknowledge that intellectual scholarship in the academic environment is only an emancipator of men if they own and live the truth of their knowledge.

Toward the end of the course, an incarcerated student gave some of the best advice I have ever heard regarding the "decisions" and "choices" that black men who are trying to escape the clutches of the counter-culture of crime contemplate. While looking directly at an "outside" student, the incarcerated student stated:

> Now . . . the most important thing I learned about myself over the past twenty years of living behind these prison walls . . . is that I am never coming back. Now . . . I don't mean that I don't think I'm coming back, or I hope that I'm not coming back, but I can guarantee that I'm never coming back. You see, I possess some skills and family support that I believe will allow me to make a *choice*. I don't ever plan on going back into crime . . . but . . . if I ever made the *decision* of going back into this culture . . . I want you to know if we come face-to-face . . . and you're a police officer . . . and your job, which I respect, is to put me back into one of these cages . . . I want you to know right now that you're not gonna make it. One of us is not going to walk away from that meeting,

and since the innocence of taking a person's life is already on my re-
sume, I will hesitate a bit on doing what I have to do. Since you don't
have that experience, I can guarantee that you will not win and just
because we know each other in this class does not mean anything to
me. I know that ultimately your people [other police officers] are going
to eventually get me, but either way, I'm never coming back to prison.
So you better be 100 percent positive that this is the career field you
want because I'm not alone in my thinking . . . there are other black
men just like me and you might meet them . . . but I really hope not.

I realize that some readers might interpret the words of this incarcerated student as a subtle threat, but I would caution against this approach,
as it is only applied through the blinded prism of white privilege. However, if one were to understand the hidden message behind his words,
which can only be found through the eyes of the collective lived black
American experience, you would be able to see what is often invisible to
the blinded masses: his *truth*. To me, it is obvious that his period of
incarceration has not been wasted by watching *Sports Center* and point-
less conversations on the latest music fad. His words resonate a clear
message for me that: (1) He has an applied knowledge of his *cultural
survival gene*. (2) He has increased his *criminal justice system IQ*. (3) He
understands the pain of victimization and the price he will pay if he
participates in the *black counter-culture of crime*. And (4) he is now prepared, for the first time in his life, to make a decision regarding his only
true duty: not to renounce his freedom through his own choices. He has
courageously chosen to transform the humiliation of criminal offender to
the humility of incarcerated student and attempt to successfully navigate
the delicate *30 percenter* transition back into owning his own respective
life, fulfilling an opportunity at cultural redemption and reconciliation.

THE DANGER OF KNOWING THE TRUTH

The foundational premise of the *Humiliation to Humility Perspective* (HHP)
has always been *owned truth*. I have attempted to confront the socially
constructed lies that choked the life out of the black American experience
for one of its most valuable commodities: the incarcerated black student. I
have focused my writings on the incarcerated black student because I
don't think there is any living person in America right now more deserv-
ing of the truth. As a black male, there is no doubt in my mind that we are
in a life and death struggle with the black counter-culture of crime and
where it fits in the black American experience.

Asante (2003, p. 64) believes there are two aspects of historical consciousness in this regard: (1) toward oppression; and (2) toward victory.
To me his words speak the truth, that when a person is able to understand and communicate the narrative of his oppression, which includes

everything that has preceded the cycle of incarceration, he has taken the first step in his freedom. However, this is not enough and only creates a hollow story. For an incarcerated black student to be able to truly emancipate himself from the bondage of the *politics of shaming, self-segregation,* and *transgenerational learned helplessness* that have served as insurmountable psychosocial obstacles for so many attempting to make the successful transition back into owning their respective lives, he must be able to consciously make the *choice* to transcend them into the "lived legacy of a victory" that only the messenger of a *black cultural privilege* (BCP) has a right to claim. Asante (2003) stated:

> The victorious attitude shows the Africans on the slave ship [ultimately] winning. It teaches that we are free because we choose to be free. Our choice is the determining factor, [for] no one can be your master until you play the part of slave . . . know your history and you will always be wise . . . the true character of a people resides in how they relate their history to the present and future . . . [for] strength is an inner attribute that cannot be bestowed by another. (p. 65)

Incarcerated black students must have the skills to own their life narrative. Although extremely important, this journey does not simply involve obtaining pre-release employment or technical training, job interviewing skills, substance abuse and mental health treatment, housing, community mentors, and seeking to re-establish family ties. Each of these is a critical component in the overall strategy for a successful prison-community transition; however, these alone are not enough for incarcerated students trapped in a black counter-culture of crime and self-destruction. They must also secure the ability to look inward and develop a *mental toughness,* one that will allow them to understand and apply the power of their owned truth, for the tangible skills noted above will not be sufficient to withstand the universal social rejections that formerly incarcerated black students often face, especially managing the invisible "three-dimensional elephant in the room," the social constructs of race, white supremacy, and white privilege.

The HHP sets aside the antiquarian recidivism model of measuring a successful prison to community transition on the *staying out of prison* (SOP) concept, and supplanting it with a paradigm shift that focuses on *building the sustainable whole person by truth,* where a "black criminal offender" transforms into an "incarcerated black student" who will be able to offer more to himself, his children, and his community than a minimum wage job and a counter-culture that is lost in shame, anger, and alienation. Only by educationally inspiring incarcerated black students on the importance of owning their own lived truths, and the truths behind their *black cultural privilege,* the criminal justice system, and the true victims of their involvement in a *black counter-culture of crime,* their own children, will they finally be able to own their life choices. Confronting the cycle of humiliation provides incarcerated black men an opportunity to liberate themselves from the politics of shaming, self-segregation, and transgenerational learned helplessness and embrace the universal power of humility by becoming incarcerated black students. Only by owning the truth will incarcerated black students be able to hear the voice of Carter Godwin Woodson (1933):

> When you control a man's thinking you do not have to worry about his actions. . . . The thought of the inferiority of the Negro is drilled into him in almost every class he enters and almost every book he studies. . . . Hopelessness is the worst sort lynching. It kills one's aspirations and dooms him to vagabondage and crime. It is strange, then, that the friends of the truth and the promoters of freedom have not risen up against the present propaganda in the schools and crushed it. This crusade is much more important than the ant-lynching movement, because there would be no lynching if it did not start in the schoolroom. However, if he happens to leave school . . . he will naturally escape some of this bias and may recover in time to be of service to his people. . . . Practically all of the successful Negroes in this country are of the uneducated type or that of Negroes who have had no formal education at all. (pp. 5–8)

After everything our nation has put them through, I only hope that incarcerated black students are ready to listen to the truth.

References

Adi, H. (2003). *Pan-African history: Political figures from Africa and the diaspora since 1787.* New York, NY: Routledge.

———. (2005). How many in the slave trade. In Halaqah Media (Producers), and Shahadah, O. A. (Director), *500 years later* [Motion picture]. London: Halaqah Films.

———. (2008). *Nelson Mandela.* London: Wayland.

Administration for Children, Youth, and Families. (2004). *Children of incarcerated parents: Research and resources.* Retrieved from http://cbexpress.acf.hhs.gov/articles.cfm?article_id=768

Africanus, L. (1896). *The history and description of Africa.* R. Brown (Ed.). London: Hakluyt Society.

Alexander, M. (2010). *The new Jim Crow: Mass incarceration in the age of colorblindness.* New York, NY: The New Press.

Allen, R. L. (2006). The race problem in the critical pedagogy community. In C.A. Rossatto, R.L. Allen, and M. Pruyn (Eds.), *Reinventing critical pedagogy: Widening the circle of anti-oppression education* (3–20). New York, NY: Rowman and Littlefield.

American Association of Suicidology. (2010). *USA suicide: 2010 official final data* [Data file]. Retrieved from http://www.suicidology.org/c/document_library/get_file?folderId=262&name=DLFE-635.pdf

American Civil Liberties Union. (2013). Prisoner's rights. *National prison project.* Retrieved from http://www.aclu.org/prisoners-rights

American Correctional Association. (2007). *Correctional employees.* Retrieved from https://www.aca.org/research/

American Council on Education. (2012). By the numbers: More black men in prison than in college? Think again. Retrieved from http://www.acenet.edu/the-presidency/columns-and-features/Pages/By-the-Numbers-More-Black-Men-in-Prison-Than-in-College-Think-Again-.aspx

Ancient Africa. (2013). *Pre-history Africa and the Badarian culture.* Retrieved from http://wysinger.homestead.com/badarians.html

Anderson, B. (1991). *Imagined communities: Reflections on the origin and spread of nationalism.* London: Verso.

Anderson, E. (1999). *Code of the street: Decency, violence, and the moral life of the inner city.* New York: NY: W. W. Norton.

Angelou, M. (1969). *I know why the caged bird sings.* New York, NY: Ballantine.

Ansari, Z. I. (2004). Islam among African Americans. In Z. H. Bukhari, S. S, Nyang, M. Ahmad, and J. L. Esposito (Eds.), *Place in the American Public Square: Hope, Fears, and Aspirations.* Lanham, MD: AltaMira.

Aos, S., Miller, M., and Drake, E. (2006). *Evidence-based adult corrections programs: What works and what does not.* Olympia, WA: Washington State Institute for Public Policy.

Armitage, S., Jasim, S., Marks, A., Parker, A., Usik V., and Uerpmann, H. (2011). The southern route "out of Africa": Evidence for an early expansion of modern humans into Arabia. *Science, 331,* 453–456.

Asante, M. (2003). *Afrocentricity: The theory of social change.* Souk Village, IL: African American Images.

———. (2005). How many in the slave trade. In Halaqah Media (Producers), and Shahadah, O. A. (Director), *500 years later* [Motion picture]. London: Halaqah Films.

———. (2007). *The history of Africa.* New York, NY: Routledge.

———. (2009). *Maulana Karenga: An intellectual portrait.* Boston, MA: Polity.

Baldwin. J. (2010). *The cross of redemption: Uncollected writings.* R. Kenan (Ed.). New York, NY: Pantheon.

Balko, R. (2006). *Overkill: The rise of paramilitary police raids in America* [White paper]. Retrieved from http://www.cato.org/sites/cato.org/files/pubs/pdf/balko_whitepaper_2006.pdf

———. (2013). *Rise of the warrior cop: The militarization of America's police forces.* New York, NY: PublicAffairs.

Balola, L. (2011). The global presence of African civilizations: An interview with Runoko Rashidi. *The Journal of Pan African Studies, 4*(8), 1–8.

Barnett, R., and Alongi, P. (2011, February 14). Critics knock no-knock police raids. *USA Today.* Retrieved from http://usatoday30.usatoday.com/news/nation/2011–02–14–noknock14_ST_N.htm

Bell, D. (1992). *Faces at the bottom of the well.* New York, NY: Basic Books.

Bennett, L. (1961). *Before the Mayflower: A history of Black America.* New York, NY: Penguin.

Bernal, M. (1987). *Black Athena.* New Brunswick, NJ: Rutgers University Press.

Bernstein, N. (2005). *All alone in the world: Children of the incarcerated.* New York, NY: The New Press.

Blackstock, N. (1988). *COINTELPRO: The FBI's Secret War on Political Freedom.* Park Ridge, IL: Pathfinder.

Boahen, A. (1969). *Topics in West African history.* New York, NY: Longmans, Green, and Co.

———. (1971). *The coming of the European (c. 1440–1700): The horizon history of Africa.* New York, NY: McGraw Hill.

Bonilla-Silva, E. (2005). Racism and new racism: The contours of racial dynamics in contemporary America. In Z. Leonardo (Ed.), *Critical pedagogy and race.* Hoboken, NJ: Blackwell.

Blustain, R. (2013, April 15). Pushing cops to consider kids when arresting parents. *City limits.* Retrieved from http://www.citylimits.org/news/articles/4781/pushing-cops-to-consider-kids-when-arresting-parents#.UeROyJTD_IU

Bougois, P. (1996). *In search of respect: Selling crack in El Barrio.* New York, NY: Cambridge University Press.

Budu-Acquah, K. (1960). *Ghana: The morning after.* London: Goodwin.

Bureau of Justice Statistics (2008). *Local police* [Data file]. Retrieved from http://www.bjs.gov/index.cfm?ty=tp&tid=71

Bureau of Justice Statistics (2010). *State Corrections Expenditures, FY 1982–2010* [Data file]. Retrieved from http://www.bjs.gov/index.cfm?ty=pbdetail&iid=4556

Burrell, T. (2010). *Brainwashed: Challenging the myth of black inferiority.* New York, NY: SmileyBooks.

Burns, K. (2006). Suicide rate for minorities much lower, census data indicate. *News Reporting and the Internet.* Retrieved from http://students.com.miami.edu/netreporting/?page_id=1285

Cann, R. L., Stoneking, M., and Wilson, A.C. (1987). Mitochondrial DNA and human evolution, *Nature, 325,* 31–36.

Carrion, V., Haas, B., Garrett, A., Song, S., and Reiss, A. (2009). Reduced hippocampal activity in youth with posttraumatic stress symptoms: An fMRI study. *Journal of Pediatric Psychology, 35*(5), 559–569.

Carrion, V., and Wong, S. (2011). Can traumatic stress alter the brain? Understanding the implications of early trauma on brain development and learning. *Journal of Adolescent Health, 51*(2), 23–28.

Center for Children of Incarcerated Parents. (2004). *CCIP Data Sheet 3a* [Data file]. Retrieved from http://www.hunter.cuny.edu/socwork/nrcfcpp/info_services/children-of-incarcerated-parents.html

Center for Constitutional Rights (2009). *Report: Racial disparity in NYPD stop and frisks* [Data file]. Retrieved from http://ccrjustice.org/learn-more/reports/report:-racial-disparity-nypd-stop-and-frisks

Center for Effective Public Policy. (2012). *Reentry*. Retrieved from http://cepp.com/reentry

Centers for Disease Control and Prevention. (2013). *Assault or homicide* [Data file]. Retrieved from http://www.cdc.gov/nchs/fastats/homicide.htm

Chamberlain, A. (1911). The contribution of the Negro to the human civilization. *Journal of Race Development, 1,* 482–502.

Chew, P., and Kelley, R. (2012). The realism of race in judicial decision making: An empirical analysis of plaintiffs' race and judges' race. *Harvard Journal on Racial and Ethnic Justice, 28,* 91–113.

Chicago Crime Commission. (2013). *Gang book*. Retrieved from https://www.chicagocrimecommission.org/util/gangseminarsummary.pdf

Chicago Police Department Annual Report 2010. (2010). *Arrest data* [Data file]. Retrieved from https://portal.chicagopolice.org/portal/page/portal/ClearPath/News/Statistical%20Reports/Annual%20Reports/10AR.pdf=

Chicago Police Department. (2013, April 9). Anti-violence initiative targets narcotics on city's west side: Supports comprehensive policing strategy to reduce crime in Chicago [Press release]. Retrieved from http://www.chicagopolice.org/MailingList/PressAttachment/releasenarcoticswestside.pdf

Children's Defense Fund. (2011). Press release: New research finds tough times for black children [Press release]. Retrieved from http://www.childrensdefense.org/newsroom/cdf-in-the-news/press-releases/2011/press-release-new-research.html

City of Chicago Official Website. (2013). *Ex-offender re-entry initiatives*. Retrieved from http://www.cityofchicago.org/city/en/depts/mayor/supp_info/ex-offender_re-entry-initiatives.html

Clarke, J. H. (1993). *African people in world history*. Baltimore, MD: Black Classic Press.

———. (1996). The power of the people. In W. Snipes (Producer), and St. C. Bourne (Director), *A Great and Mighty Walk* [Motion picture]. USA: Black Dot Media.

———. (1998). *Christopher Columbus and the African holocaust: Slavery and the rise of European capitalism*. New York, NY: Eworld.

Cleaver, E. (1968). *Soul on Ice*. New York, NY: Random House.

Clegg, L. H. (2003). *Before Columbus: Black explorers of the New World*. Retrieved from http://rense.com/general43/before.htm

Cohen, G. B., and Smith, R. (2010). The racial geography of the federal death penalty. *Washington Law Review, 85,* 425–492. Retrieved from https://digital.lib.washington.edu/dspace-law/bitstream/handle/1773.1/470/Racial%20Geography%20of%20the%20Federal%20Death%20Penalty.pdf?sequence=1

Cone, J. (2003). *Martin, Malcolm and America: A dream or a nightmare*. New York, NY: Orbis.

Congressional Record. (2007, April 12). *Recidivism reduction and Second Chance Act*. United States Senate. Section 20. Retrieved from http://beta.congress.gov/congressional-record/2013/11/13/senate-section/article/S8001−1

Cooper, R., and Jordan, W. J. (2005). Cultural issues in comprehensive school reform. In Fashola, O. S. (Ed.), *Educating African American males: Voices from the field*. Thousand Oaks, CA: Corwin.

Corcoran, F. (1985). Pedagogy in prison: Teaching in maximum security institutions. *Communication Education, 34*(1), 49–58.

Council on Foreign Relations. (2012). *Muslims in the United States*. Retrieved from http://www.cfr.org/united-states/muslims-united-states/p25927

Cureton, S. (2011). *Black vanguards and black gangsters: From seeds of discontent to a declaration of war*. Baltimore, MD: University Press of America.

Curtin, P. (1969). *The Atlantic slave trade: A census*. Madison, WI: The University of Wisconsin Press.

Curtis, E. (2002). *Islam in Black America: Identity, liberation, and difference in African-American Islamic thought*. New York, NY: State University of New York Press.

Danquah, J. (1927). *United West Africa at the bar of the family of nations*. Privately Published.

Davis, J. (1992). *Spying on America: The FBI's domestic counter-intelligence program*. New York, NY: Praeger.

———. (2001). *Who is Black?: One nation's definition*. University Park, PA: Pennsylvania State University Press.

Davis, J. E. (2003). Early schooling and academic achievement of African American males. *Urban Education, 38*(5), 515–537.

Davis, L. M., Bozick, R., Steele, J. L., Saunders, J., and Miles, J. M. (2013). *Evaluating the effectiveness of correctional education: A meta-analysis of programs that provide education to incarcerated adults*. Retrieved from https://www.bja.gov/Publications/RAND_Correctional-Education-Meta-Analysis.pdf

Davis, S. W., and Roswell, B. S. (Eds.). (2013). *Turning teaching Inside Out: A pedagogy of transformation for community-based education*. New York, NY: Palgrave Macmillan.

Delgado, R., and Stefancic, J. (2005). *The Derrick Bell reader*. New York, NY: New York University Press.

DeLisi, M., Kosloski, A., Sween, M., Hachmeister, E., Moore, M., and Drury, A. (2010, August). Murder by numbers: Monetary costs imposed by a sample of homicide offenders. *Journal of Forensic Psychiatry and Psychology, 21*(4), 501–513. http://www.soc.iastate.edu/staff/delisi/murder%20by%20numbers.pdf

Department of Justice Office of Victims of Crime. (2013). *Victim impact: Listen and learn*. Retrieved from https://www.ovcttac.gov/victimimpact/about_this_curriculum.cfm

Diouf, S. (1998). *Servants of Allah: African Muslims enslaved in the Americas*. New York: New York University Press.

———. (2003). *Fighting the slave trade: West African strategies*. Athens, OH: Ohio University Press.

———. (2004). The West African paradox. In Z. H. Bukhari, S. S. Nyang, M. Ahmad, and J. L. Esposito (Eds.), *Muslims' place in the American public square: Hope, fears, and aspirations*. Oxford, UK: Altamira.

Diop, C.A. (1974). *The African origin of civilization*. Chicago, IL: Lawrence Hill.

Douglass, F. (1995). *Narrative of the life of Frederick Douglass*. Mineola, NY: Dover.

Drug Abuse Resistance Education. (2013). *Chief Daryl Gates Founder of D.A.R.E*. Retrieved from http://www.dare.org/

Du Bois, F. (1969) *Timbuctoo the mysterious*. New York, NY: Negro Universities Press.

Du Bois, W. E. B. (1899). *The Philadelphia Negro: A social study*. Philadelphia, PA: University of Pennsylvania.

———. (1903a). The talented tenth, In *The Negro problem: A series of articles by representative Negroes of today*. New York, NY: James and Pott.

———. (1903b). *The Negro problem: A series of articles by representative Negroes of today*. New York, NY: James and Pott.

———. (1977). *Africa: Its geography, people and products and Africa: Its place in modern history*. New York, NY: KTO.

———. (1994). *The souls of black folk*. Mineola, NY: Dover.

Duke Population Research Institute (2011). *The impact of jury race in criminal trials* [White paper]. Retrieved from http://papers.ccpr.ucla.edu/papers/PWP-DUKE-2011-001/PWP-DUKE-2011-001.pdf

Dyson, M. (1996). *Race rules: Navigating the color line*. New York, NY: Vintage.

Edelman, M. W. (2000). *Lanterns: A memoir of mentors*. New York, NY: Harper Perennial.

Ely, M. (1992). *The true story of the Columbus invasion*. Chicago, IL: Revolutionary Books.

Erisman, W., and Contardo, J. B. (2005). *Learning to reduce recidivism: A 50–state analysis of postsecondary correctional education policy*. Retrieved from http://www.ihep.org/assets/files/publications/g-l/LearningReduceRecidivism.pdf

Esposito, S. (2011, June 24). Top cop Garry McCarthy likens federal gun laws to 'racism.' *Chicago Sun-Times*. Retrieved from http://www.suntimes.com/news/cityhall/6145603–418/top-cop-garry-mccarthy-likens-federal-gun-laws-to-racism.html

Fanon, F. (1952). *Black skin, white masks*. (C. Farrington, Trans.). New York, NY: Grove.

———. (1967). *The wretched of the earth.* London: Penguin.
Federal Bureau of Investigation. (2013). Operation Blue Storm selected as National Organized Crime Drug Enforcement Task Force most outstanding regional drug trafficking case of 2012 [Press release]. Retrieved from http://www.fbi.gov/omaha/press-releases/2013/operation-blue-storm-selected-as-national-organized-crime-drug-enforcement-task-force-most-outstanding-regional-drug-trafficking-case-of-2012
Federal Bureau of Investigation Uniform Crime Report. (2013a). *Crimes in the United States 2011* [Data file]. Retrieved from http://www.fbi.gov/about-us/cjis/ucr/crime-in-the-u.s/2011/crime-in-the-u.s.-2011/tables/table-1
———. (2013b). *Persons arrested 2011* [Data file]. Retrieved from http://www.fbi.gov/about-us/cjis/ucr/crime-in-the-u.s/2011/crime-in-the-u.s.-2011/persons-arrested/persons-arrested
F———. (2013c). *Federal Bureau of Investigation arrest statistics:1994–2010* [Data file]. Retrieved from http://ojjdp.gov/ojstatbb/ezaucr/asp/ucr_display.asp
Federal Bureau of Prisons (BOP). (2012). *FY 2012 budget request at a glance* [Data file]. Retrieved from http://www.justice.gov/jmd/2012summary/pdf/fy12–bop-bud-summary.pdf
———. (2013). *Quick facts about the Bureau of Prisons* [Data file]. Retrieved from http://www.bop.gov/news/quick.jsp
Ferembach, D. (1965). Diagrammes craniens sagittaux et mensurations individuelles des squelettes ibéromaurusiens de Taforalt Maroe oriental. Travaux du Centre de recherches anthropoilogiques, prehistor. et ethnograph. Paris: Arts et métiers graphiques.
———. (1985). On the origin of the Iberomaurusians (Upper Paleolothic: North Africa). A new hypothesis. *Journal of Human Evolution, 14,* 393–397.
Floyd, et al v. City of New York, et. al. 813 F.Supp.2d 457 (2011).
Forbes, C., and Kaufman, P. (2008). Critical pedagogy in the sociology classrooms: Challenges and concerns. *Teaching Sociology, 36,* 26–33.
Foster, M. (1997). *Black teachers on teaching.* New York, NY: New Press.
Foucault, M. (1994). *The archeology of knowledge.* (A. M. Sheridan Smith, Trans.). London: Routledge. (Original work published 1969)
Fox, J., and Zawitz, M. (2005). *Homicide trends in the United States.* Retrieved from http://www.bjs.gov/content/pub/pdf/htiuscdb
Frazier, E. F. (1920). *New currents of thought among the colored people of America.* Atlanta, GA: Clark University Publishing.
———. (1932). *The Negro family in Chicago.* Chicago, IL: University of Chicago Press.
———. (1957). *Black bourgeoisie.* New York, NY: MacMillan.
———. (1968). *On race relations.* Chicago, IL: The University of Chicago Press.
Freire, P. (1970). *Pedagogy of the oppressed.* New York, NY: Herder and Herder.
Frierson, H. T., Wyche, J. H., and Pearson, W. (2009). *Black American males in higher education: Research, programs and academe.* London: Emerald Group.
Frontline. (2012). *By the numbers: Childhood poverty in the U.S.* Retrieved from http://www.pbs.org/wgbh/pages/frontline/social-issues/poor-kids/by-the-numbers-childhood-poverty-in-the-u-s/
Fuller, N. (1969). *The united independent compensatory code/system concept for victims of racism.* Washington, DC: Library of Congress.
Garvey, A. J. (1986). *Philosophy and opinions of Marcus Garvey.* Dover, MA: Majority.
Gaskew, T. (2008). *Policing Muslim American communities.* Lewiston, NY: Edwin Mellen.
———. (2009a). Are you with the F.B.I.? Fieldwork challenges in a post-9/11 Muslim American community. *Practicing Anthropology, 31*(2), 12–17.
———. (2009b). Peacemaking criminology: An ethnographic study of Muslim Americans, the USA PATRIOT Act, and the War on Terror. *Contemporary Justice Review, 12*(3), 345–366.

Gates, H. L. (2013). *Life upon these shores: Looking at African American history, 1513–2008.* New York, NY: Knopf.

Gay, G. (2000). Curriculum theory and multicultural education. In J. A. Banks and C. A. McGee Banks (Eds.), *Handbook of research on multicultural education.* Hoboken, NJ: JosseyBass.

Gay, G. (2010). *Culturally responsive teaching: Theory, research, and practice* (2nd ed.). New York, NY: Teachers College.

Gorgol, L. E., and Sponsler, B. A. (2011). *Unlocking potential: Results of a national survey of postsecondary education in state prisons.* Retrieved from http://www.ihep.org/Publications/publications-detail.cfm?id=143

Grabar, H. (2013, June 7). Many of America's worst counties for racially biased marijuana arrests are urban. *The Atlantic.* Retrieved from http://www.theatlanticcities.com/neighborhoods/2013/06/americas-worst-counties-racially-biased-marijuana-arrests-are-urban/5828/

Grammy, A. P. (2011). *The underground economy* [Web log file]. Retrieved from http://www.csub.edu/kej/documents/economic_rsch/2011–11–28.pdf

Greenberg, E., Dunleavy, E., and Kutner, M. (2007). *Literacy behind bars: Results from the 2003 National Assessment of Adult Literacy Prison Survey* [Data file]. U.S. Department of Education, National Center for Education Statistics. Retrieved from http://nces.ed.gov/pubs2007/2007473_1.pdf

Greenwald, A. G., and Banaji, M. R. (1995). Implicit social cognition: Attitudes, self-esteem, and stereotypes. *Psychological Review, 102*(8), 4–27.

Guerino, P., Harrison, P. M., and Sabol, W. J. (2010). *Prisoners in 2010.* Retrieved from http://www.bjs.gov/content/pub/pdf/p10.pdf

Gundy, A. V., Bryant, A., and Starks, B. C. (2013). Pushing the envelope for evolution and social change: Critical challenges for teaching Inside-Out. *The Prison Journal, 93*(2), 189–210.

Haley, A. (1964). *The autobiography of Malcolm X.* New York, NY: Ballantine.

———. (1976). *Roots: The saga of an American family.* Boston, MA: Hall.

Hansberry, W. L. (1981a). *Africa and Africans as seen by classical writers.* J. Harris (Ed.). Washington, DC: Howard University Press.

———. (1981b). *Pillars in Ethiopian history* (Vol. 1). J. Harris (Ed.). Washington, DC: Howard University Press.

Harlow, C. W. (2003). *Education and correctional populations* [Data file]. U.S. Department of Justice, Bureau of Justice Statistics. Retrieved from http://www.bjs.gov/content/pub/pdf/ecp.pdf

Hartnett, S. J., Wood, J. K., and McCann, B. J. (2011). Turning silence into speech and action: Prison activism and the pedagogy of empowered citizenship. *Communication and Critical/Cultural Studies, 8*(4), 331–352.

Harper, S. R. (2012). *Black male student success in higher education: A report from the National Black Male College Achievement Study.* University of Pennsylvania, Center for the Study of Race and Equity in Education. Retrieved from https://www.gse.upenn.edu/equity/sites/gse.upenn.edu.equity/files/publications/bmss.pdf

Harris, K. (2009). *Smart on Crime.* San Francisco, CA: Chronicle.

Hays, J. N. (2005). *Epidemics and pandemics: Their impacts on human history.* Santa Barbara, CA: ABC-CLIO.

Henderson. C. (1901). *An introduction to the study of the dependent, defective and delinquent classes.* Lexington, MA: D.C. Health.

Hewlett, M. (2013). First black district attorney in Texas speaks to Wake Forest law students. *Winston-Salem Journal.* Retrieved from http://www.journalnow.com/news/local/article_cb3faa6a-9d90–11e2–b637–001a4bcf6878.html

Hilliard, D., and Wise, D. (2002). *The Huey P. Newton reader.* New York, NY: Seven Stories.

Hilliard, D., Zimmerman, K., and Zimmerman, K. (2006). Huey: Spirit of the panther. New York, NY: Thunder's Mouth.

hooks, b. (1994). *Teaching to transgress: Education as the practice of freedom.* New York, NY: Routledge.

Hooks, B. (2003*). Teaching community: A pedagogy of hope.* New York, NY: Routledge.

Hoskins, G. A. (1835). *Travels in Ethiopia.* London: Rees, Orme, Brown, Green, and Longman.

Hurdle, J. (2013, March 7). Philadelphia officials vote to close 23 schools. *New York Times.* Retrieved from http://www.nytimes.com/2013/03/08/education/philadelphia-officials-vote-to-close-23–schools.html?_r=0

Internal Revenue Service. (2013). *Examples of narcotics-related investigations: Fiscal year 2012.* Retrieved from http://www.irs.gov/uac/Examples-of-Narcotics-Related-Investigations-Fiscal-Year-2012

Irvine, J. J. (1988). An analysis of the problem of the disappearing black educators, *Elementary School Journal, 88*(5), 503–513.

———. (1990). *Black students and school failure: Policies, practices, and prescriptions.* San Francisco, CA: Greenwood.

Jackson, G. (1994). *Soledad brother: The prison letters of George Jackson.* Chicago, IL: Lawrence Hill.

Jackson, J. G. (1970). *Introduction to African civilizations.* New York, NY: Citadel.

Jackson, S. (2004). Preliminary reflections on Islam and black religion. In Z. H. Bukhari, S. S. Nyang, M. Ahmad, and J. L. Esposito (Eds.), *Muslims' place in the American public square: Hope, fears, and aspirations.* Oxford, UK: Altamira.

———. (2005). *Islam and the Black American: Looking toward the third resurrection.* Oxford: Oxford University Press.

———. (2009). *Islam and the problem of black suffering.* Oxford: Oxford University Press.

Jenkins, R. (1997). *Rethinking ethnicity: Arguments and explorations.* London: SAGE.

Joh, E. (2009*).* Breaking the law to enforce it: Undercover police participation in crime. *Stanford Law Review, 62*(1), 155–199.

John Jay College of Criminal Justice. (2010). *Stop, question and frisk policing practices in New York City: A primer.* Retrieved from http://www.jjay.cuny.edu/web_images/PRIMER_electronic_version.pdf

Johnson, J. E., Austin-Hillery, N., Clark, M., and Lu, L. (2010). Racial disparities in federal prosecutions: A joint project of the Brennan Center for Justice and the National Institute on Law and Equity. Retrieved from http://www.brennancenter.org/sites/default/files/legacy/Justice/ProsecutorialDiscretion_report.pdf

Justice Center: The Council of State Governments. (2013a). *Second Chance Act.* Retrieved from http://csgjusticecenter.org/nrrc/projects/second-chance-act/

———. (2013b). *Children of incarcerated parents initiative fact sheet* [Data file]. Retrieved from http://csgjusticecenter.org/nrrc/federal-interagency-reentry-council/publications/children-of-incarcerated-parents-fact-sheet/

Karenga, M. (2002). *Introduction to Black studies.* Los Angeles, CA: University of Sankore Press.

———. (2005). How many in the slave trade. In Halaqah Media (Producers), and Shahadah, O. A. (Director), *500 years later* [Motion picture]. London: Halaqah Films.

King, M. L. (1964). *Why we can't wait.* New York, NY: Signet Classics.

———. (1968a). *Where do we go from here? Chaos or community.* Boston, MA: Beacon.

———. (1968b). *I have a Dream.* Retrieved from http://www.americanrhetoric.com/speeches/mlkihaveadream.htm

Klimley, A. P., and Ainley, D. G. (1996). *Great white sharks: The biology of carcharodon carcharias.* Philadelphia, PA: Academic Press.

Kly, Y. N. (1989). 'The African-American Muslim minority: 1776–1900'. *Journal: Institute of Muslim Minority Affairs, 10*(1), 152–160.

Lafreniere, P. (2010). *Adaptive origins: Evolution and human development.* New York, NY: Taylor and Francis.

Lemonick, M. D. (1987, January 26). Everyone's Genealogical Mother, *Time,* 66.

Leaky, R. (1961). *The progress and evolution of man in Africa.* London: Oxford University Press.

————. (1996). *The origin of humankind*. New York, NY: Basic Books.

Leakey, R., and Lewis, R. (1977). *Origins*. New York, NY: Dutton.

————. (1996). *The sixth extinction: Patterns of life and the future of humankind*. Harpswell, ME: Anchor.

Leonardo, Z. (Ed.). (2005). *Critical pedagogy and race*. Boston, MA: Blackwell.

Lindner, E. (2006). *Making enemies: Humiliation and international conflict*. Westport, CT: Praeger.

Lynch, J. P. (2006). Prisoner reentry: Beyond program evaluation. *Criminology and Public Policy, 5*(2), 401–412.

Lynch, W. (2011). *The Willie Lynch letter and the making of a slave*. African Tree Press.

Lynn, M. (1999). Toward a critical race pedagogy: A research note. *Urban Education, 33*(5), 606–626.

————. (2005). Critical race theory, Afrocentricity, and their relationship to critical pedagogy. In Z. Leonardo (Ed.), *Critical pedagogy and race*. Boston, MA: Blackwell.

————. (2006). Race, culture, and the education of African Americans. *Educational Theory, 56*(1), 107–119.

Malcolm X. (1965). *Malcolm X speaks: Selected speeches and statements*. London: Pathfinder.

Mayell, H. (2005, February 16). Oldest human fossils identified. *National Geographic News*. Retrieved from http://news.nationalgeographic.com/news/2005/02/0216_050216_omo.html

Mazrui, A. (1999). Islam and the black diaspora: The impact of Islamigration. In I. Okepewho, C. Davies, and A. Mazrui (Eds.), *The African diaspora: African origins and new world identities*. Bloomington, IN: Indiana University Press.

McBride, B., Haviland, W., Prins, H., and Walrath, D. (2009). *The essence of anthropology*. Belmont, CA: Wadsworth.

McDougall, I., Brown, F., and Fleagle, J. (2005). *The oldest homo sapiens: Fossils push human emergence back to 195,000 years ago*. Retrieved from http://www.eurekalert.org/pub_releases/2005-02/uou-toh021105.php

McMillian, M. (2003). Is No Child Left Behind 'wise schooling' for African American male students? *The High School Journal, 87*(2), 25–33.

Medina, S. (2007). Measuring the great white's bite. *Cosmos Magazine*. Retrieved from http://www.cosmosmagazine.com/news/measuring-great-whites-bite/

Medwed, D. (2012). Prosecution complex: America's race to convict and its impact on the innocent. New York, NY: NYU Press.

Meredith, M. (2011). *Born in Africa: The quest for the origins of human life*. New York, NY: Public Affairs.

McCall, N. (1994). *Makes me wanna holler: A young black man in America*. New York, NY: Random House.

Minton, T. D. (2010). *Jail inmates at midyear2010 - Statistical tables* [Data file]. Retrieved from http://www.bjs.gov/content/pub/pdf/jim10st.pdf

Morris, E. (2008). *Youth violence: Implications for post-traumatic stress disorder in urban youth*. Retrieved from http://www.policyarchive.org/handle/10207/bitstreams/17613.pdf

Muhammad, K. (2010). *The condemnation of blackness: Race, crime, and the making of urban America*. Cambridge, MA: Harvard University Press.

Muhammad, W. (2009). *Black Arabia and the African origin of Islam*. Chicago, IL: A-Team.

National Association for the Advancement of Colored People. (2013). *Criminal justice fact sheet* [Data file]. Retrieved from http://www.naacp.org/pages/criminal-justice-fact-sheet

Nasr, S. H. (1994). *A young Muslim's guide to the modern world*. Chicago, IL: Kazi.

————. (1995). *Muhammad: Man of God*. Chicago, IL: Kazi.

————. (2003). *Islam: Religion, history and civilization*. San Francisco, CA: HarperCollins.

National Association of Assistant United States Attorneys. (2013). *About NAAUSA*. Retrieved from http://www.naausa.org/

National Black Prosecutors Association. (2013). *A look back at NBPA history*. Retrieved from http://www.blackprosecutors.org/index.html

National Institute of Corrections. (2013). *Offender reentry/transition*. Retrieved from http://nicic.gov/TPJC

National Reentry Resource Center. (2013). *What works in reentry clearinghouse*. Retrieved from http://www.nationalreentryresourcecenter.org/

National Urban League. (2013). *The state of Black America*. Retrieved from http://iamempowered.com/soba/2013/home

Nehusi, K. (2005). How many in the slave trade. In Halaqah Media (Producers), and Shahadah, O. A. (Director), *500 years later* [Motion picture]. London: Halaqah Films.

Newton, H. (1972). *To die for the people*. T. Morrison (Ed.). San Francisco, CA: City Lights.

New York State Office of the Attorney General. (2013). *A report on arrests arising from the New York City Police Department's stop-and-frisk practices*. Retrieved from http://www.ag.ny.gov/pdfs/OAG_REPORT_ON_SQF_PRACTICES_NOV_2013.pdf

Ohio Department of Rehabilitation and Correction North Central Correctional Complex. (2013). *The reading room*. Retrieved from http://www.drc.ohio.gov/Public/ncci.htm

Ogletree, C. (2012). *The presumption of guilt: The arrest of Henry Louis Gates, Jr. and race, class and crime in America*. London: Palgrave Macmillan.

Okpewho, I. (1999). *The African diaspora: African origins and new world identities*. Bloomington, IA: Indiana University Press.

O'Reilly, K. (1991). *Racial matters: The FBI's secret file on Black America, 1960–1972*. New York, NY: The Free Press.

Osei, I. (2005). How many in the slave trade. In Halaqah Media (Producers), and Shahadah, O. A. (Director), *500 years later* [Motion picture]. London: Halaqah Films.

Pacific Institute for Research and Evaluation. (2010). *The cost of gun violence* [Data file]. Retrieved from http://www.pire.org/more.asp?cms=963

Palmer, C. (1998). *Passageways: An interpretive history of Black America*. (Vol. 1). Belmont, CA: Wadsworth.

———. (2002). *Passageways: An interpretive history of Black America*. (Vol. 2). Belmont, CA: Wadsworth.

Parrotta, K. L., and Thompson, G. H. (2011). Sociology of the prison classroom: Marginalized identities and sociological imaginations behind bars. *Teaching Sociology, 39*(2), 165–178.

Pawasarat, J., and Quinn, L. (2013). *Wisconsin's mass incarceration of African American males: Workforce challenges for 2013*. Retrieved from http://www4.uwm.edu/eti/2013/BlackImprisonment.pdf

Pennsylvania Department of Corrections. (2013). *Office of planning, research and statistics* [Data file]. Retrieved from http://www.cor.state.pa.us/portal/server.pt/community/department_of_corrections/4604

Perry, T., Steele, C., and Hillard, A. (2003). *Young, gifted and black: Promoting high achievement among African American students*. Boston, MA: Beacon Press.

Petersilia, J. (2004). What works in prisoner reentry? Reviewing and questioning the evidence. *Federal Probation, 68*(2), 4–8.

Petrie, W. M. F. (1920). *Prehistoric Egypt*. London: British School of Archeology.

———. (1939). *The making of Egypt*. New York, NY: Sheldon.

Powell, C. (1995). My American journey: On principles and values. Retrieved from http://www.ontheissues.org/Archive/American_Journey_Principles_+_Values.htm

Price, B., and Morris, J. (2012). *Prison privatization: The many facets of a controversial industry*. Westport, CT: Praeger.

Project Implicit. (2013). *The implicit association test*. Retrieved from http://www.projectimplicit.net/index.html

Ramadan, T. (2004). *Western Muslims and the future of Islam.* New York, NY: Oxford University Press.

Rector, K. (2013, July 13). Baltimore residents trade guns for computers. *The Baltimore Sun.* Retrieved from http://articles.baltimoresun.com/2013–07–13/news/bs-md-computers-for-guns-20130713_1_northeast-baltimore-gun-exchange-exchange-event

Regoli, R., and Hewitt, J. (2008). *Exploring criminal justice.* Boston, MA: Jones and Bartlett.

Reid, G., and Hetherington, R. (2010). *The climate connection: Climate change and modern human evolution.* Cambridge, UK: Cambridge University Press.

Robbins, C. (2013, March 12). NYPD won't hire more cops, because more cops means more arrests. *The Gothamist.* Retrieved from http://gothamist.com/2013/03/12/city_council_grills_a_prickly_ray_k.php

Robinson, D. (2004). *Muslim societies in African history.* Cambridge, UK: Cambridge University Press.

Rossatto, C. A., Allen, R. L., and Pruyn, M. (Eds.). (2006). Reinventing critical pedagogy: Widening the circle of anti-oppression education. (Eds.) Lanham, MD: Rowman and Littlefield.

Ross, J. E. (2004). Impediments to transnational cooperation in undercover policing: A comparative study of the United States and Italy. *The American Journal of Comparative Law, 52*(3), 569–623.

Ryan, T. A., and McCabe, K. A. (1994). Mandatory vs. voluntary prison education and academic achievement. *The Prison Journal, 74,* 450–461.

Safer Foundation. (2013). *CARRE.* Retrieved from http://www.saferfoundation.org/

Said, E. (1978). *Orientalism.* New York: NY: Knopf Doubleday.

Schwab, G. (2010). *Haunting legacies: Violent histories and transgenerational trauma.* New York, NY: Columbia University Press.

Sanders, E., and Dunifon, R. (2011). *Children of incarcerated parents.* Retrieved from http://www.human.cornell.edu/pam/outreach/parenting/research/upload/Children-of-Incarcerated-Parents.pdf

Schott Foundation for Public Education (2012). *Given half a chance: The Schott 50 state report on public education and black males.* Retrieved from http://blackboysreport.org/urgency-of-now.pdf

Sertima, I. V. (1985). *African presence in Early Asia.* New Brunswick, NY: Transaction.

———. (2003). *They came before Columbus: The African presence in ancient America.* New York, NY: Random House.

Sesame Street. (2013). *Little children, big challenges: Incarceration.* Retrieved from http://www.sesamestreet.org/parents/topicsandactivities/toolkits/incarceration#0

SHINE for Kids. (2011). *The impact on a child when witnessing an arrest.* Retrieved from http://www.shineforkids.org.au/documents/infosheets/impact_on_child_witnessing_arrest_aug11.pdf

Shreeve, J. (2006). The greatest journey. *National Geographic Magazine.* Retrieved from http://ngm.nationalgeographic.com/print/2006/03/human-journey/shreeve-text

Simmonds, Y.J. (2009, August 27). African slave castles. *Los Angeles Sentinel.* Retrieved from http://www.lasentinel.net/index.php?option=com_content&view=article&id=5403:african-slave-castles&catid=79&Itemid=169

Smith, C. (2003). *Mandela: In celebration of a great life.* London: Struik.

Smith, R., and Levinson, J. (2012). The impact of implicit racial bias on the exercise of prosecutorial discretion. *Seattle University Law Review, 35*(3), 795–826.

Snipes, W., and Bourne. S. (1996). *John Henrik Clarke: A great and mighty walk.* USA: Black Dot Media.

SpearIt. (2013). *Growing faith: Prisons, hip-hop and Islam.* Retrieved from http://www.huffingtonpost.com/spearit/growing-faith-prisons-hip-hop-and-islam_b_2829013.html

Spycher, D. A., Shkodriani, G. M., and Lee, J. B. (2012). *The other pipeline: From prison to diploma community colleges and correctional education programs.* The College Board

Advocacy and Policy Center. Retrieved from http://advocacy.collegeboard.org/sites/default/files/11b_4792_MM_Pipeline_WEB_120416.pdf

Stephan, J. J. (2008). *Census of state and federal correctional facilities, 2005* [Data file]. U.S. Department of Justice, Bureau of Justice Statistics. Retrieved from http://www.bjs.gov/content/pub/pdf/csfcf05.pdf

Stiddem, D. (1990). *It's time we rethink our history*. Published in CALC Report.

Stringer, C. (2003). Human evolution: Out of Ethiopia. *Nature. 423,* 692–695.

Stringer , C., and McKie, R. (1996). *African exodus: The origins of modern humanity.* New York, NY: Henry Holt.

Susman, T. (2012, August 16). N.Y. support for 'stop-and-frisk' split along racial lines in poll. *L.A. Times.* Retrieved from http://articles.latimes.com/2012/aug/16/nation/la-na-nn-stopandfrisk-20120816

Tapper, J. (2009, July 11). An emotional President Obama tours former slave port with family. *ABC NEWS.* Retrieved from http://abcnews.go.com/blogs/politics/2009/07/an-emotional-president-obama-tours-former-slave-port-with-family/

Taylor, E.R.. (2009). *If we must die: Shipboard insurrections in the era of the Atlantic slave trade.* Baton Rouge, LA: Louisiana State University Press.

Terry v. Ohio, 392 US 1 (1968).

The Genographic Project (2013). About. *National Geographic.* Retrieved from https://genographic.nationalgeographic.com/about/

The Inside-Out Center. (2013). *The Inside-Out prison exchange program.* Retrieved from http://www.insideoutcenter.org/

The National Center for Children in Poverty. (2009). *Child poverty and intergenerational mobility.* Retrieved from http://www.nccp.org/publications/pdf/text_911.pdf

The Pew Charitable Trusts. (2010). *Collateral costs: Incarceration's effect on economic mobility.* Retrieved from http://www.pewtrusts.org/uploadedFiles/wwwpewtrustsorg/Reports/Economic_Mobility/Collateral%20Costs%20FINAL.pdf

The Rutherford Institute. (2011). *SWAT team mania: The war against the American citizen.* Retrieved from https://www.rutherford.org/publications_resources/john_whiteheads_commentary/swat_team_mania_the_war_against_the_american_citizen

The Sentencing Project. (2009, February). *Incarcerated parents and their children: Trends 1991–2007.* Retrieved from http://www.sentencingproject.org/doc/publications/publications/inc_incarceratedparents.pdf

———. (2013a). *The changing racial dynamics of women's incarceration.* Retrieved from http://www.scribd.com/doc/127583695/Changing-Racial-Dynamics-2013

———. (2013b). *Children in harm's way: Criminal justice, immigration enforcement, and child welfare.* Retrieved from http://www.sentencingproject.org/doc/publications/cc_Children%20in%20Harm's%20Way-final.pdf

The World Factbook. (2013). *Africa.* Retrieved from https://www.cia.gov/library/publications/the-world-factbook/

Thompkins, D.E. (2010). The expanding prisoner reentry industry. *Dialectical Anthropology, 34*(4), 589–604.

Thornton, R. (1990). *American Indian holocaust and survival: A population history since 1492.* Norman, OK: University of Oklahoma Press.

Tierney, J., Wright, L., and Springen, K. (1988). The search for Adam and Eve, *Newsweek,* 46–52.

Tricas, T. C., and McCosker, J. E. (1984). Predatory behavior of the white shark. *Proceedings of the California Academy of Sciences, 43*(14), 221–238.

United States Census Bureau. (2010). *School enrollment.* Retrieved from http://www.census.gov/hhes/school/

———. (2012). *Homicide trends.* Retrieved from http://www.census.gov/compendia/statab/2012/tables/12s0313.pdf

———. (2013a). *American native.* Retrieved from http://www.census.gov/newsroom/releases/archives/amer_indian_alaska_native/

———. (2013b). *Ohio quick facts: 2012* [Data file]. Retrieved from http://quick-facts.census.gov/qfd/states/39000.html

———. (2013c). *Pennsylvania quick facts: 2012* [Data file]. Retrieved from http://quick-facts.census.gov/qfd/states/42000.html

———. (2013d). *Population.* [Data file]. Retrieved from http://www.census.gov/compendia/statab/cats/population.html

United States Department of Education. (2010). National Center for Education Statistics. (2011). *Digest of education statistics,* [Data file]. Retrieved from http://nces.ed.gov/fastfacts/display.asp?id=61

———. (2012). *Civil rights data collection.* Retrieved from http://ocrdata.ed.gov/

———. (2013). *Public high school drop out rates.* Retrieved from http://www.ed.gov/blog/2013/01/high-school-graduation-rate-at-highest-level-in-three-decades/

United States Department of Health and Human Services. (2013). *Post-traumatic stress disorder.* Retrieved from http://www.hhs.gov/

United States Department of Justice. Federal Bureau of Investigation. *Uniform crime reports, 1930–1959.* ICPSR03666–v1 [Data file]. Ann Arbor, MI: Inter-university Consortium for Political and Social Research.

United States Department of Justice. Office of Justice Programs Bureau of Justice Statistics. (2007a). *Sheriffs' offices, 2007 - Statistical tables* [Data file]. Retrieved from http://www.bjs.gov/content/pub/pdf/so07st.pdf

United States Department of Justice Office of Justice Programs Bureau of Justice Statistics. (2007b). *Local police departments, 2007.* Retrieved from http://www.bjs.gov/content/pub/pdf/lpd07.pdf

———. (2011a). *Plea and Charge Bargaining.* Retrieved from https://www.bja.gov/Publications/PleaBargainingResearchSummary.pdf

———. (2011b). *Contacts between police and the public, 2008.* Retrieved July 5, 2013 from http://www.bjs.gov/content/pub/pdf/cpp08.pdf

———. (2011c). *Homicide trends in the United States, 1980–2008: Annual rates for 2009 and 2010* [Data file]. Retrieved from http://www.bjs.gov/content/pub/pdf/htus8008.pdf

United States Department of Justice Office of Justice Programs. (2012a). *Probation and parole in the United States, 2011* [Data file]. Retrieved from http://bjsdata.ojp.usdoj.gov/content/pub/pdf/ppus11.pdf

———. (2012b). *Correctional populations in the United States, 2011* [Data file]. Retrieved from http://bjsdata.ojp.usdoj.gov/content/pub/pdf/cpus11.pdf

United States Department of Justice. (2013a). *Organized Crime Drug Enforcement Task Forces (OCDETF) Program.* Retrieved from http://www.justice.gov/criminal/task-forces/ocdetf.html

———. (2013b). *FY 2014 Interagency Crime and Drug Enforcement Congressional Budget submission.* Retrieved from http://www.justice.gov/jmd/2014justification/pdf/ocdetf-justification.pdf

United States Drug Enforcement Administration. (2013). *DEA arrests.* Retrieved from http://www.justice.gov/dea/resource-center/statistics.shtml#arrests

United States Sentencing Commission. (2010). *Demographic differences in federal sentencing practices.* Retrieved from http://www.ussc.gov/Research/Research_Publications/2010/20100311_Multivariate_Regression_Analysis_Report.pdf

United States Sentencing Commission. (2011). *Overview of federal criminal cases: Fiscal year 2011.* Retrieved from http://www.ussc.gov/Research_and_Statistics/Research_Publications/2012/FY11_Overview_Federal_Criminal_Cases.pdf

———. (2011). *Overview of federal criminal cases: Fiscal year 2011.* Retrieved from http://www.ussc.gov/Research_and_Statistics/Research_Publications/2012/FY11_Overview_Federal_Criminal_Cases.pdf

University at Albany Sourcebook of Criminal Justice Statistics. (2013). Retrieved on from http://www.albany.edu/sourcebook/

Urban Institute Police Center. (2005). *Families left behind: The hidden costs of incarceration and reentry.* Retrieved from http://www.urban.org/uploadedPDF/310882_families_left_behind.pdf

———. (2013). *Corrections, reentry, and community supervision.* Retrieved from http://www.urban.org/justice/corrections.cfm

Van Gundy, A., Bryant, A., and Starks, B. C. (2013). Pushing the envelope for evolution and social change: Critical challenges for teaching Inside-Out. *The Prison Journal, 93*(2), 189–210.

Vedantam, S. (2005, January 23). See no bias. *Washington Post,* Retrieved from http://www.washingtonpost.com/wp-dyn/articles/A27067-2005Jan21.html

Vera Institute of Justice. (2012). *The price of prisons: What incarceration costs taxpayers.* Retrieved from http://www.vera.org/sites/default/files/resources/downloads/Price_of_Prisons_updated_version_072512.pdf

———. (2013). *Pathways from prison to postsecondary education project.* Retrieved from http://www.vera.org/project/pathways-prison-postsecondary-education-project

Von Hentig, H. (1940). The criminality of the Negro. *Journal of Criminal Law and Criminology, 30*(5), 662–680.

Walsh, L. (2000). The African American population of the colonial United States. In M. Haines and R. Steckel (Eds.), *A population history of North America.* New York, NY: Cambridge University Press.

Weatherwax, J. (1963). *The man who stole a continent.* Los Angeles, CA: Bryant Foundation.

Weiss, M. (2012, December 21). New York City arrests rose to record levels during Bloomberg era, NYPD stats show. *The Huffington Post.* Retrieved from http://www.huffingtonpost.com/2012/12/21/new-york-city-arrests-record-levels-bloomberg-era-nypd_n_2345085.html

Wells, S. (2002). *The journey of man: A genetic odyssey.* Princeton, NJ: Princeton University Press.

Welsing, F. (2004). *The Isis papers: The keys to the colors.* New York, NY: CW.

———. (2005). How many in the slave trade. In Halaqah Media (Producers), and Shahadah, O. A. (Director), *500 years later* [Motion picture]. London: Halaqah Films.

West, C. (2001). *Race matters* (2nd ed.). New York, NY: Vintage.

West, H. C., Sabol, W. J., and Greenman, S. J. (2011). *Prisoners in 2009.* U.S. Department of Justice, Office of Justice Programs, Bureau of Justice Statistics. Retrieved from http://www.bjs.gov/content/pub/pdf/p09.pdf

Whittaker, S. (2003). *Africans in the Americas: Our journey throughout the world.* Bloomington, IN: iUniverse.

Williams, C. (1974). *The destruction of African civilization, Great issues of race from 4500 B.C. to 2000 A.D.* Chicago, IL: Third World.

Williams, E. (1964). *Capitalism and slavery.* New York, NY: Capricorn.

———. (1963). *Documents of West Indian history (Vol. 1), 1492–1655: From the Spanish discovery to the British conquest of Jamaica.* Trinidad: P.N.M.

———. (1984). *From Columbus to Castro: The history of the Caribbean: 1492–1969.* New York, NY: Vintage.

———. (1942). *The Negro in the Caribbean.* New York, NY: Negro Universities Press.

Williams, S. (2004). *Blue rage black redemption.* Pleasant Hill, CA: Damamli.

Wilson, J. (2009). *More than just race: Being black and poor in the inner city.* New York, NY: W.W. Norton.

———. (2012). Race. In Ackerman, R., Alcaro, D., and Barnes J. (Producers), and Jarecki, E. (Director), *The House That I Live In* [Motion Picture]. USA: Charlotte Street Films.

Winters, C.A. (1978). Afro-American Muslims: From Slavery to Freedom. *Islamic Studies, 7*(1), 187–203.

Wisconsin Department of Corrections. (2013). *Employment.* Retrieved from http://doc.wi.gov/Employment

Wise, T. (2010*). Colorblind: The rise of post-racial politics and the retreat from racial equity.* San Francisco, CA: City Lights.

———. (2011). *White like me: Reflections on race from a privileged son.* Berkley CA: Soft Skull.

———. (2012). *Dear white America: Letter to a new minority.* San Francisco, CA: City Lights.

Woodson, C. G. (1918). *A century of Negro migration.* Washington, D.C.: Association for the Study of Negro Life and History.

———. (1925). *Free Negro heads of families in the United States in 1830.* Washington, D.C.: Association for the Study of Negro Life and History.

———. (1933). *The Mis-education of the Negro.* New York, NY: Tribeca.

———. (1947). *The Negro in our history.* Washington, D.C.: Association for the Study of Negro Life and History.

Woodward, H. (2005). How many in the slave trade. In Halaqah Media (Producers), and Shahadah, O. A. (Director), *500 years later* [Motion picture]. London: Halaqah Films.

Worthington, E. L. (2007). *Humility: The quiet virtue.* Philadelphia, PA: Templeton Foundation.

Wroe, S., Huber, D. R., Lowry, M., McHenry, C., Moreno, K., Clausen, P., Ferrara, T. L., Cunningham, E., Dean, M. N., and Summers, A. P. (2008). Three-dimensional computer analysis of white shark jaw mechanics: How hard can a great white bite? *Journal of Zoology, 276*(4), 336–342.

Zuberi T. (2005). How many in the slave trade. In Halaqah Media (Producers), and Shahadah, O. A. (Director), *500 years later* [Motion picture]. London: Halaqah Films.

———. (2011). *Perspectives on Africa and the world.* Thousand Oak, CA: SAGE.

———. (2013). Timbuktu before the storm. *Huffington Post Black Voices*, March 1. Retrieved from http://www.huffingtonpost.com/dr-tukufu-zuberi/timbuktu-photos_b_2784472.html?view=print&comm_ref=false.

Zuberi, T., and Bonilla-Silva, E. (2008). Toward a definition of white logic and white methods. In T. Zuberi, and E. Bonilla-Silva (Eds.), *White logic, white methods: racism and methodology.* Lanham, MD: Rowman and Littlefield Publishers.

Index

About the Author

Tony Gaskew, PhD, is associate professor of criminal justice and director of the Criminal Justice Program at the University of Pittsburgh (Bradford). He also serves as the Chair of the President's Advisory Committee on Diversity and the Board President of the Consortium for Educational Resources on Islamic Studies (CERIS). He received his doctorate from Nova Southeastern University within the Graduate School of Humanities and Social Sciences, with a research emphasis on crime and justice. He was awarded a Fulbright Hays Fellowship, an FDD Fellowship, and a University of Pittsburgh Faculty Diversity Fellowship, where he conducted ethnographic research in Egypt and Israel examining issues of social justice, political, structural, and direct violence. He is a Human Dignity and Humiliation Studies (HumanDHS) research team member, and also served on the FBI-sponsored Global Hostage-Taking and Analysis Project. He is a graduate of the Inside-Out Prison Exchange Program Instructor Institute at Temple University. He is also the principal investigator on a Pennsylvania Commission on Crime and Delinquency (PCCD) Prisoner Reentry Grant. Dr. Gaskew is involved in numerous social justice outreach projects, including serving as a member of the McKean County Criminal Justice Advisory Board and the Federal Bureau of Prisons (BOP) Federal Correctional Institution (FCI) McKean Community Relations Board. Since 2007, he has been actively involved in creating prison-based educational initiatives at FCI McKean. In 2010, he received the Volunteer of the Year Award from FCI McKean. Dr. Gaskew is also a former police detective at the Melbourne Police Department, where he was assigned to the Special Operation Unit as a ten-year member of the United States Department of Justice, Organized Crime Drug Enforcement Task Force (OCDETF), working with the U.S. Attorney's Office, Drug Enforcement Administration, Internal Revenue Service, Immigration and Customs Enforcement, Federal Bureau of Investigation, and the Florida Department of Law Enforcement, conducting wiretap and conspiracy investigations targeting violent criminal organizations within the Middle District of Florida. He is a court-certified expert in drug trafficking investigations, and in 2001, he was awarded the Region IV Florida Narcotic Officer of the Year.

Lightning Source UK Ltd.
Milton Keynes UK
UKOW02n0619031014

239499UK00006B/47/P